Praise for The New Turkish Republic

"A Turkey rejected by Europe will bring the Middle Eastern problem into Europe. Fuller's incisive analysis of this dilemma is truly of great and even immediate geopolitical import."

—**Zbigniew Brzezinski**, Counselor and Trustee, Center for Strategic and International Studies

"Timely and lively, Graham Fuller's latest book makes a valuable contribution to the debate about Turkey and its role in the world. Drawing on a range of interviews in Turkey and the region, it reflects on recent events and trends in a way that is not found in other works on Turkish foreign policy. It is an essential read for those looking to understand the new Turkey—and its meaning for others."

—**Ian Lesser**, Senior Transatlantic Fellow at the German Marshall Fund of the United States, and Public Policy Scholar at the Woodrow Wilson Center in Washington, D.C.

"In this very timely study of Turkey, Graham Fuller provides an objective and balanced assessment of Turkish domestic and foreign policy. Factoring in the country's unique social, economic, political, and cultural dynamics, he presents a multidimensional perspective often missing in other studies of Turkey. Written in a highly readable, easy flowing style, this is an excellent study of Turkey for a wide audience."

—**Omer Taspinar**, Brookings Institution

"Graham Fuller is one of the most sensible analysts of Turkish politics in particular and political Islam in general. This high-quality work makes a valuable contribution to the study of Turkey and Islamic politics and breaks new ground by stressing the transformation of Turkey and its role in the region."

—**Hakan Yavuz**, University of Utah

D0060449

The New Turkish Republic

The New Turkish Republic

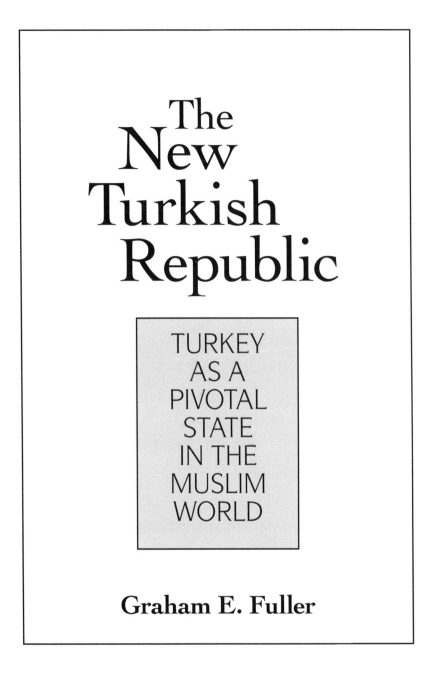

TURKEY
AS A
PIVOTAL
STATE
IN THE
MUSLIM
WORLD

Graham E. Fuller

UNITED STATES INSTITUTE OF PEACE PRESS

WASHINGTON, D.C.

UNITED STATES INSTITUTE OF PEACE
1200 17th Street NW, Suite 200
Washington, DC 20036-3011
www.usip.org

First published 2008

To request permission to photocopy or reprint materials from USIP Press, please contact copyright clearance center at www.copyright.com.

Printed in the United States of America

The paper used in this publication meets the minimum requirements of American National Standards for Information Science—Permanence of Paper for Printed Library Materials, ANSI Z39.48-1984.

Library of Congress Cataloging-in-Publication Data

Fuller, Graham E., 1937-
      The new Turkish republic : Turkey as a pivotal state in the Muslim world / Graham E. Fuller.
         p. cm.
      Includes bibliographical references and index.
      ISBN 978-1-60127-019-1 (pbk. : alk. paper)
      1. Turkey—Foreign relations—21st century. 2. Turkey—Politics and government—21st century. 3. Turkey—Strategic aspects. I. Title
      DR477.F85 2007
      327.561—dc22
                        2007037704

Contents

Foreword

Momentous changes have been under way in Turkey for two decades, and as the Turkish Republic continues to define its role in international politics, there is little doubt that more change lies ahead. Turkey is an important member of NATO, and it has been a valued ally of the United States since World War II. But the U.S. invasion of Iraq in 2003 exposed some of the fundamental contradictions in U.S.-Turkish relations. With little consultation with its ally, U.S. war planners simply assumed that Turkey would serve as a land and air bridge to northern Iraq. In fact, the invasion was profoundly unpopular in Turkey, and the democratically elected parliament rebuffed the United States. This action prompted Deputy Secretary of Defense Paul Wolfowitz—a proponent of democracy in Iraq—to suggest that the Turkish government could have short-circuited the democratic process. But, as Graham Fuller reveals in this volume, democracy is alive and well in Turkey.

Democracy is only sixty years old in Turkey, and the military, which sees itself as the guardian republic, has regularly intervened to counter threats to Kemalism, the ideology espoused by the founder of the republic, Mustafa Kemal Atatürk. Inspired by French laicism, Kemalism insists on a subordination of religion to state authority. Atatürk, a military hero and the dominant political personality of his generation, was a giant of Turkish history, but he was no democrat. His vision of Turkey insisted on an autocratic state that dominated both politics and the economy. Turkey's democratic experiment began in 1950, a dozen years after Atatürk's death. The first democratically elected leader of the republic, Adnan Menderes, was hanged by the army in 1961. Since then, Kemalists have periodically—without intending irony—called upon the military to intervene to "save democracy."

A key twenty-first century debate is whether Muslim societies will embrace democracy. To that debate Turkey, where Muslims accounts for over 98 percent of the population, brings a very hopeful example. In the course of three short generations, Turkey has developed a vibrant, exciting, and responsive democracy that is now dominated by a competent political party with a decided Islamic personality. It is noteworthy that the Turkish democratic experiment is being closely watched in Muslim societies.

The ruling Justice and Development Party (often known by its Turkish acronym, AKP), led by Prime Minister Recep Tayyip Erdogan, spurns the label "Islamist." AKP embraces secularism, which, as Fuller reveals, privileges the individual's right to religious freedom, in contrast to the trademark laicism espoused by the Turkish military elites and fervent Kemalists. In

contrast, some of the Kemalists reveal a fundamentalist obsession with laicism, which is no less exclusionary than the perspectives of mirror-image
Islamists. In any case, AKP has found a modus vivendi with the military. In
2007, when the generals vetoed the parliament's selection of Abdullah Gul, a
leading AKP figure, to become president of the Republic, Erdogan called for
new elections. AKP won a resounding victory. Gul is now the president.

AKP has been buoyed by the rise of an Anatolian middle class, which
is more socially conservative than many of the Kemalist entrepreneurs but
is deeply committed to Turkey and to the model of the republic. The party's constituents evince "Muslimhood," tempered by Turkish nationalism.
Many of these people participate in the Nur (light) movement, which is the
largest social movement in Turkey. As Fuller explains, this movement, which
takes the premise of a strong Turkish state more or less for granted, is based
in Islamic modernism.

While military intervention in politics is still possible, it has been less
plausible, particularly so long as Turkey is vying for membership in the European Union. AKP has been leading the Turkish campaign for EU membership. During the cold war, Turkey's key relationship was arguably with the
United States, but, as Fuller emphasizes, Turkey now is pursuing interests in
Europe, Eurasia, and the Middle East. Turkey's agenda does not necessarily
coincide with the agenda of the United States, as Washington policymakers
are discovering. While the embassy in Washington remains keenly important to Ankara, the end of the cold war, the growing salience of the European
Union and Europe in politics and trade, and the changes and opportunities
that inevitably come with Turkey's geopolitical setting dictate a *toutes directions* foreign policy for Turkey.

Turkey turned its back on the Middle East after the founding of the
republic, which Fuller refers to as a product of the "Kemalist historical
lobotomy." Well into the 1990s, neither Turkish officials nor scholars paid
much attention to the Middle East, despite the centrality of the region to the
former Ottoman Empire. Now Turkey is reconnecting to the region after a
long hiatus in Turkish-Arab relations. It is instructive that Turkey's border
with Syria was officially recognized by Ankara only in 2004, in conjunction
with Prime Minister Erdogan's visit to Damascus in 2004.

While Turkey has developed an important strategic relationship with
Israel, it balances that orientation with a variety of other developing relations
in the Middle East. Perhaps most indicative of the Turkey independent
foreign policy is its relationship with non-Arab Iran, an important trading
partner and neighbor. After years of tense relations, particularly in the
decade following the toppling of the shah of Iran in 1979, the two countries
have developed reasonably cordial relations.

Restive Kurdish minorities are found in both Turkey and Iran. Violent
Kurdish nationalists, benefiting from sanctuary in Iraqi Kurdistan, have

grown more active in both countries. With U.S. occupation forces consumed by the challenges of civil war and insurgency in Iraq, an ineffectual Iraqi government in Baghdad, and few incentives for Iraqi Kurdish authorities to act against popular nationalist groups, the challenge of Kurdish nationalism now preoccupies and unites many in Turkey. Turkey and Iran have found they have some common security interests as well, despite Washington's dismay.

As the "new Turkish republic" finds its way and its voice, there will be no turning back to the simpler dynamic of the cold war. Thus the quality of U.S.-Turkish relations will inevitably be maturing and evolving, just as Turkey is doing. This timely book is an indispensable primer to the challenges that lie ahead and the context in which those changes are occurring.

Augustus Richard Norton
Professor of Anthropology and International Relations
Boston University

Acknowledgments

This book draws on a lifetime of interest in and involvement with Turkey, specifically its history, politics, culture, language, and society. Therefore, I wish to express thanks to the United States Institute of Peace for the grant to write this book. I am especially pleased to have had the chance to explore the role of Turkey in the Middle East and the broader Muslim world for two principal reasons: it is a topic that has received relatively little attention from Turkish, Western, and Arab analysts; and Turkey's relations with its neighbors and coreligionists will only grow in importance in the decades ahead, particularly as many parts of the Muslim world lurch toward further instability and turmoil. I also wish to thank the Earhart Foundation for an earlier grant to explore the character of contemporary religious movements in Turkey—in particular, the Fethullah Gülen movement—which has greatly helped inform this book.

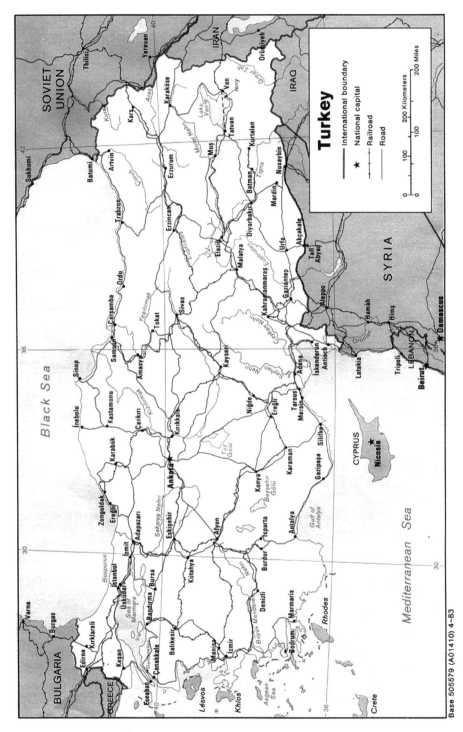

Source: Map produced by the CIA, 2003. Perry-Castañeda Library Map Collection, University of Texas Library, www.lib.utexas.edu/maps/turkey.html.

The New Turkish Republic

Introduction

Is Turkey in the Middle East?

Ten years ago, while traveling through a town in central Anatolia, I visited a historic Seljuk mosque. There, I struck up a friendly conversation with a local Turk who eventually asked me how I learned Turkish and what I did for a living. I replied that I was a Middle East specialist. "Then what are you doing in Turkey?" he replied, with no trace of irony. Indeed, what was I doing there? Was I simply spending a few weeks on vacation in Turkey while away from the Middle East? Or was I on the job, seeking insights into a key part of a diverse Middle East?

Whether Turkey is a part of the Middle East has been the subject of emotional debates for well over a century. Responses have varied depending on the era or the political juncture in which the question was asked. Furthermore, definitions of the Middle East itself have changed. It is, after all, a construct, making generalizations difficult and imprecise. For Ankara, the term "Middle East" represents Turkey's immediate Muslim neighbors, most all of whom fell outside the mainstream focus of Turkish foreign policy for much of the twentieth century. It also represents an agglomeration of regional states of differing character enjoying inconsistent relations among themselves. But if Turkey is indeed linked to the Middle East, however defined, how so? Today's Arabs, Turks, and Westerners all have different perspectives on the matter.

The question of Turkey's "real" orientation is multilayered, involving a range of variables, such as geography, history, culture, ethnicity, geopolitics, nationalism, religion, tradition, psychology, and identity. The simple answer, of course, is "yes": Turkey is indeed part of the Middle East—just as it is also part of Europe, the Mediterranean, the Balkans, and the Caucasus in geopolitical and geographic terms. But the question goes well beyond geography: it also probes issues related to identity, orientation, and aspirations. Among Turks the question itself is a sensitive one—how individuals respond often says much about their own personal politics.

But the question of Turkey's place in the Muslim world is determined not only by the Turks' own perceptions of themselves but also by the perceptions of others. For example, today Turkey is struggling to convince European states that it is indeed a Western country that deserves admission into the European Union. And until the 1960s, the U.S. State Department bureaucratically handled Turkey within the Bureau of Near Eastern Affairs. When Turkey joined NATO, it was transferred by the stroke of a pen into the Bureau of European

Affairs. Turkey was quite simply reclassified—dare we say upgraded?—to the status of a European country, both to gratify the Turks' own Western aspirations and for bureaucratic convenience. Were the State Department ever to bureaucratically redesignate Turkey back into the Bureau of Near Eastern Affairs, Turks would undoubtedly perceive it as a serious insult, fraught with negative cultural, political, and psychological significance.

Even if Turkey is part of Europe, its geographical location in the Middle East invariably thrusts it into the heart of Middle Eastern politics, whether the Turks like it or not. But from the founding of the modern Turkish Republic in 1923, its relations with most former Muslim regions of the Ottoman Empire have been limited and strained. Only relatively recently has Turkey's involvement in the Middle East begun to change course dramatically.

Turkey in a Snapshot

Turkey has been a country of exceptional importance throughout the history of the Muslim world and has existed in two dramatically differing incarnations, first as the Seljuk/Ottoman Empire and later as the modern Turkish Republic.

- Founded by Turks, the Ottoman Empire stood at the center of the Muslim world for six centuries. The largest, longest-lasting, and most powerful empire in Islamic history, its rule extended far north into the Balkans, throughout Anatolia, and across almost all of the Arab world, including North Africa at one point. Additionally, it was one of the most successful and stable models of a multiethnic and multicultural empire of its time, and it was the seat of the Islamic Caliphate—the supreme religious office for the entire Sunni world.
- Arising out of the ruins of the defeated Ottoman Empire, the modern Turkish Republic, led by the brilliant, autocratic, and westernizing leader Mustafa Kemal Atatürk, went on to form what has become the most advanced, powerful, secular, and democratic state in the Muslim world. A member of NATO, it is now a candidate for membership in the European Union in 2015.

In 2002, Turkey made history by freely electing—for the first time in Muslim history—an Islamist party to national power. Still in power in 2007, this government seeks to harmonize the legacy of Kemalism and Turkey's forced march toward westernization with the more traditional and Islamic elements of Turkish culture. Just as the country bids to play an expanded international role between East and West, it also seeks to create a new domestic synthesis between traditional and modern values.

In this context, Turkey's global strategy is undergoing considerable revision under multiple influences both domestic and foreign. Ankara increasingly perceives its own interests in independent terms and as somewhat divergent from Washington's regional agenda. There are clear signs that Turkey, touted for decades as a loyal ally of the United States, can no longer be counted on to routinely demonstrate its loyalty. To be sure, some of these shifts in Turkey parallel the changes in attitude toward Washington that are occurring in other countries.

Turkish and American interests are most troubled when it comes to issues related to the Muslim world. Turkey, as an emerging regional power, is no longer comfortable with interventions by the United States, particularly when they complicate Ankara's own initiatives and damage its own interests. In fact, today Turkey sees the United States as the chief destabilizing factor in the Middle East. As a result, there is an increasing prickliness, wariness, and even suspicion across most of the Turkish political spectrum toward U.S. policies and actions.

These frictions are becoming more prominent and have begun to sink into Turkish political consciousness. As evidence, consider the striking results from a survey of Turkish perceptions that was conducted by Turkey's International Strategic Research Organization (ISRO) in 2004:

- The United States ranked as the number one *threat* to Turkey, followed by Greece, Armenia, and Israel. Russia ranked seventh and Iran ninth.
- The United States ranked number seven among the countries friendliest to Turkey.
- As a potential long-term partner for Turkey, the European Union ranked first and the United States fifth, one place lower than the "Islamic world."
- The United States was overwhelmingly ranked number one as the country most believed to threaten to world peace, followed by Israel and the United Kingdom.
- Yet interestingly, the United States ranked number one as the country Turkey could most count on for aid in time of crisis (earthquake, civil war, etc.) [1]

This book will argue that Turkey's new search for independence in its foreign policy, however complicating or irritating for the United States, will nonetheless ultimately serve the best interests of Turkey, the Middle East, and even the West. In the coming decade, Turkey—for the first time in its modern history—is becoming a major player in Middle East politics. Its evolving sense of its own identity and increasing recognition of its historical role within the Muslim world is catching the attention of other Muslims, who themselves are beginning to perceive Turkey as a potentially important

---

1. ISRO, "ISRO Second Foreign Policy Perception Survey," October 2004, www.usak.org.uk.

ally to their own interests. The importance of the Turkish role will likely only grow as authoritarian regimes all across the region slide toward deepening crises of leadership and legitimacy and face eventual collapse.

In such an environment of swirling and uncontrolled change, few Muslim states have successfully or positively undergone such wrenching transition. Indeed, at this point in its history, perhaps only Turkey can demonstrate a positive record on multiple levels: it has managed to enact successful economic policies; it has created a largely stable political order with a tested democracy; it has a vibrant Islamic culture; it has demonstrated an ability to reach some form of reconciliation with political Islam in a way that few other Muslim states have; it has demonstrated a growing realism in the way it treats its own multiethnic problems; it has maintained a close working relationship with the West in the political, economic, and military spheres and continues on a (controversial) course toward EU membership; and it has a strong military and a powerful sense of sovereignty and independence. These are qualities greatly sought after and critically needed by other Muslim societies. As a result, in its new, more independent mode, Turkey is no longer perceived regionally as a mere Western "wannabe"; it is now for the first time being viewed positively within the Muslim world as a state worth watching—and maybe even emulating.

Additionally, with a GDP of $627 billion in 2006 and a real growth rate currently at 7.4 percent, Turkey's economy is one of the largest in the Middle East.[2] And although Turkey is one of the biggest countries of the Middle East, with a population of more than 70 million, its birth rate currently stands at 1.09 percent, meaning the social infrastructure crises that plague so many other developing countries with higher birth rates will likely be avoided.

Turkey also presents a diverse religious and ethnic makeup, similar to many other states in the region such as Iran, Iraq, Afghanistan, and Pakistan. In religious terms Turkey's population is 99.8 percent Muslim, but in sectarian terms there is a sizeable (30 percent) Alevi (heterodox Shiite) community that has its own strong sense of communal identity. Additionally, Turkey is distinctly multiethnic: the single largest ethnic minority in the country are the Kurds, who represent roughly 20 percent of the population and speak a non-Turkic language akin to Persian. The Kurdish population has presented the modern Turkish Republic with serious issues of insurgency and separatism, especially in recent decades, but Ankara is slowly learning to manage these issues with more wisdom. While the situation has improved, Turkey's "Kurdish problem" is far from resolved and is now complicated by the politics of Kurds in post-Saddam Iraq.

---

2. CIA, "The World Factbook—Turkey," www.cia.gov/library/publications/the-world-factbook/geos/tu.html.

Significance of Turkey to the United States

Ever since the founding of the modern Turkish Republic, Turkey's dominant elite has identified itself with the West for strategic, cultural, economic, and psychological reasons. This identification eventually led Ankara to form a close military-strategic relationship with both Europe and the United States, which understood Turkey's geopolitical importance, particularly after World War II with the rise of the Soviet threat. A neighbor to the Levant, the Balkans, Mesopotamia, Iran, and the energy-rich Caucasus, Turkey is a Mediterranean and Aegean power that controls the Bosphorus, the straits that cut through Istanbul, dividing Europe and Asia, and that control Russian egress out of the Black Sea. Turkey's orientation and strategic geography ultimately led to Turkish membership in NATO, and its involvement in Western strategic planning in the Eastern Mediterranean and Black Sea regions.

With the Iranian Revolution of 1979 and the rise of political Islam, the West came to prize Turkey's strong secularism and pro-Western commitment. As Islamic movements spread through the Middle East, Turkish government hostility to any form of political Islam contributed to its image as a bulwark against Islamic radicalism. Additionally, after the fall of the Soviet Union, Turkey's ethnic ties with the newly independent Turkic states of Central Asia added to its strategic importance, as did plans to make Turkey a hub for the transit of Caspian and Central Asian oil and natural gas. Around this time, Turkey also intensified its military relations with Israel.

After September 11, 2001, Washington expected Turkey to be a natural partner and source of support in the Global War on Terrorism (GWOT), to back U.S. military operations in the region, and to continue to be an enduring symbol of anti-Islamist ideology. Yet these expectations did not materialize as Washington had hoped. Indeed, bilateral relations have changed markedly and shown signs of dramatic deterioration in recent years. The reasons behind this change—and the implications of this change for Turkey and the United States—is a key issue explored in this book.

Turkey's Changing Role

Turkey's own role in the Middle East has been rather modest in past decades. But since 2001, its role there has greatly expanded for two key reasons. The first relates to the impact of 9/11 and the subsequent GWOT, which led to U.S. military and paramilitary engagements across large segments of the Muslim world, including on Turkey's doorstep. The second relates to Turkey's 2002 national elections and the rise to power of the Justice and Development Party (JDP, or Adalet ve Kalkınma Partisi [AKP]), Turkey's own highly moderate Islamist party. Turkey's response to the

GWOT and the emergence of the JDP represent a new stage in the ongoing evolution of Turkey's identity and role in the Middle East, a stage that raises a number of interesting questions:

- What role can or will Turkey play in a period of increasing turbulence and dramatic change in the Middle East?
- What relevance does the election of a moderate Islamist government in secular-minded Turkey have for other Muslim countries? And how does the large, moderate, and largely apolitical Islamist movement of Fethullah Gülen contribute to the development of a new moderate Islam in Turkey?
- Can Turkey's JDP serve as a model or an important body of political experience to the rest of the Middle East?
- How will Turkey's emerging role in the Middle East impact Turkey's membership bid in the European Union?
- What is behind Turkey's growing anti-American attitudes, at both the official and the popular level? How "permanent" is this development and what does it mean for the Middle East?
- What will be the future determinants of Turkish policies in the Middle East, and how will they affect U.S. interests and policies?

The Argument

With these and other questions in mind, a key thesis of this book is that the modern Turkish Republic—after a long period of abnormal isolation from the Middle East and Eurasia—is now in the process of becoming a part of Middle Eastern politics once again. This process is tied to Turkey's growing vision of its new geopolitical place in the world. Thus, the Turkey that the West has grown comfortable with over the past half century actually represents a transient geopolitical aberration from a long-term norm to which it is now returning. While this "return of history" partially dilutes and complicates Turkey's relationship with the West, it also enriches and complements it.

A long succession of U.S. administrations grew comfortable with the "old" Turkey—the faithful, reliable, and strongly pro-Western ally whose interests appeared to differ little from America's, a country that was ready and willing to assist in fulfilling most every U.S. geopolitical goal in the region. But for multiple reasons, we are witnessing a gradual global reaction within the international order that seeks to restore some degree of multipolarity to the world, much at Washington's expense. This trend is related both to global geopolitical changes since the end of the Cold War and the impact of Washington's turn toward more unilateral and hegemonic policies under the administration of George W. Bush. As a result, onetime faithful U.S. allies in many regions of the world can no longer be described as just that. Turkey is part of this trend.

But we are also witnessing a historic trend toward the forging of renewed interrelationships between Turkey and the Middle East. The consequences of this trend are not yet fully clear but are likely to be generally positive for most parties. This trend transcends the vision of the JDP alone and represents a slowly emerging Turkish national consensus of sorts. As a powerful, stable, advanced, and democratic Middle Eastern state, Turkey is now moving—indeed, compelled to move—toward more independent involvement in a troubled region where it has vital interests. In the end, it is the complex interplay between the United States, the European Union, and Turkey's non-Western interests that will define what Turkey does in the Middle East and broader Muslim world.

As an extension of this thesis, this book will also argue that Turkey's relationship with the United States is now in the process of permanently losing much of its earlier closeness for three main reasons. First, the collapse of the Soviet Union and the reordering of European politics removed the primary strategic geopolitical threat to Turkey. Second, at roughly the same time, Washington's regional agenda in the Middle East came to be increasingly perceived as being at odds with Ankara's own interests in the region. Third, Ankara has increasingly developed new strategic openings to the Muslim world, Eurasia, Russia, and China that offer alternative political and economic options to the country. Although these openings have greatly accelerated under the JDP, I view this particular shift as a long-term geopolitical one that will irrevocably change Ankara's links to Washington.

From Washington's vantage point, Turkey is now a much more difficult and independent-minded ally that is far less reliable than it was in previous decades—some might even say it has been lost. To be sure, today Turkey's geopolitics are diversifying, expanding, and coming of age. In the future, therefore, far more complex skills and mutual sensitivities will be required on both sides to better manage and navigate the Turkish-American relationship. This book will examine the implications of Turkey's current trajectory and recent developments within Turkey and across the region for both U.S. and Turkish goals and interests in the Muslim world.

The Organization of the Book

There is an inherent tension between a topical and chronological presentation of a country's evolving identity and strategic outlook, but this book tries to straddle both. The historical legacy of the Ottoman and early Republican (Kemalist) periods are extremely important in revealing two essentially contradictory visions of what Turkey was and is. Therefore, the first part of this book explores these contradictory visions and argues that Turkey's future will represent a fusion of these two powerful legacies. After all, an understanding of the key legacies of Turkey's past is essential for understanding what the psychological and cultural foundations of the country are—and for understanding where the country is coming from and what its future trajectory might then be.

Specifically, I will identify the key political, cultural, and psychological events that have influenced the tumultuous ride Turkey has experienced over the last hundred and fifty years and that continue to affect Turkish foreign policy thinking. To do so, I will highlight four eras: the late Ottoman era, the Kemalist reform era, the early Cold War era and Turkey's strategic embrace of the West, and the present era in which Turkey has made gradual but accelerating moves toward greater independence in foreign policy.

With this understanding of Turkey's past historical trajectory, I will then examine Turkey's sources of influence and its present relations with the Muslim world. As I will argue, Turkey's relationships with its neighbors are colored by their respective histories, meaning the past continues to have a hold on the present, but there are signs that this is changing. Thus, the middle part of this book addresses some of Turkey's key bilateral relations, such as with Syria, Iraq, Iran, Israel, the United States, and many others, and examines how and why the weight of the past is diminishing.

The last part of this book examines alternative futures for Turkey in the Muslim world, particularly as they affect relations with the United States, the European Union, and power centers in the Middle East and Eurasia. It concludes with a set of policy recommendations for the United States in dealing with an increasingly independent-minded and evolving Turkey.

Part I

Turkey's Historical Trajectory

1

The Historical Lens

Turkish Attitudes toward the Middle East

Turks have felt divorced now from the Middle East for at least four generations. Few great-grandmothers are left in Turkey who can share personal memories of the Ottoman Empire with their families. Decades of Kemalist-oriented history instruction indoctrinated the country to think negatively about the Islamic world in general and the Arab world in particular. Turks have been socialized to associate the Muslim world only with backwardness and extremism. Yet these Turkish views are based more on ideology and prejudice than on genuine knowledge of the area. As Turkish scholar Bülent Aras argues, Turkey's perception of the Middle East has been in part a mirror image of Turkey's own self-image as created by the Kemalist elite. Although this self-image is being challenged by a diverse and broad spectrum of domestic views and interests, this self-image—and the often paranoid tendency of the elite to perceive threats to itself—has played a central role in the formulation of traditional Turkish foreign policy.[1]

As a result, even among Turkey's highly professional diplomatic class, the Middle East has been viewed negatively. Many Turkish diplomats are uncomfortable serving in the region and see postings there as an unfortunate reality of diplomatic life. For them, most "real" diplomacy is conducted with the West, not with the East. Indeed, Turkish diplomats—highly educated, professional, and polished in European languages—know virtually no Arabic, nor are they taught it. In the face of growing regional cataclysms, however, such a situation may be on the threshold of change; linguistic and cultural knowledge of the region will become increasingly important for Ankara and its diplomatic corps. Interestingly, the Turkish military, with a far more realistic eye, already has training institutes in which non-European languages are taught to select officers.

Conflicting Views of History

There are at least three basic lenses for viewing the trajectory of Turkey's course: Kemalist, historical, and cyclical/dialectical. Each of these lenses offers much truth, but none by themselves captures the whole story.

---

1. Bülent Aras, *Turkey and The Greater Middle East* (Istanbul: Tasam Publications, 2004), 17–24.

Although the view of Turkey's trajectory differs significantly depending on the lens employed, one thing is clear across all lenses: Turkey's strategic identity is still in the process of formation.

The Kemalist View: Turkey's Radical Break with History

The traditional view of Turkey's trajectory reflects the classic foundational ideology of Kemalist—or Atatürkist—Turkey. In its most orthodox form, this view is still embraced by a large, though diminishing, portion of Turkish elites; until recently, it represented the *sole* view of Turkish history known to most Westerners. This Kemalist narrative portrays the foundation of the Turkish Republic in 1923 as a radical turning point in Turkish history, taking the country in a dramatic new direction following the collapse of the decaying multicultural empire of the Ottomans. In this view, the Kemalist period transformed the post-Ottoman state into a westernized, homogeneous, ethnically based nation-state. Perceived to be a natural part of advanced Western civilization, this new nation-state rejected the backward and repressive nature of its Islamic past.

This westernizing vision was vouchsafed to a Kemalist elite that would shepherd Turkey out of its dark Ottoman past and into a brighter and enlightened westernized future. With Turkey's modern national narrative and founding myth shaped to meet the goals and needs of this Kemalist elite, this vision has been safeguarded by the army, which serves as the primary guardian of the Kemalist legacy. In fact, it is designed to protect the country from any element that threatens a return to an Islamic-based polity or that advocates the promotion of non-Turkish ethnic identities. While committed to democracy in principle, the army's guardianship role has compelled it in the past to intervene in the face of ideological threats. As a result, over the past eighty years, it has periodically acted to restore the country to the path set forth by Atatürk—"democracy on training wheels," as one wag observed.

In the classic Kemalist view, then, Turkey is profoundly committed to facing West, and the Middle East is seen as a dangerous and subversive force from which Turkey must be protected in order to preserve the purity of Atatürk's westernizing legacy. Many Turks still speak of Turkey's Western "calling," implying an instinctive, near mystical, and even inherent Turkish orientation toward Western institutions and civilization. This view of Turkey is also popular in the West for at least two reasons: (1) it is flattering to the Western self-image, and (2) it reaffirms a commitment to close Turkish strategic cooperation with the West in fulfillment of the Western political and security agenda.

But what, exactly, is meant by the term "westernization" in the Turkish context? From the earliest days of westernizing reforms in the nineteenth-century Ottoman Empire, westernization did not refer to a cultural project as such but rather to the acquisition of the West's power—particularly for defensive purposes to better fend off the encroachments of Western imperialism. In fact, the history of modernization in the developing world as a whole demonstrates that westernization was generally perceived as a form of modernization and self-strengthening and not as a form cultural emulation. This was true even of nineteenth-century Meiji Japan, a country that pursued its own quite distinctive form of modernization while consciously preserving its Japanese character. All of this came at a time when the West represented the only extant model(s) of modernization.

Thus, Muslims have worked for centuries to divine the true "secrets" of Western power that have allowed it to dominate the rest of the world. Westerners have flattered themselves in the belief that this whole process shows "they want to be like us," when in reality they want to be "powerful like us." Westernization in this light is really a defensive process, a form of nationalism, a quest for the most efficient means to match the West's success in order to fend it off and to reduce dependency upon outsiders for national security. While this kind of westernization undeniably represents a kind of acknowledgment of the success of the Western model, its adoption became almost a weapon by which to resuscitate local power. Failure to grasp this essential point is to misread much of the history of westernization in the Muslim world.

Even Mustafa Kemal Atatürk's own westernizing process reflected suspicions about Western intentions toward Turkey and its interests. Furthermore, his approach to reform, while filled with vitality during his lifetime, congealed into an -ism after his death. As a result, reforms have been implemented by his successors in ways that Atatürk himself might not have necessarily approved. Significantly, Kemalism has branched into several different schools, including nationalist, leftist, and even Islamic, with each competing ideological school claiming him as its own.

From this perspective, then, a dual view of the West exists in Turkey, even within the Kemalist tradition. The West is admired as a powerful, advanced, and accomplished civilization, but it is also recognized as a long-standing source of imperialist aggression that was a key force in the dismantling and destruction of the Ottoman Empire. Western powers even sought to dismember the newly emerging Turkish Republic and might have been successful were it not for Atatürk's brilliant generalship that drove forces from four countries out of Anatolia. Thus, the West is admired more for *what it is*, including for being powerful, than for what it does in the world.

While there are indeed many elements of truth to this Kemalist view—particularly concerning Atatürk's role as national savior and his bold and visionary role in building a strong new state—it tells only part of the story.

The Historical View: The Role of Continuity in Turkish History

A second view of Turkey's trajectory starts not with the formation of the new Turkish Republic but rather with a much longer reform process that began with the *tanzimat* (administrative reforms) of 1839. This reform process—which included liberalization, the adoption of many aspects of Western law, a rationalization of administration, exposure to Western techniques of governance, and greater centralization of state power—proceeded with fits and starts through the nineteenth century and into the Young Turk period (1908–1918), World War I, and the early modern Turkish Republic.

This view, accepted by a broad range of foreign scholars, emphasizes with greater historical accuracy the threads of continuity between the late Ottoman Empire and the Kemalist reform period. Proponents of this view point out that the Kemalist reforms—as vital, powerful, and significant as they were—had clear antecedents in the previous century; they did not spring out of nowhere or represent a total about-face in Turkish history. However, this view in no way diminishes the extraordinary impact of Atatürk as reformer and savior. But it sees him as representing the culmination and institutionalization of a long- and well-established elitist bureaucracy and reformist tradition that had its ultimate victory with the republic's formation.

In this view, therefore, the Kemalist reforms are not seen as being totally "revolutionary," particularly given their antecedents that stretched back nearly a century. And Atatürk's import rests not so much on his revolutionary vision but in his skill and ability to codify Turkey's reformist past, to bureaucratize reforms under a committed elite, and to impose them on the new state with extraordinary results. Although the transition from multinational empire to ethnically based nation-state did lead to dramatic shifts in Turkey's borders, structure of government, ideology, and public culture, Atatürk's authoritarian approach was remarkably enlightened for its time considering so many of his contemporaries: Franco in Spain, Hitler in Germany, Mussolini in Italy, Stalin in Russia, and Chiang Kai-Shek in China.

This perspective has understandably been less popular among Kemalist ideologues than historians because it grants importance to pre-Kemalist intellectual, political, legal, psychological, and social reform in an era generally viewed in quite negative terms in Kemalist thinking. Over time, however, educated Turks have increasingly come to recognize that the Ottoman period was not as dark and primitive as popularly portrayed in early Kemalist writing, that there were many Ottoman accomplishments and developments about which Turks can be proud, and that modern Turkey need not be cut off from this historical continuum.

The Cyclical/Dialectical View

A third view of Turkey's trajectory, one that I personally espouse, accepts both the centrality of Kemalist institutionalized change and the grand continuity of reformist tradition going back to Ottoman times. But this view believes that the Kemalist reforms introduced a number of authoritarian innovations and forms of discrimination into Turkish political, social, and ideological life; some of these reforms, in the light of history, can now be seen as harmful excesses, breaking too sharply and unrealistically with mainstream Turkish culture. In harsher terms, we might say that Atatürk performed a kind of "cultural lobotomy" on Turkey that produced a national amnesia about the country's Islamic and Ottoman past. This was done with the aim of creating a new nationalism through a racially oriented rereading of pre-Islamic Turkish history. (This race-related rewriting of history paralleled similar trends in German, Hungarian, Greek, Iranian, Slavic, Zionist, Japanese, and many other ethnoracial movements of the period.)

As a result, modern Turkish history from 1950 on has demonstrated a gradual process of redressing Kemalist ideological excesses and returning to a more comfortable and "normal" relationship with the nation's prerepublic past. With traditional cultural values gaining strength within Turkey, a new synthesis that marries elements from both the Kemalist tradition and the country's Islamic Ottoman past is being created. In turn, this synthesis is beginning to heal three key psychological and cultural wounds from the Kemalist nation-building process. These wounds include

- a legacy of authoritarianism that has not been fully abandoned even today by portions of the Kemalist elite and that is represented particularly by the persistence of a major military voice over aspects of national policies;
- the exclusion and suppression of non-Turkish ethnic identities (mainly Kurdish) in the process of building the new European-style and purportedly "ethnically homogeneous" nation-state;
- the vilification of Islam and Islamic traditions implicit in the Enlightenment-driven reforms of the Kemalist period, which alienated huge sections of the more traditional social classes that take pride in their Islamic and Ottoman past, even while accepting the need for reform and change in strengthening the nation, and that are now entering the mainstream Turkish body politic.

This psychological and cultural healing process is being spurred by increased democratization within the country, a growing acceptance of the multiethnic and multicultural character of Turkish society and the place of religion within it, a greater acknowledgment of the country's Islamic Ottoman past, and a better understanding of Turkey's place in the Muslim world. The process is not only well advanced, but it is also psychologically extremely healthy: contrary to Kemalist fears, it will actually strengthen the fabric and resilience of modern Turkish society.[2]

---

2. Graham E. Fuller, "Turkey's Strategic Model: Myths and Realities," *Washington Quarterly* (Summer 2004).

The New Turkey and Foreign Policy

How we perceive today's events, then, depends greatly on how we view Turkey's past. Will Turkey recommit to Kemalism's full ideological program, with all its strengths and weaknesses? Or are the country's Kemalist roots evolving, diversifing, and offering alternative paths of development? Equally important, must Turkey continually bolster and "prove" its Western orientation through fulfillment of Western, and especially U.S., policy preferences? Or is Turkey's identity now strong enough that it can afford to seek an independent path on many key regional issues, particularly when Ankara sees Washington's policies as being unwise or unhelpful to its interests?

In the end, the power and cultural weight of history cannot be denied; it has tugged insistently on modern Turkish culture and society. Although it was mostly unseen and underground during the early Kemalist period, it began to emerge more boldly as Turkey democratized and opened up in the second half of the twentieth century. As a result, the country's Islamic Ottoman past is regaining a position of respectability across Turkish society, to the special satisfaction of more traditionalist religious and conservative circles. In turn, this reemergence is leading to a greater cultural and political balance within Turkey that embraces both the country's extraordinarily rich past and its (sometimes bumpy) EU-bound future. But to fully understand Turkey's present and future trajectory, we must first more fully understand its past.

2

The Ottoman Era

The Ottoman Experience: Good or Bad?

It is cliché to say that Turks do not like Arabs. In popular Turkish parlance, Arabs are variously described as lazy, dishonest, backward, treacherous, and fanatic. For their part, the Arabs popularly describe Turks as slow-witted, harsh, imperious, stubborn, fawning toward the West, and confused about their own self-identity. In a world in which few peoples have flattering views of their neighbors, Turks and Arabs are no exception. But most Turks today have also never met an Arab, do not speak Arabic, and have never set foot in an Arab country. Yet, over many centuries during the Ottoman period, both peoples had a more balanced and respectful view of each other, largely because they shared a common space and had greater interaction.

Serious enmity between Turks and Arabs has not been a historical constant, was not foreordained, and only began to emerge in the last days of the Ottoman Empire, when the multinational state gave way to a collection of ethnically based, nationalistic, and rival nation-states. But this almost century-long stage of Arab-Turkish political hostility may be waning, opening up prospects for new and more productive relationships. In turn, the Ottoman legacy may now be viewed with greater balance on all sides.

Ottoman Legitimacy—and Its Legacy

The longevity of the Ottoman Empire rested to a great extent upon the legitimacy it held among Muslims. In an age of shifting rulers, borders, and empires, the extension of Ottoman power across the Arab world contained few ethnic overtones: its extension of power was carried out in the name of the Faith. Like the Seljuk Turks before them, the Ottomans established new urban orders replete with charitable institutions, educational establishments, and Islamic courts. Ottoman military power shared a commitment to the expansion of Islam, the defense of the sharia, and concern for the basic interests of the Muslim community.[1] Local rulers, usually selected from the local elites or "notables," enjoyed considerable autonomy

---

1. Ira Lapidus, *A History of Islamic Societies* (New York: Cambridge University Press, 1988), 310–22.

as long as they met their tax obligations to Istanbul, maintained basic order, and acknowledged the suzerainty of the Ottoman Court.

"Ottomanism"—Back to the Future

In the nineteenth century, the Ottoman Empire began facing a triple threat: European imperial designs on its territory; uprisings and rebellions among Christian populations of the Balkans who had been infected with ideas of European ethnonationalism and who were often provoked by Europe; and internal reformist ideas and demands to make the empire more efficient, more capable of resisting European threats, and more equitable and representative.

As the Ottoman administration cast about for remedies to these multiple threats, it developed an interesting fusion of Islamic concepts, reformist initiatives, and Western nationalism in the form of the doctrine of *Ottomanism*—an ideology that was meant to create a new sense of "national" loyalty to the multinational empire. Ottomanism represented a conscious effort to synthesize Islamic ideas with those of the Western Enlightenment. It called for loyalty not to the sultan or to one's *millet* (ethnoreligious community), but to an Ottoman *vatan* (homeland or nation) that was the common property of *all* peoples within the Ottoman state and that superceded traditional local, ethnic, and religious identities. This was a new concept of common Ottoman citizenship that promised legal equality for all.[2] This ideology called for a spirit of modernization within the framework of existing Ottoman culture and not through wholesale adoption of Western practices and culture—as the Kemalists reformers would later do.[3]

In the end, Ottomanism, as a "nationalist" expression of loyalty to the empire, did not succeed in diverting rising local nationalism among the Christian regions of the Balkans, but it did have much resonance among the Muslim population, including Arabs. While innovative, this new ideology could not save the empire; the rush of world events would eventually bring World War I and the empire's breakup.[4]

The Arabs and the Breakup of the Empire

Contrary to popular myths on both sides, Turks and Arabs have not been longtime foes. If relations between them are to improve, both sides need to revisit the past to gain a clearer understanding of what actually did and did not happen between them as the empire moved toward collapse. The essential reality is that the Arab populations of the empire remained loyal

---

2. Dietrich Jung and Wolfango Piccoli, *Turkey at the Crossroads: Ottoman Legacies and a Greater Middle East* (London: Zed Books, 2001), 44–5.
3. Erik J. Zürcher, *Turkey, A Modern History*, (London: L.B Tauris, 1997), 132.
4. See Serif Mardin's masterful *The Genesis of Young Ottoman Thought* (Princeton, N.J.: Princeton University Press, 1962) for the definitive treatment of this period.

to it in principle almost up to the moment of its breakup. Yet in the popular Turkish view of today, the empire's Arab population "stabbed Turkey in the back" by siding with the English and French. Similarly, modern Arab nationalism tells of deep Arab longing for liberation from Turkish colonialism. Neither of these views are in keeping with actual historical events.

While the empire's Balkan Christian minorities did engage in a series of rebellions and calls for national liberation against the Ottoman state beginning in the nineteenth century, the empire's Arab population was largely committed to the state's continued functioning virtually to the end of World War I. The Arab populations had elected representatives in the early Ottoman experiments in parliamentary government, and many Arab politicians and leaders joined hands with their Turkish counterparts in calling for reforms within the empire. But as Ottoman reformers sought to strengthen and modernize the state, they inevitably turned to greater centralization, a goal often not appreciated by local notables and provincial authorities seeking to preserve maximum local autonomy. Although these reforms produced some friction, Arabs fully accepted the empire's legitimacy.

Local grievances were perceived as something to be negotiated within the political order and not as grounds for rebellion against the Ottoman state. For most Muslims, membership in a multiethnic Muslim empire was in keeping with the character of Muslim history and was entirely appropriate. Thus, the Ottoman state, its parliament, and administrative order were broadly accepted by Arabs right on into World War I, despite British and French efforts to undermine Ottoman authority in the Arab world. Even the Arab ulema remained almost unanimously loyal to Ottoman power and institutions during this period.[5]

Arab Versus Turkish Nationalism

Today's familiar concepts of Arab and Turkish nationalism were still inchoate during most of the nineteenth century; local identities provided the primary distinguishing features among Muslims. Although Turkish and Arab nationalism would powerfully emerge over time, nationalism was not the proximate cause of the breakup of the empire in its Muslim regions.[6] As Middle East historian Rashid Khalidi points out,

> For most of its adherents before 1914, Arabism did not mean Arab separatism, nor did it conflict with loyalty to the Ottoman Empire or to its religious legitimizing principle. . . .

5. Ernest Dawn, "The Origins of Arab Nationalism," in *The Origins of Arab Nationalism*, ed. Rashid Khalidi et al., eds, (New York: Columbia University Press, New York, 1991), 19.
6. See, in particular, the discussions in Khalidi et al., eds., *The Origins of Arab Nationalism*.

There were ideological differences between Ottomanists and Arabists in the Arab provinces of the Ottoman Empire, but these involved the concrete political issues of the day, such as the best means of resistance to imperialism or the proper balance of centralization versus decentralization, rather than whether the Arabs should remain part of the empire. This was simply not an issue for most Arabists before 1914.[7]

The romantic concept of the "Arab revolt" of 1916 against Ottoman rule, popularized by Lawrence of Arabia, had little to do with Arab nationalism. It was mostly due to the Hijazi quest for a local hereditary empire, the desire to maintain sharia law, and the fear of Ottoman taxes. The "revolt" itself played a strategically trivial role in the empire's fate.[8] The forces of ethnic Arab nationalism really only achieved supremacy after the collapse of the empire and the takeover of the Arab world by British and French colonial powers. As scholar William Cleveland notes,

"The Ottoman Empire still viewed itself as the universal protector of Islam. And the support the vast majority of Ottoman Muslims gave to the empire's war effort demonstrated that even though the [Young Turk] government was not particularly well liked, its devotion to the defense of the Ottoman-Islamic order against European ambitions was shared by the population at large.[9]

The Emergence of Pan-Islamism

To maintain the integrity of vast Muslim parts of the empire, Sultan Abdülhamit II turned to the ideology of pan-Islamism, issuing a broad warning that the seat of the Muslim world was under threat from Western unbelievers and calling for Muslim unity against the European Christian enemy invader. As an ideological counterstrike, he also called for liberation of all Muslim minorities who were under British, French, and Russian colonial control and oppression.[10] The very concept of a pan-Islamic policy today is of course absolutely anathema to modern Turkey's Kemalist ideology and secular values; nonetheless, history reveals how widespread pan-Islamic thinking was in Istanbul barely a decade before the foundation of the Turkish Republic.

---

7. Rashid Khalidi, "Ottomanism and Arabism in Syria before 1914: A Reassessment," in *The Origins of Arab Nationalism*, ed. Khalidi et al., 62–3.
8. William Ochsenwald, "Ironic Origins: Arab Nationalism in the Hijaz, 1882–1914," in *The Origins of Arab Nationalism*, 190–4.
9. William Cleveland, *A History of the Modern Middle East*, 2nd ed. (Boulder, Colo.: Westview, 2000), 150.
10. Jung and Wolfango, *Turkey at the Crossroads*, 48; and Jacob M. Landau, *The Politics of Pan-Islam* (Oxford: Clarendon Press, 1994), 81–3, 94.

Although a pan-Islamic ideology almost certainly will never be adopted as a basis for foreign policy in contemporary Turkey, the reality is that today's Muslim world is still in search of a leader. In view of its present leadership deficit—there is hardly a single leader who commands broad respect across the region—Turkey is being listened to more carefully as an increasingly respected, independent, and successful Muslim voice. Many Turks likely have minimal interest in filling such a leadership role, and many Muslims are unlikely to call upon Turkey to play this role, but as long as this vacuum exists, Turkey may ultimately be more qualified and capable of exerting its influence across the region than almost any other Muslim state. At the least, Turks and Arabs may soon come to revisit their centuries-long experience of fruitful cultural and political interaction that ended with World War I.

3

The Kemalist Experience

The Kemalists Break with the Muslim World

The period following World War I was one of intense turmoil and change for Turkey. It witnessed the empire's collapse, the defeat of Western imperialist attempts to curtail and marginalize the fledgling Turkish state, and Atatürk's determination to reform, westernize, and construct a new Turkish identity. Yet, as dramatically reformist as the Kemalist mission was, this reforming instinct did not emerge from a vacuum. As discussed in chapter 1, the Kemalist reforms represented a culmination of and moment of triumph for the reform movements of the nineteenth-century Ottoman Empire.[1]

Recreating the Turkish State and Nation

The Kemalists sought to create a new Turkish nation-state founded explicitly on Turkish ethnic nationalism and a new set of nationalist values that would replace the multiethnic, multireligious, and Islam-oriented values of the Ottoman Empire. In one of his first acts, Atatürk quickly displaced the traditional religious class. Although it had already been disempowered and intellectually impoverished by an increasingly secularizing Ottoman state in the areas of law and education,[2] the Kemalists confiscated the ulema's extensive endowment lands (evkaf), the traditional institutional source of its economic power. As a result, total state control was extended over all aspects of religious institutions, practices, and personnel, and sweeping cultural changes were implemented.

Additionally, history was rewritten to bolster the new ethnically based nation-state: Turkish glory began not with Islam but in the eras long before Islam; some writers suggested that Turkish history had become bogged down in Islam. Even the Turkish language was radically reworked: a massive purge of Arabic and Persian loanwords at the heart of Ottoman Turkish gave way to the creation of a broad new vocabulary created out of old Turkish root words, and the Arabic alphabet itself was abolished in

---

1. Jung and Piccoli, *Turkey at the Crossroads*, 200.
2. Serif Mardin, *The Genesis of Young Ottoman Thought* (Princeton, N.J.: Princeton University Press, 1962), 127, 408.

favor of the Latin. In one stroke, these changes shut down for subsequent generations routine access to the entire corpus of the Ottoman literary past. In politics, the sultanate was abolished in favor of a republic. Further, select Western legal codes were adopted wholesale and all vestiges of Islamic law scrapped. Western clothing became the new and required norm, and women were discouraged from using any kind of veil.

Abolition of the Caliphate and Its International Impact

Turkey delivered the most significant blow of all to its relationship with the Muslim world in 1924 when Atatürk abolished the very institution of the caliphate itself, the supreme religious office of the entire Sunni world. This was an act of extraordinary importance. While Atatürk certainly was free to implement reforms within Turkey, the abolition of the caliphate was an act that affected Muslims everywhere. It was roughly akin to a snap decision by an Italian prime minister to abolish the papacy without consultation with the worldwide Catholic community.

In the waning days of the Ottoman Empire, the sultan had vigorously sought to play the pan-Islamic card to rally support for the empire against European imperialist attacks. Many Muslims around the world had responded to this call, fearful that Western imperialists would take advantage of Ottoman weakness and come to dominate the Muslim world. In fact, this was just what European imperialists were in the process of doing, extending imperial control over nearly all of the Muslim dominions of the Ottoman Empire, most notably the Arab world.

Thus, abolition of the caliphate came as a body blow to Islam itself, at once depriving the Muslim *ummah* of both its central institution and supreme religious figure, a potent symbol of Islamic identity, power, and legitimacy that had existed for more than thirteen hundred years. Today, the Muslim world still finds no champion in its midst, and the continuing absence of a caliphate has found new resonance among many Islamist movements of the twenty-first century. Indeed, this absence is perceived by many as symptomatic of the overall weakness and division of Islam today. And with the creation of the GWOT, fear among Muslims of a new Western anti-Muslim crusade is especially powerful today. As a result, the caliphate remains a key symbolic and political office that may be awaiting the emergence of some enterprising religious leader—not necessarily a fire-breathing radical. All of this highlights the fatefulness of the Turkish decision of 1924 and informs the Muslim world's attitude toward Turkey—past, present, and future.

Muslim Sense of Rejection

For Muslims, especially Arabs, Kemalist Turkey represented a total rejection of Islam, of the Arab and broader Muslim world, of their long-standing ties with the Turks, and of their shared culture. Furthermore, it represented a denigration of Islam as a religion, a strategic abandonment of the Arabs to imperialist powers with whom Turkey quickly fell in league, and an overall sapping of Muslim power at a time when Turkish power had never been more needed to face growing Western threats.

Atatürk was not alone in rewriting history: it was to come on the Arab side as well. As Turkish foreign policy scholar Ahmet Davutoğlu points out, the Arab nationalist movement that became mainstream only after World War I retroactively came to perceive its years of inclusion within the empire as representing a removal of Arabs from the historical stage (*tarihsizleşme*). In this view, Arab history "ended" in 1258 with the fall of the Abbasid Caliphate to the Mongols. Thereafter, the Arabs ceased to be independent players on the international scene due to their subordination first to the Seljuk Turks and later to the Ottoman Turks. Arab nationalists came to believe that if they had been able to maintain their independence and to develop their own institutions and power over those centuries, they might have been better prepared to resist European imperialism—just as Turkey did after World War I.[3]

Davutoğlu also points out that Turks do not employ their own rich Ottoman archives in formulating their views of the Arab world; they rely on Western sources and train few of their own Ottoman historians. Thus, the Kemalist historical lobotomy performed on the Turkish public—the expunging of Turkey's Ottoman past—has had lasting impact: both Arabs and Turks are now operating off prejudices, pumped-up nationalist myths, and skewed historical understandings of each other that prevent mature mutual recognition, much less close cooperation.[4] Perhaps now that the two worlds have been sharply isolated from each other for three-quarters of a century, they may have developed secure enough identities to return to a new, mature, and productive interrelationship. The artificial barriers of their respective founding nationalist myths may be giving way to the new realities of the region.

From an Arab perspective, Islam is still seen as one of the key commonalities that could bridge the fateful gap between them. Many Arabs hope that the legacy of past cooperation could lead the Turks to be more sympathetic toward and supportive of the Arab world in its current plight. For this reason, many Arabs have been delighted at the JDP's ascension to power in Ankara—however moderate and depoliticized its Islamic roots may be. The JDP's electoral success is interpreted as an indicator that Turkey is rediscovering its roots and becoming interested in the broader Muslim

---

3. Ahmet Davutoğlu, *Stratejik Derinlik: Türkiye'nin Uluslararası Konumu* [*Strategic Depth: Turkey's Place in the World*] (Istanbul: Küre Yayınları, 2001), 406–9.

4. Davutoğlu, *Stratejik Derinlik*, 409.

world. Few Arabs expect that growing interest should come at the expense of Turkey's ties with the West. Rather, they see it as something that could complement Turkey's Western ties, allowing Ankara to bring its strength to bear to help facilitate East-West ties.

These sentiments have grown considerably since the launch of the GWOT, which is perceived to have delivered a body blow to Arab dignity, independence, strength, and stability. Of course no Arab wants to go back to Turkish domination of the region, but many of them would welcome a powerful new ally who could help in breaking current Arab isolation and weakness. Arab expectations may outrun reality in this regard, but new Arab interest in Turkey is in itself highly notable. In turn, Turks are slowly becoming aware of this Arab interest.

Turkish Denigration of the Arab World

After World War I, the Arab world lay well outside Turkish foreign policy thinking for multiple reasons: (1) the Arab world had ceased to be part of the Turkish state; (2) neighboring Arab states were under European mandate control and could therefore play no real role on the international scene or pose any threat to Ankara; (3) Turkey was internally absorbed with its new nation-building tasks; and (4) Turkey's priority was to build new ties with its erstwhile European enemies. Additionally, a pronounced Kemalist denigration of Arab and Islamic culture dominated Ankara's thinking. Islamic culture was seen as the source of Turkish backwardness and weakness, the "other" out of which an enlightened new Turkey would arise. As a result, study of Arabic and Arab culture nearly disappeared within Turkey, except among a small minority engaged in religious studies.

The Internal "Islamic Threat"

Turkey's strategic paranoia—or "Sèvres complex," which refers to the humiliating treaty of defeat the empire was forced to sign after World War I and later rejected by Atatürk—is not just an exercise in nervous Turkish imagination. To invoke "Sèvres" today is still an emotive call for remembrance and a reminder to never again permit foreigners to act in ways that might dismember or cripple Turkey. (The Kurdish problem is viewed particularly in this light.) Gaining Western recognition of the republic's sovereignty, therefore, was key to Turkey's survival as an independent nation. After all, the empire's territories had been constant prey to endless nibbling annexation by Europe and Russia, and the new republic had only just recently repelled British, French, Italian, and Greek military efforts to seize significant portions of Anatolia, to control the Bosphorus, and to grant large national homelands in Anatolia to Kurds and Armenians.

As a result, the early Kemalist state feared potential internal dissidence—religious and ethnic—that could constitute a fifth column exploitable by external powers. While large numbers of clerics fully supported Kemal's struggle to save Turkish soil from infidel aggression, few were comfortable with the new secularizing measures that ended the caliphate and stripped Islamic institutions of all power. In the eyes of many fervent Turkish nationalists, Islam and the clerics became the antithesis of Turkish patriotism, a highly suspect if not traitorous element within the Turkish polity. The Kemalists quickly propagated the view that the Arab world was not only the source of Ottoman backwardness but also threatened to drag Turkey back into the "dark ages." In short, it came to represent an anti-Turkish force in the region.

While the republic did face genuine external enemies, Kemalist ideology tended to incorporate a fear of external powers and conspiracies as a key element in its world outlook. This paranoia toward the outside world helped both to preserve Turkey's domestic power and to justify an authoritarian approach to guarding the nation against external threats. The most telling feature of this outlook was Turkey's poor relations with virtually every single one of its neighbors for more than five decades. Until recently, in speaking to Western policymakers, Turkish officials commonly justify their hard-line views with the quip, "We live in a bad neighborhood." This line—also used by many Israelis—usually evinces chuckles among Westerners, but its intent is meant to win Western acceptance of hard-line Turkish views and Turkey's security-driven foreign policy.

Yet even in the Kemalist period, Ankara needed to regularize its new borders with Iraq, Syria, and Iran. While Atatürk established the firm principle of neutrality, irredentism, and noninterference in the region, exceptions were made when it came to Turkey's unresolved territorial disputes, particularly with Iraq and Syria, which further contributed to worsening relations between Turkey and its Arab neighbors.

Iraq and the Dispute over Mosul

Following the collapse of the Ottoman Empire, the delineation of the Turkey-Iraq border remained in question for some eight years and included often intense diplomatic negotiations with Britain and even hints of force. In 1926, Turkey finally gave in, reluctantly giving up the Mosul region to British-ruled Iraq.[5] (Oil was not struck in the area until 1927.) As a result, the Mosul issue remains a historical memory for both sides, and Iraq remains suspicious of Turkish intentions there. The issue still figures prominently in today's diplomacy over the future of the Iraqi city of Kirkuk.

---

5. Hale, *Turkish Foreign Policy,* 71–2.

Syria and Hatay/Alexandretta

After the collapse of the empire and the Ottoman withdrawal from its province of Greater Syria, the area lay open to the mercy of European imperial powers. It was carved up into the new "artificial" states of Lebanon, Palestine, Jordan, and Syria—each of which became a mandate of either Britain or France. For Arab nationalists, the process was a bitter disappointment. Although it hoped for independence as promised by the British before World War I, post-war Syria found its province torn asunder. Furthermore, Ottoman overlords had simply been replaced by European imperial administrators who were far less culturally linked to Arabs than the Ottoman Turks.

Although the new Kemalist government renounced all claims to ethnic Arab territory, one key area of dispute with Syria remained: the region of Alexandretta (Hatay in Turkish) in Syria's then-northwestern Mediterranean border. Although a part of French-controlled Syria, Turkey claimed the region on the grounds that its Turkish population constituted the region's largest single ethnic group—in what was, in reality, a highly multicultural and multireligious area. In June 1939, following a referendum, France ceded control of Alexandretta to Turkey over the strong objection of the Syrians. Syria remained bitter about what it viewed as a Turkish land grab blessed by imperialist France, and the Alexandretta issue became symbolic of the deeper frictions yet to come between the two states in the Cold War period. Not until December 2004, when Turkish prime minister Recep Tayyip Erdoğan visited Damascus, did the two countries agree to officially recognize the border between them in the context of a broader rapprochement.[6]

Iran

Turkey initiated the 1937 signing of the four-power Saadabad Pact with Iran, Afghanistan, and Iraq. The pact called for noninterference in one another's affairs, nonaggression, and a commitment to consultation on common problems. Scholar William Hale attributes this pact to the desire of these four states to demonstrate solidarity and a new unity of purpose against any would-be European aggressors. The pact also focused on common firmness to control their respective large Kurdish minorities (except in Afghanistan) and to discourage manipulation of the Kurds as a foreign policy instrument.[7] Despite these commitments, however, the Saadabad Pact was not enough to prevent Britain and Russia from carving up Iran

---

6. Yoav Stern, "Turkey Singing a New Tune," *Haaretz*, January 9, 2005, www.haaretz.com/hasen/spages/524517.html.

7. Hale, *Turkish Foreign Policy*, 62; and Safa A. Hussein, "Turkish-Iranian Relations: Competition over Iraq," *Bitter Lemons Middle East Roundtable* 4, no. 18 (May 18, 2006), www.bitter-lemons-international.org.

during World War II, an act to which Turkey and the other signatories were powerless to respond.

Conclusion

Up until World War II, the Muslim world played an extremely modest role in Turkish foreign policy calculations. The new republic remained preoccupied with the more urgent issues of European imperial politics, while most of the Arab world lay under European imperial mandate. As a result, Ankara showed a distinct political coolness if not disdain toward the region and a cultural rejection of it. At the same time, however, Ankara demonstrated a pragmatic recognition of the need to establish normalized bilateral relations with the newly formed Arab states and renounced territorial claims on non-Turkish parts of the Middle East, with the exception of certain border areas of Syria and Iraq. All the while, the creation of new national founding myths and identities on both sides further alienated Turks from Arabs and Arabs from Turks, but global geopolitics would soon drive an even deeper wedge between them during the Cold War.

4

The Cold War Interlude

Turkey Aligned

The Cold War rapidly took on Middle Eastern dimensions, leaving Turkey and the Arab world on opposite sides of the East-West divide. Shaped by the rising Soviet threat, the introduction of Turkey as a new element in Western defense, and increasing Turkish ideological hostility toward the Arab world, it represented a high-water mark in the history of U.S.-Turkish relations. But the Cold War also marked a singularly narrow and unsuccessful era in Turkish foreign policy toward the Middle East.

The Impact of the Rising Soviet Threat

From 1917 to World War II, the Soviet Union was preoccupied with consolidating its power internally and thus posed no threat to Turkey. But historic Turkish-Russian tensions were quickly rekindled with the advent of the Cold War and a series of aggressive acts by Joseph Stalin that directly affected Turkey: he declared Soviet territorial designs on northern Iran; he unilaterally abrogated the 1921 Turkish-Soviet Friendship Pact that had once settled Turkish-Soviet borders; he resuscitated Soviet claims on Turkey's eastern provinces of Kars and Ardahan; he renewed demands for a voice over the control of the Bosphorus; and he called for the establishment of Soviet bases on Turkish soil. Further, as Russia extended its empire into all of Eastern Europe, Soviet forces moved into Bulgaria, Turkey's neighbor.

Ankara quickly abandoned its decades-long Kemalist neutrality and sought protection through close security association with the West. In fact, Ankara declared its willingness to assume a defensive role in the Middle East in return for NATO membership.[1] By 1952, Turkey had become an integral part of the Western security system and was bureaucratically reclassified in Washington as "part of Europe." After centuries of falling victim to European imperial ambition, Turkey had actually achieved protection within the European system.[2] Additionally, Turkey had secured "permanent" and institutionalized security against its most likely adversary—the Soviet Union. All of its other foreign policies flowed from this strategic cornerstone.

---

1. Hale, *Turkish Foreign Policy*, 125.
2. Ibid., 120

.

Turkey as a Western Element in Middle East Defense

In support of Western strategy, Turkey's policies toward the Middle East in this period were limited primarily to quite unsuccessful promotion of anti-Soviet alliances. This partisan approach, often quite overbearing and counterproductive, won Turkey much hostility in the region.[3] Ankara did, however, reap strategic rewards via much increased Western economic and military aid. Ironically, as analysts Dietrich Jung and Wolfango Piccoli write, Turkey had "[re-]inherited the Ottoman task of counterbalancing Russia's political power in the Eastern Mediterranean."[4] Beyond its efforts at strategic pact-making, Turkey did not develop any meaningful bilateral relations with Arab states.

After two failed American- and British-led anti-Soviet security schemes for the Middle East, the United States created the Baghdad Pact in 1955, which was adopted by the United Kingdom, Turkey, Iran, Pakistan, and Afghanistan, and also monarchical Iraq—the sole Arab member. This pact was part of a broader strategy to contain and encircle the Soviet Union. But Turkish and Iraqi governmental support for this pact angered the Arab public, which perceived not Soviet military aggression but the continuing Arab-Israeli military confrontation as the greatest strategic threat facing it.

In 1958 the British-supported Iraqi monarchy was overthrown in a bloody military coup. The new nationalist leadership in Iraq promptly abandoned the pro-Western camp and joined the Arab nationalist camp that looked to Moscow for support. Soon thereafter, the West scrambled to create a new strategic arrangement—the Central Treaty Organization (CENTO)—which included no Arab member states and was limited entirely to the northern tier states of Turkey, Iran, Afghanistan, and Pakistan.

From 1957 to 1967, during the period of Turkey's first democratically elected government under Adnan Menderes, Turkey's foreign policy was almost completely aligned with Western interests.[5] In fact, the degree to which Turkey staunchly aligned itself with the West was dramatically demonstrated in a number of ways:

- In 1955, Turkey told the Jordanian government that if it did not join the Baghdad Pact (it never did) Turkey might find itself one day fighting on Israel's side against Jordan. Following this threat, Washington and London warned the Turks against alienating essentially pro-Western Arab leaders.[6]
- In 1955, Turkey shocked the developing world by casting its vote in the United Nations *against* the independence of Algeria during its

3. Ibid., 129.
4. Jung and Piccoli, *Turkey at the Crossroads*, 137.
5. Ibid., 138.
6. Hale, *Turkish Foreign Policy*, 128

brutal anticolonial war with France. Ankara was presumably suspicious of any national liberation wars.
- In 1957, when communists appeared positioned to seize power in Damascus, Ankara massed troops on Syria's southern border. Although Turkey threatened to unilaterally invade the country, it was cautioned against doing so by the United States and the United Kingdom.[7]
- In 1958, Turkey unsuccessfully called for Western military intervention in Iraq to restore the monarchy after its overthrow.[8]

As a result, this period created the deep and enduring impression that Turkey's strategic orientation was indistinguishable from that of the West. Furthermore, Turkey's actions were not always productive. Comments political scientist Philip Robins, "Turkey's heavy-handedness . . . drove a weak and unstable Syria, a country with an already acute 'Turcophobia', into closer relations with Moscow. To this day the Baghdad Pact saga represents the greatest foreign policy debacle of republican Turkey."[9] Davutoğlu finds a supreme irony in the impression Turkey generated through its actions: although Mustafa Kemal Atatürk had been one of the Muslim world's greatest anti-imperialist strugglers, within two decades of his death, Turkey had come to be viewed by the developing world not as a leader or even as a supporter of national independence but as a diplomatically isolated instrument of Western policy goals.[10]

The Crises of Alignment with Washington

Despite its close ties with the United States, Ankara did undergo two major crises with Washington in the 1960s. The Cuban missile crisis and U.S. policy toward Cyprus both created doubt in Ankara about the reliability of U.S. security guarantees and the degree of U.S. sensitivity to Turkish interests. Both incidents, as well as Turkey's growing diplomatic isolation in the developing world, prompted Turkey to reevaluate its policy of total alignment with the United States.

Ideological Confrontation with the Arab World

While Turkey moved solidly into the Western camp, the Arab world faced a dramatically different strategic situation and began moving in the opposite direction for quite understandable reasons. Most Arab states had only recently gained independence—Algeria as late as 1962. It was a heyday of global anti-

---

7. Ibid., 128–9; and Jung and Piccoli, *Turkey at the Crossroads,* 138.
8. Hale, *Turkish Foreign Policy,* 129; and Jung and Piccoli, *Turkey at the Crossroads,* 138.
9. Philip Robins, *Suits and Uniforms: Turkish Foreign Policy since the Cold War,* (Seattle: University of Washington Press, 2003), 99.
10. Davutoğlu, *Stratejik Derinlik,* 411.

colonial struggle and rising "Third World" consciousness during which the Arab world experienced the impact of the new state of Israel in its midst and the movement of large numbers of Palestinian refugees. Additionally, the Arabs suffered humiliating military defeat at Israel's hands with their ill-conceived declaration of war against the fledgling Jewish state in 1948.

Traumatized by the rising Palestinian refugee problem and successive Arab defeats at the hands of Israel, the Arab states in this period began evolving into "security states" ruled by authoritarian—often military—regimes. In this atmosphere of rising nationalist emotions and anti-imperial consciousness, many Arab leaders increasingly turned to the Soviet Union as a source of arms procurement and as a broader diplomatic counterweight to Western power. Among Moscow's key client states were Syria and Iraq—which sit on Turkey's borders—as well as Algeria, Libya, Egypt, and Yemen. Even pro-Western Arab leaders adopted some degree of neutrality on many international issues, principally because they lacked the ironclad Western security guarantees that NATO-member Turkey had. For the Arabs, balance-of-power policies were the safest to adopt, and Turkey was perceived as having sold itself to the Western camp, as being committed to serving Western strategic needs, and as remaining hostile to Arab needs and aspirations.

Regional State Relationships

Iran. In contrast to Ankara's rather confrontational relationship with the Arab world, its ties with Pahlavi Iran during this period were good. Although the shah often viewed Turkey as a bit of a rival, these ties were based on a shared geopolitical fear of the Soviet Union and a common desire for Western backing, and were maintained up until the Iranian Revolution in 1979. Both states had also shared membership in the Baghdad Pact, CENTO, the Region for Cooperation and Development, which later became the Economic Cooperation Organization (ECO), and other regional organizations, although member states never viewed these cooperative arrangements with any serious importance.

Syria. Turkey's negative relationship with Syria intensified during the Cold War. In the broader context of geopolitical hostility, both Turkey and Syria sought instruments through which to exert pressure on the other: Turkey's main instrument lay in its control of Euphrates water into Syria, while Syria had one in the provision of aid to Kurdish rebels operating against the Turkish state. For example, beginning in the early 1980s, Damascus gave refuge to Kurdish Workers Party (PKK) leader Abdallah Öcalan and provided guerrilla training camps and logistical support to his organization.

Iraq. After the shattering of the Baghdad Pact, Iraq's relations with Turkey remained tense until the Iran-Iraq War in 1980, when Iraq became deeply dependent upon Turkey economically.

Conclusion

By the late 1960s, Ankara had come to recognize the costs of its single-track commitment to Western policies. As the immediacy of the Soviet threat receded, Turkish foreign policy centered increasingly on new economic interests, Greece, Cyprus, and the Kurdish problem. In confronting these issues, Turkey had received almost no diplomatic support from the developing world. To meet its own regional priorities, Ankara was thus compelled to acknowledge the necessity for a more differentiated and textured foreign policy. As a result, the high-water mark of Turkey's single-minded strategic commitment to the United States began to recede.

5

New Openings to the Muslim World

B y the mid-1960s, Ankara had come to realize the considerable costs of its exclusive strategic orientation toward the West, in which it sometimes appeared more pro-Western than the West itself. As a result, Ankara gradually moved to improve ties with the Middle East, the Soviet Union, and the developing world in hopes of gaining economic benefits and greater international support for its foreign policy goals. Over the course of thirty years, a number of major economic, political, and geopolitical developments marked Turkey's gradual if sometimes erratic opening toward the Muslim world.

Increased Economic Involvement in the Middle East: 1970–1980

For the first time, starting in the 1970s, Turkey developed an economic component to its foreign policy. This was driven by a major economic crisis that included triple-digit inflation, industrial production operating at half capacity, and an inability to meet hard currency interest payments on foreign loans following the dramatic rise in oil prices in 1973.[1] Turkey could no longer meet the costs of its own Middle East energy dependence by maintaining statist, autarkic economic policies that were based on import substitution, that ignored an export market, and that kept Turkish markets closed to the outside world.

As a result, Ankara shifted away from an exclusive focus on security in its dealings with the Middle East. While Turkey had tended to treat the region as a somewhat hostile bloc, it began to build new bilateral relationships based on mutual state interests. For example, in 1977, Ankara negotiated the opening of a pipeline from Iraq to Turkey's Mediterranean coast that ultimately brought Turkey revenues of up to $1.2 billion dollars a year.[2] Concurrently, Ankara grew far more cautious about lending generalized support to U.S. policies in the region unless it was vital to the NATO alliance or had a clear humanitarian purpose.[3] Thus, Turkey remained

---

1. "Turkey," Country Studies, www.country-studies.com/turkey/growth-and-structure-of-the-economy.html.
2. Phebe Marr, "Turkey and Iraq," in *Distant Neighbor, Turkey's Role in the Middle East,* ed. Henri Barkey (Washington, D.C.: United States Institute of Peace, 1996), 49–50.
3. Hale, *Turkish Foreign Policy,* 170.

neutral in the 1967 Arab-Israel war and denied the United States use of Turkish bases for refueling or resupplying Israel. The same was true during the 1973 Yom Kippur War. Turkey also supported UN calls for Israeli withdrawal from occupied Palestinian territories on the West Bank and Gaza Strip, recognized the Palestine Liberation Organization (PLO) in 1976, and later permitted the PLO to establish an office in Ankara. Ankara also refused support to the ill-starred U.S. effort to rescue American hostages in Iran in 1980 and resisted involvement in Washington's plans to set up a U.S. Rapid Deployment Force in the Middle East.[4]

The Iran-Iraq War

Harking back to old Kemalist principles of neutrality, Turkey remained neutral throughout the entire Iran-Iraq war and pointedly refused to support the trade embargo the United States imposed on Tehran after the hostage crisis. As a result, Ankara was the prime beneficiary of the war because both warring states developed a high degree of economic dependency upon Turkey during the conflict; Turkey was one of their few outlets to the West and a source of local goods. In fact, Turkish trade with Iraq increased by a factor of seven during the war, topping off at some $961 million or 12 percent of all Turkish exports. These economic gains greatly helped offset the ongoing Turkish economic crisis, although the scope of this trade dropped considerably after the end of the war, when relations between Turkey and the two countries cooled.[5]

The Özal Era

The impact of the remarkable leadership of Turgut Özal—first as economic czar, later as prime minister, and then as president before his untimely death in 1993—cannot be overestimated. It was under his authority that economic policy became a driving force in Turkish foreign policy. He led a strategic export-oriented program that unlocked the Turkish economy, opened the country to foreign investment, and allowed the entrepreneurial skills of the Turkish public to blossom—skills that had never before in history been associated with the traditionally military-oriented Turks. This expansion of foreign economic relations in turn paved the way to a broadening of diplomatic relations throughout the region.[6] Subsequently, the collapse of the Soviet Union opened up additional new economic options

---

4. Hale, *Turkish Foreign Policy*, 169–171.
5. Henri J. Barkey, "Hemmed in by Circumstances: Turkey and Iraq since the Gulf War," *Middle East Policy Council Journal* 7, no. 4 (October 2000), www.mepc.org/public_asp/journal_vol7/0010_barkey.asp.
6. Robins, *Suits and Uniforms*, 209–12.

for Turkey in the newly liberated republics of the former Soviet Union, including in the vital energy field.

The 1991 Gulf War

Despite full Turkish neutrality during the Iran-Iraq war and the economic benefits Turkey gained from this stance, Özal dramatically changed course at the outbreak of the 1991 Gulf War, when he firmly aligned Turkey with the broader U.S.-led coalition in the fight against Saddam Hussein. Among other reasons, Özal wanted to demonstrate the continuing geopolitical indispensability of Turkey to the United States after the collapse of the Soviet Union. Nonetheless, the Gulf War proved to be extremely costly— even disastrous—to most Turkish regional interests. First, in accordance with the newly minted UN embargo on Iraq, Turkey was required to close down its oil pipeline with Iraq and curtail much of its trade there, costing its economy up to $1.2 billion a year. Second, the war sparked a massive flow of Iraqi Kurdish refugees out of Iraq, creating a major humanitarian crisis and leading Washington to create a no-fly zone—a protected Kurdish region in northern Iraq. Creation of this zone marked the establishment of a de facto autonomous Kurdish region under Western protection—a political development well on the road toward realizing one of Turkey's greatest fears: an independent Kurdish state. This experience greatly increased Turkish ambivalence about the costs and benefits of close strategic support for U.S. policies in the region.

Islamists as Policymakers: Round One

As part of Turkey's continued political evolution, the Islamist Welfare Party (Refah Partisi) gained a plurality in national elections for the first time in 1995. This development shocked the Kemalist establishment, but it grudgingly acquiesced to the Islamists' participation in a coalition government with the secular-conservative True Path Party (Doğru Yol Partisi). The ascension of Welfare Party leader Necmettin Erbakan to head of the coalition cabinet demonstrated how far the Turkish establishment, and particularly the army, had come in tolerating Islamist participation in politics, even if it demanded that the Islamists formally accept Turkey's secular character.

As Turkey's grand, charismatic, old-style Islamist politician par excellence, Erbakan was always a source of continuing and justifiable controversy, and his outlook and political power were only eclipsed later with the emergence of the JDP. Although he was educated as an engineer in Germany, Erbakan's rhetorical calls reflected many of the classical themes of mainstream Islamists in other parts of the world. He had long railed against the imperial character of the Christian West, denounced the European Union as a "Christian club"—a view mirrored by some EU spokesmen—opposed Turkish plans to seek EU membership, and urged a Turkish pullout from NATO. Additionally, he consistently articulated his standing suspicion of the role of Jewry in influencing international politics and his strong criticism of Israel's regional policies, including Turkey's alliance with it. He also sought closer relationships with other Islamist leaders across the Muslim world, most notably the Muslim Brotherhood. Robins deftly summarizes Erbakan's long track record as "a mixture of pious Islamism, 1950's style Third World struggle, and truculent, xenophobic Turkish nationalism."[7]

Erbakan sometimes demonstrated an interest in direct party-to-party ties with foreign Islamists that transcended traditional state-to-state ties with Muslim states, reflecting an Islam-directed ideological orientation, even if moderate by Muslim world standards. His close ties with the Muslim Brotherhood won him the criticism of Egyptian president Husni Mubarak and strained Turkish bilateral relations with Egypt. By some accounts, Erbakan received funding from Libya and Saudi Arabia,[8] but such charges were never pursued, even by the hostile military. Erbakan also demonstrated a deep suspicion of U.S. strategic intentions toward Turkey—suspicions shared by many Kemalists, leftists, and nationalists—and consistently urged greater Turkish independence of action in foreign policy.

Erbakan's ideological leanings were fully demonstrated in a 1996 Islamic Communities Association meeting, supported by the Welfare Party in Istanbul, that was attended by many world Islamist leaders, including important Muslim Brotherhood figures from Syria, members of Hamas from Palestine, and figures from Afghanistan, Pakistan, and Lebanon.[9] In terms of normal Muslim world politics, such a gathering resembled business-as-usual mainstream political Islam. But in the Turkish context, such contacts represented a worrisome precedent and strengthened the impression that Erbakan was flirting with radical international Islamist politics. Erbakan also unsurprisingly maintained close ties with the European branches of the Millî Görüş, an Islamist movement he had started in the 1970s that had grown to more than a thousand public branches, providing a direct source of funding for the Welfare Party from Turkish immigrant communities throughout Europe.[10] This ideological legacy is what that the founders of the JDP wished to erase, even though many of them had politically grown up under Erbakan and worked closely with him in earlier periods.

---

7. Robins, *Suits and Uniforms*, 209–12.
8. Ibid., 150.
9. Ibid., 151.
10. Ibid., 152–3.

It is instructive to see what did and did not happen under the Erbakan prime ministry. After rotating into the position of prime minister under the coalition government, he became more circumspect when faced with the actual responsibilities of power, with pressures from coalition partners, and with the intense scrutiny of a military poised and waiting for a misstep. Nonetheless, Erbakan quickly launched an unprecedented new opening toward the Muslim world, beginning with official state visits to Iran and Libya.

Although Turkey has a multiplicity of bilateral interests with Iran (trade, energy, Kurdish issues) that merit serious discussion, Erbakan's high-profile visit there upset Washington, particularly given its desire to isolate Iran and Erbakan's clear desire to break away from the restrictions of a Washington-centric view of the region. In Libya, meanwhile, the quixotic Mu'ammar Qadhafi took the occasion to publicly denounce Turkey's oppression of the Kurds and Turkey's close ties with Israel, embarrassing Erbakan and tarring the trip with political fiasco. Other key Erbakan destinations included Egypt, Malaysia, Pakistan, Indonesia, and Nigeria, where Turkey had quite legitimate and potentially important economic interests to develop.

In the course of this travel, Erbakan called for the establishment of a Developing 8 (D-8) organization, a pointedly Muslim parallel to the Group of Seven (G-7) of the West. The D-8 was to represent the economic interests and power of key emerging Muslim countries.[11] Robins sees its boldness of vision as "a foreign relations initiative worthy of Özal."[12] However, the D-8 organization at this juncture of world politics remained moribund, partly because it lacked the needed cohesive character and sound structural economic foundations for close economic cooperation. Despite the often clumsy and poorly executed nature of these visits, they represented an important early precedent.

As a proponent of a broad and independent foreign policy for Turkey, Davutoğlu argues that these early initiatives to Asia were an important first step in developing a necessary new Asian "axis" of economic partners. Given the Asian character of the Turks' origins and Ankara's continuing interests in the broader Turkic world, which extends into China via the Uyghur Turks, Davutoğlu maintains that Asia should be an important complement to the exclusively Western and Atlantic trade patterns of the past.[13] Davutoğlu further argues that Ankara requires a strongly grounded psychological and cultural understanding of the Muslim world—and a firm presence within it—if it is to be a regional force. Turkey's ties with the Middle East have always been primarily designed to meet defense or

---

11. Jung and Piccoli, *Turkey at the Crossroads*, 132.

12. Robins, *Suits and Uniforms*, 66.

13. Davutoğlu, *Stratejik Derinlik*, 281.

short-term diplomatic needs, with Ankara generally holding the region at arm's length. Davutoğlu states that Ankara must move away from its classic "threat assessment approach" in which it views the Muslim world principally as a political and cultural threat to Turkey's secularism. He further states that only when Turkey overcomes its own internal historical and psychological hang-ups about Islam and begins to understand the Middle East in its own psychological terms can Turkey develop effective relationships there that complement Ankara's policies in other regions.[14]

Although Erbakan was ultimately forced from office in 1997 when the military ratcheted up domestic tensions and demanded his resignation, this extralegal action, which violated democratic procedures in Turkey, drew little comment from Washington. While the Islamists received no more than 20 percent of the vote in 1996 and did not represent a dominant political force, the Welfare Party's modest popularity had been principally due to the party's active social welfare programs that helped fill economic and social gaps opened by Özal's liberal reforms.[15] The Islamists had also shown themselves capable of good municipal administration and were noted for their lack of corruption.

Islamic Banking

Any discussion of Ankara's opening to the Middle East would not be complete without an examination of the fascinating, significant, and controversial Islamic banking phenomenon in Turkey. Under Islamic law, the charging of interest is prohibited. Islamic banking, therefore, involves making loans and providing dividends based on risk- and profit-sharing at mutually negotiated rates. Nearly all observers agree that Islamic banking forces lenders, borrowers, and investors to forge close relationships with one another in order to properly negotiate and monitor the terms and operation of a loan, encouraging greater transparency and heightened social involvement and responsibility—key Islamic values.

But the very thought of Islamic banking within Turkey raised alarms in Kemalist circles, which saw it as a potentially dangerous regression from Western to Islamic ways. It took the clout and financial and leadership genius of President Özal to ram through special legislation in 1983 to permit it. Özal had two goals: (1) to grow the economy by bringing into circulation locked-in, unused capital held by those opposed to interest-bearing banking; and (2) to develop economic ties with the wealthy Gulf states and to encourage them to invest in Turkey. (While Özal had his eye on the financial benefits of this system, he was also known to have personal links with

---

14. Ibid., 262–4.

15. Jung and Piccoli, *Turkey at the Crossroads*, 118–9.

Turkish Sufi brotherhoods—a not unusual phenomenon among Turkish politicians even in secular Turkey.) From a financial standpoint, the legislation has been extremely successful. As analyst Ji-Hyang Jang points out, "Turkish Islamic banks have been clearly growth-oriented in terms of their balance sheets, market shares, and numbers of branches and employees and have shown solid performances compared to the conventional banks."[16]

If the Islamic basis of the concept was not controversial enough for Kemalist Turkey, the early associations of these banks with Saudi and Gulf capital further upset staunch secularists. Chartered in 1985, the first two Islamic banks in Turkey were al-Baraka Finance House (Dar al-Mal al-Islami in Arabic) and the Faysal Finance House, both of which were the products of a joint Saudi-Turkish venture. A third Arab-linked joint venture was the Kuwait-Turkey Finance House, which was tied to the Turkish Vakıf Bank that historically had ties to Turkey's religious endowments. Most of these banking establishments were connected to the major financial interests of conservative and religious business circles close to Turkey's Islamist parties and movements. A major insurance company involved in one of these investments was Işık Sigorta, which is affiliated with the Fethullah Gülen community.

Because there is a high degree of correlation among the Islamic banks, Gulf funding, and Turkey's Islamist business circles,[17] the military and radical secularists perceived these developments as a scheme by Saudi and other conservative Gulf leaders to strengthen Islamist forces in Turkey through the provision of capital within the Turkish system. The linkages are undeniably there and there can be no doubt that Islamic circles have been financially strengthened through these banks, but whether these linkages are illegal or contrary to Turkish law is another question. The banks have withstood close, even hostile, state scrutiny. Furthermore, economic activism by traditional Anatolian conservative and religious businessmen long preceded Islamic banking. It grew out of the opening of Turkey's economic, political, and social order, which essentially liberated broad social elements formerly marginalized by the early elitist Kemalist system.

Indeed, as Jang points out, a major benefit of the Islamic banking system—and one of the many goals of Özal at the time—was to encourage Islamists to break from their old-fashioned statist and sometimes conspiratorial view of the world and to enter into a transparent, profitable, and open partnership with the existing Turkish system. As he argues, "The steadily growing Islamic banks may offer a way for the political Islamists to acquire

---

16. Ji-Hyang Jang, "The Politics of Islamic Banks in Turkey: Taming Political Islamists by Islamic Capital," paper prepared for the 2003 annual meeting of the Midwest Political Science Association, Chicago, Ill., 2–3, www.gov.utexas.edu/content/research_papers/midwest_903/jangmpsa03.pdf.

17. Ibid., 4

new financial stakes and to discard old radical behaviors or anti-system stances in order to secure predictable capitalist interests. In doing so, the Islamic banks might strengthen more liberal, moderate forces among the political Islamists."[18] In fact, it was the new, young, more moderate leaders of the JDP that embraced Islamic banking most strongly, thereby strengthening Islamic voices within the financial system and allowing themselves to become better integrated into the system on a political, economic, social, and financial level.

Although controversy still surrounds Islamic banking in Turkey, it is an important part of the Islamist political movement—by 1999 more than 120 Islamic bank branches had been opened—and serves as a source of support and finance for Islamists. The branches are particularly well represented in cities where the JDP is strong.[19] Overall, Islamic banking in Turkey has brought about radical changes in the position of the Islamists, both strengthening and "domesticating" them. It has also loosened rigidities among the Kemalist secularists, who are now obliged to accept the phenomenon as legitimate—even if it is unwelcome—particularly when urged to do so by the World Bank and the IMF as part of overall banking reform.[20] Over time, the capital sources of the banks have relied far less on the Gulf states and more on the extensive financial circles of the broader Islamic community in Turkey.

The Organization of the Islamic Conference

Turkey never attributed much importance to its long-time, low-key, and unofficial membership in the Organization of the Islamic Conference (OIC), an international Muslim organization originally formed under Saudi sponsorship that seeks to represent and promote the interests of all Muslim states. For many years, Turkey's parliament would not even ratify Turkish membership in a strictly Muslim organization. It was only in 1969, when Turkey's foreign minister first attended an OIC summit in Rabat, that Turkish membership became a domestic political issue and the source of objections from radical secularists. But Turkey's membership in the OIC led the organization to support Ankara's fight against the persecution of the Turkish minority in Bulgaria in the mid-1980s.[21] As Turkey started to place greater emphasis on its relations with the Muslim world, it began to look upon the OIC with greater interest as a useful diplomatic tool, particularly during the Bosnian crisis.

---

18. Ibid., 2.
19. Jang, "The Politics of Islamic Banks in Turkey."
20. Ibid., 2.
21. Hale, *Turkish Foreign Policy*, 171.

Syria Yields

One of the most significant breakthroughs in Turkey's relations with the Arab world occurred in 1999, when the Turkish military publicly threatened war with Syria over its support to the PKK. Isolated following the collapse of the Soviet Union and concerned by Turkish-Israeli strategic cooperation, which had blossomed in the 1990s, Syrian president Hafiz al-Asad uncharacteristically yielded to Turkey. This virtual surrender by Damascus, which coincided with several other internal and foreign issues, opened the door to a dramatically new and promising relationship between Syria and Turkey and added to the overall architecture of Turkey's newly emerging Middle East policy.

Conclusion

Over the course of three decades, Turkey underwent a gradual but clear process of moving toward greater involvement in the Middle East, first in the economic arena and later in the political and strategic arenas. Regular and substantive dealings with the Muslim world increasingly became a central part of Turkey's foreign policy process. While often wary, even the Turkish military began to recognize the pragmatic strategic benefits of new openings to neighbors and overcoming the past tensions of the Cold War.

Today, such policies toward the region enjoy a considerable degree of national consensus. By the close of the century, Turkish policymakers even began to speak more openly about the need to transform the country's foreign policy environment and to create for the first time a "zone of peace" (barış çemberi). This long-gestating notion has been prominently supported by leading Turkish think tanks, such as TESEV (Türkiye Ekonomik ve Sosyal Etüdler Vakfı), and was explicitly raised by the speaker of Turkey's parliament on the eve of the U.S. invasion of Iraq.[22] Seen in this light, current JDP policies simply represent a culmination of major initiatives to strengthen Turkey's ties and clout in the Muslim world. But because Turkey's role in the Muslim world has always been directly affected by the changing place of Islam in Turkey—and by Muslim world perception of Turkish attitudes toward it—it is important to understand the nature of the reemergence of Islam within Turkey and its relevance for the broader Muslim world in the twenty-first century.

---

22. Press Statements of the Turkish National Assembly, www.tbmm.gov.tr/develop/owa/tbmm_basin_aciklamalari_sd.aciklama?p1=2169.

6

The Reemergence of Turkish Islam

M any Muslims have long considered Turkey's break with its historical and cultural past to be so radical as to make its experience irrelevant to them; after all, most Muslim societies have sought to retain an Islamic identity even while undergoing a modernization process. Yet, despite the strong bias of the modern Turkish state structure against Islam, Turkey has produced two dynamic Islamic movements that have significant importance not only for Turkey but also for contemporary Islam in general: the decidedly political JDP and the largely apolitical communitarian movement of Fethullah Gülen. As a result, the new face of Turkish Islam, particularly within its evolving political context, is increasingly intriguing Muslims everywhere.

The Justice and Development Party

The JDP did not emerge from thin air; it grew out of a series of Islamist movements and parties in Turkey that evolved, learned, and changed over a thirty-five year period. But the JDP is the first party to break free of the more traditional Islamist influence of Necmettin Erbakan, who led four successive Islamist parties from 1970 to 1997, with each one in turn eventually being banned. As we have seen, Erbakan espoused radical views—at least by Turkish standards—of the West, Israel, the European Union, secularism, and the Kemalist legacy. Although his party shared power in three different coalition governments, it never came to power in its own right.

The growing strength of Islamist parties in Turkey has reflected the gradual political, social, and economic democratization of the country. This process included Özal's economic opening in the 1980s, which increased foreign investment, Islamic banking, foreign trade, private entrepreneurial opportunity, and general domestic prosperity. These changes empowered at least three groups: a new and growing Anatolian business class, traditional lower classes in the cities, and a new and growing Islamic professional and intellectual class that, while modern, still finds meaningful identity in Muslim tradition.[1] These groups have increasing impact on Turkey's character, identity, and future foreign policy orientation. While the new, traditionally minded Anatolian business class honors Atatürk as a reformer and as savior of the

---

1. Jenny B. White, *Islamist Mobilization in Turkey* (Seattle: University of Washington Press, 2002), 114–5.

nation from Western imperialism, it retains a deep identification with the Ottoman past and is uncomfortable with Kemalism's inherent disparagement of the country's Ottoman and Islamic past. This new class has proven to be a key source of financial support both for Turkey's Islamist parties and the nonpolitical Gülen movement.

The eighties saw a proliferation of Islamic media in Turkey that included new books on Islam, translations of classic twentieth-century Islamist works from the Arab and Muslim world, new religious newspapers and journals, and Islam-oriented radio and television stations. All attracted new followers and stimulated serious intellectual debate about Islam and the relevance of Islamic values to social and political life. This debate, thanks to Turkey's democratization, has been more open and creative than would be possible in the relatively closed atmospheres of most other Muslim states. In the 1980s, even the Turkish military opportunistically encouraged the fusion of religious and patriotic identity in an attempt to combat a radical and violent left.

The mid-1990s witnessed growing Islamist representation in parliament and Islamist electoral victories in key municipalities around the country, including in Ankara and Istanbul. Although the Welfare Party was closed after Erbakan was forced out of power by the military in 1997, it was quickly reincarnated as the Virtue Party. In turn, younger and more liberal Islamist reformers within this party broke away from Erbakan to form the JDP. An old Erbakan Islamist rump then formed the Felicity Party (Saadet Partisi) that has had limited influence.

Founded in August 2001 under the leadership of Recep Tayyip Erdoğan, a former successful mayor of Istanbul, the JDP is by far the most moderate, professional, and successful of this long series of Islamist parties in Turkey. Indeed, by absolute standards, it has been more skillful in managing foreign policy, the economy, and reform issues than almost all other mainstream Turkish parties in recent decades. And it has wisely learned from the mistakes of earlier Islamist parties, which, admittedly, had to operate under more difficult political circumstances imposed by the military. As a result, in 2002, the JDP came to national power on its own by winning a clear plurality in free elections—a first for Islamists anywhere in the world. But the JDP has defined itself in sharply different terms than have past Islamist parties in Turkey.

First, and most dramatically, the JDP officially distances itself from any formal relationship with Islam and acknowledges secularism or "laicism" as a fundamental prerequisite for democracy and freedom. However, it pointedly insists that secularism be defined as "the state's *impartiality* towards every form of religious belief and philosophical conviction" and that "the state, rather than the individual, is restricted by this."[2] This interpretation thus rejects Kemalism's standing definition of secularism, which calls for state

---

2.   Jenny B. White, *Islamist Mobilization in Turkey*, 274.

domination of religion. Additionally, the JDP defines itself as a "democratic conservative party" and avoids any use of the term "Islamic" or "Islamist" in describing itself. This stance is, of course, politically astute, given the highly negative views the military has toward Islamists.

Second, under the JDP, Ankara has moved toward an interesting dual foreign policy that simultaneously aims at both EU membership *and* greater attention to Muslim world politics. This dual strategy raises an important question: will serious Turkish involvement in Middle Eastern regional politics hinder or improve Turkey's prospects for integration into the European Union? Certainly those Europeans already opposed to Turkish membership will present Turkey's policy activism in the Middle East as a drawback. But, as Turkish foreign minister Abdullah Gül argues, Turkey's leadership role in this sphere should ultimately enhance its position in applying for EU membership: "At a time that people are talking of a clash of civilizations, Turkey is a natural bridge of civilizations. All we are trying to do is to use our position to bring Islam and the West closer together."[3]

Yet the JDP's dramatic turn away from longtime Erbakan policies has nonetheless still been received with suspicion by parts of the Turkish electorate, particularly because of the continuing leadership of many key figures from the old Erbakan ranks, such as Erdoğan and Gül. But this turn does not represent a "religious dissembling" *(takiye)* by Erdoğan, as is sometimes charged; rather, it represents a considered shift in policy. Moderate Islamists have long been committed to an agenda of democratization in Turkey: they perceive themselves as direct beneficiaries of any steps that lessen the arbitrary power of the military and radical secularists who for so long curtailed Islamist political rights and civil liberties. The JDP's embrace of the European Union has been one of the wisest and most successful aspects of the JDP's platform. It contributed greatly to its electoral support in the country and to its reputation abroad, although more recently this policy has begun to lose some support due to EU foot-dragging on Turkey's membership application and the resultant souring of Turkish public opinion on the topic.

Yalçın Akdoğan, a senior adviser to Prime Minister Erdoğan, defines the JDP as a "mass party at the national level, conservative in values, with an appreciation of past history, culture and religion." That is, it is not a single-issue party, it does not view issues from a religious perspective, and it does not seek to spread Islam. In its foreign policy, he argues, the JDP has no special mission in the Middle East other than furthering Turkish national interest. In fact, he points out that the JDP is not linked to any religious or ethnic group inside Turkey, or to any external regional group or organization. This, he claims, is the source of its broad support within Turkey. As a result, the

---

3. Amir Taheri, "Turkey's Bid to Raise Its Islamic Profile and Court Europe May Backfire," *Arab View*, www.arabview.com/articles.asp?article=471.

JDP does not formally seek to be a model for the rest of the Muslim world, although he acknowledges that it could serve as a useful example for how to manage modern politics.[4]

Is the JDP Islamist?

Distinguished Islamic scholar, academic, and JDP state minister for religious affairs Mehmet Aydın similarly states that the party does not consider itself to be "moderate Islamist" but rather sees itself as a party comprised of "moderate Muslims."[5] He and many other JDP members speak of a new concept of "Muslimhood" (Müslümancılık) that is embraced by many JDP members "whose religious ethics inspire their public service as individuals but cannot be construed as part of their identities as political actors."[6] While agreeing that religion is basically personal, the JDP argues that "[religion] can be incorporated into the public and political spheres without compromising the secular state system."[7] Indeed, as social anthropologist Jenny White points out, the debate ultimately comes down to "redefining the boundaries of the private and the public, the personal, the civil, and the political." As she further states, the religious identity of an individual "may even benefit the political realm by inserting personal ethics and a moral stance."[8]

Scholar Hakan Yavuz goes further, arguing that the JDP has now passed beyond being a party based on Islamic identity to being one based on service. That is, it no longer seeks to embody an ideology or specific identity but rather simply seeks to win votes by meeting generalized public needs across the board.[9] This view raises a significant question: what determines whether a party qualifies (or disqualifies) as an Islamist or Islamic party? In my view, "Islamist" is a broad term that applies to a wide spectrum of activists who believe that the Koran and the life of the Prophet offer important principles about Islamic governance and society.[10]

In this context, I do consider the JDP to be a form of Islamist party—one that is not only moderate but, more important is also exploring the very concept of what it means to combine religious values with political life. As party members point out, these religious principles need not be formalized. Rather, they can be internalized in the thinking and action of the individual politician. Indeed, the JDP is writing a new chapter in the evo-

---

4. Yalçın Akdoğan, interview by author, Ankara, Turkey, September 2004.
5. Mehmet Aydın, interview by author, Ankara, Turkey, September 2004.
6. Jenny B. White, "The End of Islamism? Turkey's Muslimhood Model," in *Remaking Muslim Politics: Pluralism, Contestation, Democratization*, ed. Robert W. Hefner (Princeton, N.J.: Princeton University Press, 2005), 87–8.
7. White, *Islamist Mobilization*.
8. White, "The End of Islamism? Turkey's Muslimhood Model," 87–8.
9. Hakan Yavuz, "The Transformation of a Turkish Islamic Movement," *American Journal of Islamic Social Sciences* 22, no. 3 (2005): 105–8.
10. See Graham E. Fuller, *The Future of Political Islam* (New York: Palgrave, 2003).

lution and thinking of Islamist parties. Its concept of Muslimhood is a creative one that removes an explicitly religious agenda from its political program but does not remove the inherent values of Islam from it. I consider the JDP to be a form of Islamist party for a multitude of other reasons as well.

First, a large portion of the JDP leadership comes directly out of Turkey's broader Islamic movement and was closely associated with Erbakan and his Welfare/Virtue Party in the past. Although there is evolution here, there is also continuity.

Second, in describing itself as a "conservative" party, the JDP is in fact responding to a broad desire among many Turkish believers that Islam and Turkey's Ottoman heritage be acknowledged and honored rather than suppressed. While not a formal part of the JDP platform, this desire is widely implicit in the actions and words of a large number of the party's supporters.

Third, the party is strongly supported by Muslim believers—although JDP support is by no means limited to that group, as its success at the polls attests—and, as some leading Turkish businessmen protest, it focuses too much on polarizing religious issues at the expense of needed reforms.

Fourth, the JDP has pursued several socioreligious policies: it supports (so far unsuccessfully) overturning the government ban on headscarves for women working in state offices, universities, public service, and politics; it flirted briefly with and then abandoned the idea of criminalizing adultery (to be punishable by fines in the belief that, like narcotics, it is destructive to the country's social fabric); it has called for maximum integration of the *imam-hatip* (prayer leaders and preachers) schools into the broader academic system; it seeks greater freedom for the expression of Islam in public life; it has worked closely on Islamic banking; and it has shown support for elements of historic Islamic Ottoman symbolism.

Fifth, JDP members generally demonstrate public piety and religiosity. Radical secularists claim that the JDP is being disingenuous in describing itself merely as a democratic conservative party and that it is in reality concealing a deeper agenda geared toward Islamicizing Turkey and imposing sharia law, even if this latter goal is quite far-fetched.

Sixth, JDP leaders stress the urgent need to establish good relations with other Muslim countries and to stop isolating and radicalizing them. For the JDP, this highly pragmatic policy comfortably acknowledges Turkey's deep historical and cultural ties to the Muslim world and expresses a desire to play some kind of leadership role in the region without diminishing the importance of Turkey's ties with the West.

Thus, by the standards of the broader Muslim world, the JDP clearly falls into the moderate Islamist category. Of course the JDP strives to garner broad national support and to respond to the articulated needs of the entire population. In Muslim terms, serving the community's welfare is a key requirement of good governance. Additionally, that is what political parties do in all democracies if they hope to be successful. To simply call the JDP a service party, then, is to strip it of any distinctiveness whatsoever beyond being an efficient administrator. Furthermore, to refer to a moderate, successful Islamist party as a service party is to relegate the term "Islamist" to its most radical, frozen, extreme, and violent forms, leaving us with no term by which to describe the great majority of other moderate Islamist movements that do not practice violence. The term "Islamist" should not be reserved for only when referring to the "bad guys"—in the Western view—but it should also be used when referring to the positive end of the spectrum as well.

To be sure, by no means do all Muslims believe that an Islamist party must automatically give top priority to application of sharia law, as if this were the highest contribution to the Islamic community that an Islamic party could make. Attending to social justice, respecting religious tradition, acknowledging religious values, and striving for the education, health, national strength, and prosperity of the society is viewed by many Islamists as part of a grander, more holistic vision of sharia, one that serves the broad welfare of the Islamic *ummah* more immediately and directly than any narrow debate over specific laws and appropriate Islamic penalties.

Turkey's Islamists, for decades cut off from contemporary global thinking on Islam, are now broadly familiar with Islamist politics elsewhere and have demonstrated an interesting evolution toward a more realistic and sophisticated view of Islam and politics. Indeed, negative developments in the Muslim world pushed Turkish Islamists—and those elsewhere—to reevaluate an earlier Islamist focus on gaining control of the state and imposing an Islamic agenda from above. As a result, Turkish Islamists have moved away from emphasizing the role of the state in stimulating Islamic consciousness and moved toward working within civil society. This evolution reflects an old debate among Islamists—that is, whether they should enter politics or seek power at all. Because to do so successfully, they would likely need to compromise with non-Islamist parties and deal with the implications of possible voter rejection at the polls.

Having witnessed firsthand the negative aspects of state interference with Islam under Kemalism, Turkey's Islamic intellectuals now have a greater interest in working within society and in inculcating personal responsibility for moral decisions than in looking to a state-imposed legal approach. As one Islamist intellectual, Mehmet Metiner, believes, "The state cannot impose personal morality. We must be allowed the freedom to sin (*günah işlemek özgürlüğü*). We are answerable only to God. Entry into the gates of hell should not be forbidden."[11] In discussing the concept of Muslimhood, Metiner further states that Islam cannot be reduced simply to a commitment to sharia law, however it is interpreted. According to him, Islam is not just a system

---

11. Mehmet Metiner, interview by author, September 2004.

of personal belief and code of action; it also provides a sense of identity and belonging, a moral and communal orientation, and a personal connection, offering a far broader historical and philosophical vision than simple pieces of legislation. Although these views stand in stark contrast to the stifling legal edifices found in Iran and Saudi Arabia, they are shared by many other liberal Islamists in the Muslim world.

While not all Islamists necessarily concur with all of these interpretations of Islam's role in public life, they represent interesting collective advances in Turkish Islamic experience and thinking. Under the JDP, even the longtime Kemalist bastion of state control of religion, the Office of Religious Affairs (Diyanet İşleri), has exhibited creative thinking and change. Its director, Ali Bardakoğlu, is a qualified religious judge with an impressive academic background and a determination to renew religious understanding. His office is currently completing a long-term project that will provide a new interpretation of the Koran (tafsir). As Bardakoğlu comments,

> Every society and individual transmits religion from on high down into his/her own particular world and actualizes his own sense of religiosity within the context of his own world and its possibilities. . . . There is no reform of religion itself, there is only a renewal of our religious understanding, a constant renewal. . . . Except for the basic religious sources, we must not adopt religious interpretations from the past as a model to be taken literally today. Every period has its own understanding of religion, meaningful for that age and its own conditions, from which we can draw ideas and gain experience.[12]

The emergence of a creative new understanding of Islam in Turkey in its political, social, and personal context stems from a few factors:

- Turkey's overall degree of development, modernization, democratization, and openness to the world;
- The tensions between Kemalism and Islam, which have inadvertently compelled Turkish Islamists to develop more rapidly new ideas and understandings of the role of Islam in a democratic society;
- Turkey's relative insulation from the bloody and polarizing geopolitical and military confrontations with the Muslim world by Western powers over the past half century.

The rest of the Muslim world is now watching Turkey with immense interest, not just for what it is saying but also for what it is doing. The approach of the JDP offers much of value to other Islamists. The JDP will not peddle its

---

12. Ali Bardakoğlu, "Dindarlığımızın Güncelleştirilmesi" [On Up-Dating Our Religious Understanding], interview in *Hürriyet*, September 10, 2004.

own program elsewhere, but it is quite ready to share its relevant experiences with groups in other Muslim societies.

The Fethullah Gülen Movement

The second major phenomenon in current Turkish Islamic thought and action is found in the apolitical communitarian movement of Fethullah Gülen—the largest religious movement in Turkey.[13] Its roots lie in the late Ottoman period, which produced one of the most remarkable intellectual and socioreligious movements of the early twentieth century: the Nur (Light) movement. The roots of the Nur movement itself emerged from the political turmoil, setbacks, and moral crises of the declining days of the empire.

The Ottomans, like so many other Muslim societies then and now, desperately sought formulas that could provide both modernization and protection from Western domination. The Nur movement's founder, Bediüzzaman Said Nursi, was a remarkable Islamist modernist thinker. Although his ideas are still not well known outside of the Turkish context, they are of direct relevance not just to Turkey but to all Muslim societies. He unquestionably deserves inclusion in the ranks of other great Islamic reformist thinkers of the early twentieth century.[14] Said Nursi sought to make Islam's message fully relevant to contemporary life so as to help Muslims deal with the grand questions facing them in their everyday lives, especially in an era of turmoil and change.

The Gülen movement emerges out of the Nur movement. It is more modern and influential than any other Islamic movement in Turkey today. Reinforced by the markedly modest and humble lifestyle of Gülen and by the immense worldly success of his movement, Gülen's charismatic personality makes him the number one Islamic figure of Turkey. The Gülen movement has the largest and most powerful infrastructure and financial resources of any movement in the country, exerting major impact upon public life. The movement has also become international by virtue of its far-flung system of schools that offer primary, secondary, and, in some places, even university education in more than a dozen countries, including the Muslim countries of the former Soviet Union, Russia, France, and the United States.

The Gülen movement is characterized by its particular fusing of Islam with a sense of nation. Unlike most other Islamic movements, it has been

---

13. For more detailed information on the movement see, in particular, Bülent Aras, "Turkish Islam's Moderate Face," *Middle East Quarterly*, September 1998; M. Hakan Yavuz, "Towards an Islamic Liberalism?: The Nurcu Movement and Fethullah Gülen," *Middle East Journal* (Winter 1999); and M. Hakan Yavuz and John Esposito, eds., *Turkish Islam and the Secular State: The Gulen Movement* (Washington, D.C.: Georgetown University Press, 2002).

14. For detailed information about Said Nursi and for translations of his works into English, see www.sozler.com.tr/eng/.

highly accommodationist toward the state, even when repressed by it, and it is supportive of the broad goals of Turkish foreign policy. Furthermore, it has always spoken tactfully and positively about the Turkish military, despite the deep hostility and suspicion that the army leadership has toward the movement. The movement focuses on bringing about gradual social change in Turkish life through propagation of Islamic values at the grassroots level rather than through political or other top-down means. Additionally, the movement is decentralized and communitarian in focus. In fact, Gülen's willingness to accommodate the state has been the object of criticism among some Islamists in Turkey. Yet his state critics and enemies refuse to accept the reality of his accommodationist policies and accuse him of subterfuge and dissembling, stating that he is masking his supposed real goals of seizing the state and imposing sharia law.

The Gülen movement offers a modernist understanding of the world even while emphasizing the centrality of Islamic belief to traditional community values. It seeks to build a community of educated and prosperous believers who are actively engaged in worldly life—making it almost Calvinist in character. Some of the movement's key initiatives, beliefs, and activities are summarized below.

Education

The Gülen movement sees education as the preeminent means of bringing about social change and community renewal. It insists that religion can be fully understood only against the backdrop of knowledge as a whole and that only through broad education is the community strengthened and able to advance. The movement asserts that science and technology are fully compatible with Islam and that a knowledge of physical sciences and the universe is indispensable, generating awe in its revelation of God's handiwork.

As an extension of these beliefs, the Gülen movement has launched a flagship program that has built a network of hundreds of schools. Funding comes from within the community and from wealthy businessmen for whom building a school has become the modern pious equivalent of building a mosque. Although entrance is highly competitive, the schools are open to any and all who wish to enroll; their secular curriculum is based entirely on that of Turkish state schools. The schools are popular because of their quality of education, their sense of order, and their staffs' commitment. Drawn mostly from within the Gülen community, the closely monitored instructors teach Islam in accordance with the Islamic studies directives of the Turkish state education curricula.

The movement believes that the schools and their instructors should serve as a model to the community at large and inspire respect for the broader values of the movement. Educational work is complemented by the frequent availability of boarding houses or dormitories operated by the movement, especially for students far from home with limited financial resources. Gül-en's opponents accuse him of pursuing a hidden agenda and brainwashing students who live in these boarding houses into acceptance of religious doc-trines, allegedly violating Turkish laws on secularism. While the community certainly seeks to promote a religious vision of life and Gülen has much to say about religious issues across a wide spectrum of life and thought, it is hard to credit the attacks against the schools leveled by a few radical secular-ists. In court, Gülen has regularly been acquitted, although in some instances the case against him has simply been "suspended"—in what Gülen members say is scarcely veiled harassment. Despite consistent failures by a series of radical prosecutors to make a credible case against him, Gülen, whose health is problematic, has been in self-imposed exile in the United States for nearly a decade to avoid further legal harassment.

Violence and Extremism

The movement rejects extremism and violence of any kind, stating that they are incompatible with the true message of Islam, and emphasizes the devel-opment of tolerance among religious communities. In the past, Gülen has taken the lead in arranging much-publicized ecumenical meetings between himself and the Greek Patriarch, Jewish leaders, and the pope, among oth-ers. Tolerance among religions remains a major theme for Gülen. Critics of Gülen point out that he is less receptive to non-Sunni forms of Islam, such as the large Alevi (heterodox Shiite) community in Turkey.

The Use of Media

The Gülen movement has distinguished itself through its mastery of modern media, a characteristic of many other Islamic movements throughout the world. It has created a significant media empire that includes *Zaman*, probably the largest and most independent daily newspaper in Turkey, an influential television station, numerous radio stations, and a range of journals, including a popular weekly one. These media vehicles are focused more on questions of values rather than on religion per se, presenting discussions on personal and social issues of relevance even to secular-minded Turks.

Is the Movement Really Apolitical?

The Gülen movement eschews politics in the belief that it leads to social divisiveness and distraction from the essential issues of values and principle. In fact, the movement opposes the creation of political parties founded on religion in general, believing that they end up compromising or contaminat-ing religion and that they only serve to create social strife damaging to the position of religion in society. The movement is comfortable with living within the secular strictures of modern Turkish society—as long as "secularism" is not taken to mean state license to persecute the community's members or enact legislation hostile to religion.

However, Yavuz, among others, has suggested that the Gülen movement cannot really be described as "apolitical" at all and that the movement's every action is, in the end, intensely political. After all, the movement has huge communications enterprises, educational and financial institutions, and major media outlets all able to influence society. There is no doubt that the movement quite explicitly aspires to transform society through transformation of the individual, a process that could ultimately lead to collective calls for the creation of national and social institutions that reflect belief in a moral order. In a very loose sense, it is possible to call this a political project if we consider any attempt to transform society to be a political project. But I would argue that it is just as much a social or moral project. Indeed, the term "political" loses its meaning if applied equally to all efforts to transform society, regardless of means. Promotion of change through teachings, education, and information does not really become political until it formally and institutionally enters the political process. In this sense, it is correct to describe the Gülen movement as apolitical. But there can be no doubt that it is strong, influential, and active on the public scene and clear in its principles, which it publicizes broadly and transparently.

Acceptability at a High Level

Opponents of the movement claim that it is simply dissembling and concealing its "real agenda"—a sweeping and unanswerable charge. Many in the military fear the movement's size and social influence and believe it ultimately aspires to overthrow the Turkish Republic's secular order. As a result, Gülen members are barred from the military and the intelligence and security services. However, the movement has gained a major voice within the ranks of the police force, from which its members have not been excluded, a fact that disturbs the military. Ironically, the movement's abstention from politics is in itself sometimes presented by the military as a possible danger because the movement cannot be held liable to usual political party laws. In this sense, it is believed to be working underground to subvert Turkish secularism and Kemalist principles. Yet, far from involving dissimulation, the major public efforts of the Gülen movement—such as promulgating public meetings, seminars, conferences, debates, and colloquia and distributing publications on the grand issues of contemporary civilization, Islam, secularism, globalization, and tolerance—suggest a serious commitment to openly examine questions of societal value in a manner acceptable to large numbers of people.

Despite the sometimes virulent attacks against it, the Gülen movement has been viewed positively by a number of leading Turkish politicians, prime ministers, and presidents over the years on both the right and left. Some of the country's top military leaders even looked upon it favorably as an Islamic bulwark against communism during the Cold War, and others still see it as a nationalist-minded source of religious values that can combat the radical left and other extremist movements. This was the source of the Islam-Turkish synthesis of the early 1980s in which the values of Turkish nationalism and Islam were seen to be mutually reinforcing in a nationally oriented Islamic practice.

A Vision of National Islam

The Gülen movement consciously acts within the context of Turkish society and not as part of a pan-Islamic movement. It accepts the vital importance of the role of the state in creating and maintaining the conditions for the preservation of society, without which there would be anarchy. Thus, the movement is not antistate or antisystem. It views Turkish nationalism as compatible with the values of the movement as long as the state operates within the framework of tolerance and intellectual and religious freedom. Indeed, it is this strong Turkish orientation—a kind of "Turkish Islam"—that may account for the movement's limited familiarity among or attraction to Muslims outside of the Turkic world, at least so far.

Is There a "Turkish Islam"?

Some transnational Islamic movements believe Islam's message must totally transcend the state. Thus they reject in principle the Gülen movement's willingness to work within contemporary Turkish state values as in effect creating a special local form of what might be called "Turkish Islam." But is there really such a thing as Turkish Islam? If so, how much relevance could the Gülen movement ever be expected to have outside Turkey's borders? Put another way, is there enough Islamic universalism within the Gülen movement to make it relevant for non-Turkish Muslims?

Gülen's own writings show a belief in the genius of Turkish history and the role of Turks in spreading Islam and creating the Ottoman Empire. Patriotism to the state is fully compatible with his vision of Islam. Gülen perceives the evolution of global Islam as moving along diverse and well-identified historical paths and as working through the intermediacy of specific individuals and peoples throughout history. Some Turkish Islamists criticize Gülen for having a near-mystical sense of the role of Turks in Islam, almost as if the Turks were chosen for a leading role in Islamic history. If this is indeed the message imparted outside Turkey, it would place real limitations upon the movement's relevance and appeal to other Muslim peoples.

Gülen would, in fact, reject any notion that Turkish Islam exists as a different branch of Islam, much less as a different form of religion; he refers to it only as a particular body of cultural and historical experience. Thus, there is such a thing as a Turkish expression of Islam, drawn from the cultural and historical conditions of the Seljuk Turkish and Ottoman Turkish periods, which witnessed the encouragement of religious tolerance and the active involvement of Sufi orders in society. But even these cultural and historical conditions are distinctive to Turkey only in a matter of degree.

Turkish scholar Sedat Laçiner suggests that Turkish Islam had the advantage of developing within an Ottoman state that was never under European imperial control—unlike other Muslim countries, most of which were under imperialist control for long periods in the modern era. Thus, Turkish Islam could freely develop its own thinking about Islam and the world—at least until the intellectual shutdown of Islam in the Kemalist era. The Ottoman Empire was also forced to face the challenge of modernity as a state earlier than other Muslim societies. Laçiner sees Turkish Islam as more culturally secure because of the Ottomans' relative equality as an independent state within the Western geopolitical order, giving it a greater worldliness.

Additionally, Turkish Islam has never fallen under a specific leader or been the project of a specific movement—such as the Wahhabis—but has evolved organically within the broader culture. Its development within the multiethnic and multireligious Ottoman context has made it more tolerant and open to other religions as well as to other Islamic schools of thought. As a result, religion was always a pragmatic part of the state under the Ottomans. Although Turkish Islam in the Ottoman period had a number of specific cultural and historical advantages, the conclusions of that experience can be of relevance to other Muslims who were deprived of the same opportunities for independent development.[15]

It would therefore be regrettable if the particular Turkish historical roots of the Gülen movement caused other Muslims to believe the movement was irrelevant to their needs. The Gülen vision of the Turkish experience represents a belief in the compatibility of the state, faith, and modernity. This reality differs from the experience of many other Muslim states, particularly within the Arab world, where there has been no meaningful independent state tradition and where the modern state is often viewed as an imperialist creation in terms of its borders, institutions, and unrepresentative, externally supported leadership.

In principle, the Gülen movement offers a form of Islam that allows for national forms of expression and that does not deny the universal character of Islam. In this sense, Egyptian, Pakistani, and Indonesian forms of Islam clearly exist, each of which uniquely flows from their respective cultural, linguistic, geographical, and historical experiences. Taken together, they make up the mosaic of the world of Islam and its essentially single body of faith and creed.

---

15. Sedat Laçiner, "Turkish Islam and Turkey's EU Membership," *Journal of Turkish Weekly*, July 15, 2005.

A form of nationally expressed Islam—one that accepts but is independent of the state structure and its often state-controlled ulema—may be of particular relevance to other Muslim countries. Local and national expressions of Islam are not comfortable with rigidly transnational, one-size-fits-all expression of Islam. The transnationalists tend to produce a greater degree of ideological radicalism, a pan-Islamism that recognizes no local forms of expression, that is not shaped or constrained by any particular historical experience, that is largely an abstraction, that insists upon uniformity in practice, and that is beyond the purview of any state or society. This kind of Islamic vision can readily fall prey to self-appointed suprastate leaders who are out of touch with the grassroots and their specific cultural-historical practices.

I am well aware that many Islamists legitimately fear that the concept of "national Islam" can be used to weaken a sense of Islamic unity and solidarity of action in the face of Western dominance and divide-and-conquer policies: indeed, the West often reflexively opposes transnational Islam for that very reason. Islamists express the additional concern that national forms of expression often represent local non-Islamic accretions to the faith that can twist or compromise the basic premises of Islam. But even local Islam can produce quite radical forms of expression—for example, take the Taliban or hard-line Wahhabi clerics in Saudi Arabia who are not representative of the overall Islamic mainstream. Yet ironically many of the proponents of pan-Islam somehow seek "genuine" expression of the faith through embrace of Arab forms of Islamic practice, such as an insistence on Arab dress and manners that are neither universal nor relevant to the faith but are somehow seen as more Islamic.

Much of the discrediting of national expressions of Islam stems from the seeming illegitimacy of the modern Muslim state, that often lies within borders created for imperial convenience under rulers who were never democratically elected, whose policies fail to serve the people or Islam well, and whose governance is reinforced by repressive state institutions and often bolstered by external Western support. Thus, establishment clerics are often seen as hirelings who are subservient to the needs of the particular regime and employed to preserve its hold on power. Understandably, many Islamists and others reject this kind of state. Under such conditions, Islamism can easily become an antistate movement, particularly if the state is perceived to be un-Islamic, unjust, and repressive.

The task of the Gülen movement in Turkey is much facilitated by the view of most Turks that their state is quite legitimate—regardless of the shortcomings of any particular party in power—and reflects an honest and free electoral procedure. While the Gülen movement itself is unhappy with the discrimination that it suffers from the antireligious secularists within the state, the movement in principle fully accepts the legitimacy of the Turkish state and only seeks to develop greater religious freedom within it. (It is precisely this quest for change—and the implicit class rivalry within—that worries Turkish radical secularists: the new bourgeois Islamists represent a rising class competing against the old Kemalist elite.)

Curiously, Gülen is harshly criticized by both right- and left-wing nationalist circles, which portray him alternately as an instrument of foreign control, of the CIA, and of Jews and Christians, as a reactionary response to Kemalist nationalism, and as an instrument to destroy Turkish nationalism. His heavy focus on ecumenical outreach can only partly explain this peculiar virulence.

The Gülen movement was long at odds even with Turkey's Islamist political parties, particularly with the succession of Erbakan parties and even initially with the JDP. Gülen insists that Islamic movements should stay out of politics and objects to even being described as Islamist at all; he argues that the movement only seeks to further Islamic values and their practice at the personal and social level and not at the political level. In fact, the Gülen movement sees danger to itself when Islamists engage in politics, since they regularly bring down Kemalist wrath not only upon themselves but also indirectly upon the Gülen movement. Relations have thus been cool or even negative between Gülen's followers and political Islamists, although Gülen has occasionally let it be known which of the current political parties he personally believes best serves Turkey's interests—and it has not usually been an Islamist party.

Since the JDP came to power, however, and its adoption of a highly moderate, pragmatic, and productive political platform, the Gülen movement has greatly reduced criticism of it. As a result, relations between the two are much better now than in the past. Given the JDP's experience in working successfully within the political system, Islamic thinking has evolved perhaps more rapidly within the ranks of the JDP than anywhere else. The JDP is also largely an urban phenomenon, while the Gülen movement has had stronger roots in the countryside and towns. Many members of the Gülen community have now joined the JDP, not as an alternative to the Gülen movement but as a political complement to it. This improvement of ties between the two has in turn raised darker suspicions among the hardline Kemalists.

Intellectual Tolerance and Inquiry: The Abant Forum

One of the Gülen movement's greatest accomplishments—and a demonstration of its search for greater universalism—has come through a remarkable process of intellectual outreach, a series of annual roundtables called the Abant Forum. These roundtables have brought together Turks of diverse intellectual backgrounds—Muslims, secularists, traditionalists, modernists, atheists, Christians, leftists, and conservatives—to hammer out some common positions on key contemporary societal issues. The product of these forums, which have continued annually into 2007, has been remarkable and is of particular relevance to intellectual debates raging across the Muslim world.

The first two roundtables, held in 1998 and 1999, hammered out pioneering bulletins on a few key concepts and concluded the following:

- There is no contradiction between intellect *(akil)* and divine inspiration *(vahi)*. Both are valid as foundations for action. Thus, rational discourse and religious vision must complement each other and neither can trump the other in determining the validity of a chosen religious position.
- In Islam, reason permits us to understand what divine inspiration has told us. Inspiration is a divine means of conveying knowledge, while reason is a human vehicle for obtaining knowledge. If we accept the idea of discordance between divine inspiration and reason, we create tension between knowledge and religion, between the state and religion, and between life and religion.
- No individual can claim divine authority on the matter of understanding and interpreting revelation.
- Religion is one of the main components of life and culture; it is a basic source of common values. As long as it works within the law, efforts to organize religious life within society should not be prevented. Indeed, one of the key elements of democracy is to create a space where differences can coexist.
- Just as there is no uniform model of modernization, there is also no absolute conflict between religion and modernization. Not all reactionaries are religious, and not all religious people are reactionary.
- Muslims possess the authority to resolve their own religious issues. Thus, religious figures must not place any issues off limits for discussion. *Ijtihad,* or interpretation of religion, is essential in the resolution of intellectual crises. Islam is open to rational consideration as a means of reaching solutions.
- In the view of believers, God is the absolute sovereign of the world with His knowledge, will, mercy, justice, and power. This religious concept of sovereignty should not be confused with the political concept of sovereignty in which there is no political power higher than the national will. (Here we have reconciliation between the religious and secular view of the nature of power and sovereignty.) The conviction of most believing Muslims to acknowledge God as the supreme sovereign in no way binds anyone else to accept it.
- The state is a human and not a sacred institution. (This statement very deftly cuts two ways. It denies to any religious group the right to view an Islamic state as a sacred goal or institution, while it weakens the tendency of the statists in Turkey to "worship" the state as an entity in itself or as an institution above the people.)

- Islam leaves the details of operating a political regime to society. The state must remain neutral on issues of religious belief. In the end, the state must be a vehicle for facilitating and not blocking the intellectual and spiritual development of the individual and society.
- Throughout history, there have always been tensions between religion and the state. The essence of Atatürk's reforms did not reflect an attitude against the essence of religion itself but against traditions, appearances, and worn-out institutions that passed as religion.
- Under secularism, there should be no intervention on individual lifestyle. (This statement is meant to prevent the state from dictating clothing codes or banning any kind of personal dress, head covering, or expression of religious belief. It also means that religious believers cannot impose their own beliefs on nonbelievers.)
- Women should not be restricted by traditions that are presented as religiously based or by ideologically imposed political views (such as Kemalist bans on women wearing headscarves while in public service or in educational institutions.)
- Islam is no obstacle to the existence of a democratic state ruled by law. [16]

These key principles drawn from early sessions demonstrate how the annual Abant Forum process represents a historic and remarkable reconciliation and concordance of views among secular and religious segments across society. Its platform advocates a modern, democratic, pluralistic, decentralized, tolerant form of government based on people's will and not on any ideological group. Its strictures fall most heavily at first upon a Kemalist elite (or any authoritarian secularist regime) that has gained dominance over the state, but the strictures have equal application to any other ideological group that seeks to impose its beliefs, whether Islamist, nationalist, or leftist.

Acceptance of these principles by Islamist parties such as Welfare, Virtue, and JDP would represent an extremely important commitment. While the Gülen movement is known for opposing the establishment of any religious parties, its sponsorship of these principles should help dispel any belief that the movement seeks to impose an Islamic or sharia state in the long term. The Abant Forum is performing a signal service in setting forth a basic set of principles capable of directing Turkey through the shoals of internal change, religious and secular debate, and reform and democratization. These principles are of direct relevance to debates in other Muslim countries.

As the distinguished religious scholar Mehmet Aydın points out, the most striking thing about this process and its conclusions is that a religious community initiated them. In fact, it is remarkable that in Turkey today such

---

16. These are a summary of key points from the pamphlet *The Abant Platform: Final Declarations* (Istanbul: Journalists and Writers Foundation, Istanbul, 1999 and 2000).

crucial theoretical and ideological discussions—about Islam, secularism, Islamist evolution, the view of the past, modern values, and relations with the Muslim world—are discussed and debated more widely by Islamists than any other political or social group.[17] These very ideas and discussions are seen as suspect by the orthodox Kemalists, who seek to ignore this process entirely and do not even want conceptual reconciliation with Islam in any form. It is imperative that Turkey and the Muslim world as a whole engage in a broad discussion of such important themes if there is to be political evolution in the future.

Conclusion

At this point, the Islamists represent—even if by default—the most creative intellectual force in the country on these conceptual questions. While Turkey will almost certainly remain a "secular" state, the meaning of secularism within Turkey is already evolving and the country is slowly developing a new and more comfortable relationship with its own Ottoman past and cultural and religious traditions. The joint phenomena of the JDP and the Gülen movement are emblematic of this fact and demonstrate the emergence of a creative and vibrant Islamist community within Turkey. This, in turn, has significant bearing on Turkey's relationships with the Middle East and broader Muslim world.

---

17. Mehmet Aydın, interview with the author, Ankara, September 2004.

Part II

Turkey's Relations with the Muslim World and Beyond

7

JDP Policies toward the Muslim World

With the emergence of a consensus in Turkey for a foreign policy based on "no enemies" in the region—a return to a more classic form of Kemalist neutrality—the JDP has vigorously moved toward reviving and broadening Ankara's long-atrophied relations with the Middle East and Muslim world. This is evident in its active willingness to serve as an intermediary in crises between the United States and Middle Eastern countries, to broaden bilateral relations with regional Muslim and non-Muslim neighbors, and to assume leadership of the Organization of the Islamic Conference.

JDP officials acknowledge that a continued opening to the Middle East will require, among other things, a much greater official focus and training in Middle East studies and languages. But the JDP has been wary of intensely promoting such a program, because the military could interpret it as representing a special Islamist agenda. Thus, the JDP has hesitated to move too quickly or boldly on new Middle East initiatives to avoid sparking military distrust. Nonetheless, through advocacy of these multilateral Middle East processes, Turkey is heading in the direction of greater foreign policy independence and stronger regional institutions. To be sure, in the short term, this process will not be helpful to the Bush administration's agenda in the Middle East. But the process is a long-term one. Over time, Turkish-generated calls for reform, political liberalization, and a tempering of regional confrontations in the Middle East will come from a credible, strong, and independent regional voice; such calls may ultimately facilitate changes that are in the long-term interests of the West as well.

The Arab States

During Turkey's October 2005 negotiations on entry into the European Union, the Arab League was among those organizations and states that made diplomatic representations to Brussels in support of Ankara's case. This striking Arab identification with Turkish interests represented a dramatic change from past decades when Turkey had no support from the Arab world. Not only was the Arab League taking a special initiative on Turkey's behalf but it was also involving itself in a process concerned with the accession of a Muslim state to Europe. This initiative demonstrated the Arab world's hope that Turkey can become a backdoor for it in developing closer ties with Europe. It also may have reflected the increasing number of positive contacts Ankara has been having with the Arab world.

Over the past several years, Prime Minister Erdoğan has tirelessly visited every country in the region except Armenia, where he has brought to bear the Turkish perspective on regional issues. At an Arab Economic Forum in Beirut in June 2005, for example, he called for closer ties with Arab countries and expanded commercial relations, which have nearly doubled in recent years, and simultaneously touted Turkey's own economic progress. He also called for surplus earnings from soaring oil prices to be increasingly directed into investment in regional countries.[1] In March 2006 in Khartoum, Erdoğan became the first Turkish prime minister to attend and address an Arab League summit, and Turkey was granted the status of "permanent guest." Although unheard of in public speeches in Turkey, Erdoğan opened his talk with a traditional Koranic invocation.[2]

A regular Arab commentator for the *New Anatolian*, Abdel Halim Ghazaly, commented in 2006 on changes in Arab thinking toward Turkey. He noted that Erdoğan—shortly after becoming prime minister—laid great emphasis on the development of strong economic ties with the Arab world and on practical steps rather than on simple rhetoric about Islamic brotherhood. Ghazaly stated that Erdoğan had, in fact, delivered on this. He pointed out that while Turkey's new independent policies and diplomatic openings to the Arab world all had major impact, "The change began with the landslide victory of the JDP in the Turkish parliamentary elections. . . . Arab intellectuals seem to be fond of the new combination created by the party mixing Islamic conservatism with democratic ethics. As the Islamic trend is spreading in the Arab world, the policies of the JDP government have given a more positive message."[3]

This comports with the accounts of Cengiz Çandar, a leading Turkish journalist and long-time Middle East hand, who reported his impression in March 2006 that Turkey's position in the Middle East has never been higher. As evidence, he pointed to the visit of Foreign Minister Gül to Saudi Arabia, where he presented in a public forum his views on Islam in the twenty-first century. According to Çandar, Gül set forth Turkey's accomplishments as relates to Islam, and they were admired—which in itself represented a very new development.[4] In fact, some have suggested that the Sunni Arab world

1. Pakistan International News Service, June 18, 2005.
2. Cengiz Çandar, "What Is Erdogan Doing at the Arab Summit?" *New Anatolian*, March 29, 2006, www.thenewanatolian.com/opinion-3669.html.
3. Abdel Halim Ghazaly, "The Bright Image of Turkey in the Arab World (I)," *New Anatolian*, February 23, 2006, www.thenewanatolian.com/opinion.
4. Cengiz Çandar, "'Maşallah'—'İnşallah'," *New Anatolian*, February 13, 2006, www.thenewanatolian.com/opinion-590.html.

may now come to view Turkey as an important potential bulwark against rising Iranian and Shiite power in the Middle East.

Such a role would, of course, represent something of a throwback to Ottoman leadership of the Sunni world. Yet it is unlikely that the JDP, or even Turkey, thinks in such stark sectarian terms; it will probably prefer to remain neutral in any Sunni-Shiite conflicts by keeping a strong foot in each camp. In March 2003, for example, Turkey's Office of Religious Affairs—with the support of the Turkish Foreign Ministry—arranged a peacekeeping trip to Iraq through the Turkish-founded Eurasian Islamic Council to try to broker an end to clashes between Shia and Sunni communities there. Ankara convened both Sunni and Shiite clerics from Central Asia and the Caucausus in what was a first for Turkey in engaging in intersectarian mediation.[5] Only in the event of serious deterioration of Turkish relations with Iran might Ankara begin to consider association with a broader Sunni anti-Shiite agenda.

Iraq

Prior to the U.S. invasion of Iraq, the prospects of an impending war energized the JDP to launch an initiative that brought together six of Iraq's neighbors—Turkey, Egypt, Iran, Jordan, Saudi Arabia, and Syria (Kuwait demurred). In turn, this led to the Istanbul Declaration, which was explicitly aimed at heading off a U.S. military attack on Baghdad. As Davutoğlu points out, this was something of a first for Turkey; it jointly met not once but five times with these regional neighbors, all with diverse interests, to discuss a major regional crisis.[6] Although the initiative was hardly welcomed in Washington, similar initiatives from Ankara on other regional crises have been ongoing and are likely to characterize Turkish foreign policy in the future. They are based not so much on any Islamist ideology as on an evolving view of the Turkish national interest.

Then, the JDP-dominated parliament voted to deny the United States use of Turkish soil for the invasion of Iraq, fearing—presciently—that little good would come of it for Turkey. Since the end of the war, Turkey has moved away from viewing Iraqi events entirely through a Kurdish prism and has developed ties with other players in Iraq, including various Sunni and Shia Arab groups. In fact, Turkey has established ties with Muqtada al-Sadr, and it invited Iraqi prime minister Ibrahim Ja'fari to visit Ankara just before he was scuttled as prime minister under strong U.S. pressure. Furthermore, Turkey has taken a somewhat more realistic attitude toward the reality of a highly

5. "Irak'taki Mezhep Çatışmasını Önlemek için Diyanet Devrede," *Zaman*, March 3, 2006, www.zaman.com.tr/?bl=dishaberler&alt=&trh=20060303&hn=261762.

6. "Ahmet Davutoğlu İle Türk Dış Politikası Değerlendirmesi" [An Evaluation of Turkish Foreign Policy with Ahmet Davutoğlu], Turkish CNN, February 17, 2003.

autonomous Kurdistan within Iraq and has moved to establish itself as an economic power there through investment, greatly increased trade, and the provision of professional training to the Kurds. Although the dislocations of war have greatly affected Turkish bilateral trade with Iraq, it reached $2.3 billion in 2004, or 3.4 percent of overall Turkish trade.[7]

Syria

Turkish-Syrian relations have continued to improve dramatically under the JDP, particularly with a series of high-level visits. In 2004, for example, Erdoğan traveled to Syria where he signed economic, security, and free-trade agreements with Damascus. Following this, Turkish president Ahmet Sezer visited the country. His trip faced explicit remonstrances from the U.S. ambassador in Ankara, who claimed it was contrary to U.S. policies that seek to isolate Damascus.[8]

With a virtual end to the intense Turkish-Syrian frictions of the past—particularly those related to the PKK, border questions, water problems, and Turkey's close ties with Israel—Damascus has warmed to the new strategic options that Turkey might be able to offer. For most Arabs, the election of a moderate Islamist party in Ankara sent a signal (accurate or not) that a commonly shared historical and Islamic heritage can perhaps once again help bring the two countries together—even though utilization of joint Islamic heritage is precisely what the Turkish generals do not want. The elections further suggested to Arabs that Turkey may have overcome its wayward past and come to appreciate the place of the Muslim world on Ankara's broader strategic horizon. Such a rapprochement would suggest that Turkey could perhaps help bridge the gulf between the Arab world and the West. It would also demonstrate that even a Muslim state aspiring to gain entry into the European Union can maintain an important role in the Middle East, suggesting that the door of rapprochement with Europe might be open even to Syria or other regional states down the road.

In a dramatic cultural turnabout, Turkey and Syria held a publicly televised academic conference in September 2005 that led to the formation of a commission to oversee the rewriting of the historical treatment of the four-hundred-year period when Syria was part of the Ottoman Empire. The commission was formed partly under the auspices of the OIC and is designed to bring Turkish, Syrian, and other scholars together to review in a balanced light their record of historical interaction.[9]

---

7.   DEIK (Bureau of Foreign Economic Relations), www.deik.org.tr.
8.   K. Gajendra Singh, "A New Age for Turkey-Syria Relations," *Asia Times*, April 14, 2005.
9.   Ibrahim Balta, "Suriye, Osmanlı'yı Türkiye'ye danışıp yazacak" [Syria Will Write Its Ottoman Period History in Consultation with Turkey], *Turkistan Newsletter*, October 5, 2005.

There is almost a palpable sense of relief and hope among many Syrians that perhaps its isolation from the West is reaching an end, without capitulation to U.S. policy demands. Yet these Syrian expectations may not be fully realistic. Syria, of course, seeks maximum diplomatic support from any source against U.S. and Israeli pressures, and hence welcomes any seeming switch of Ankara from the enemy to the friend column. But Damascus itself has been slow to undertake necessary reforms, such as those related to democratization and political liberalization, and the JDP has stated so publicly.

Although Turkey has repeatedly offered its good offices to broker Syrian-Israeli dialogue, the JDP has been realistic and outspoken to the Syrians in regard to all relevant issues. In meetings held in 2005, both Foreign Minister Gül and President Sezer emphasized to Damascus the need for domestic reform, for the withdrawal of Syrian forces from Lebanon (which took place), and for the need to ensure that international jihadists do not enter Iraq from Syrian territory. The improved tenor of bilateral relations has permitted Ankara to speak with candor on these issues and others that are of particular importance to not only Turkey but also the United States.

Overall, Ankara now speaks with a more independent voice and hence with greater credibility in Damascus. But can Turkey really draw an isolated and weak Syria more closely into its own economic and political orbit? So far changes in Syria's policies have been limited, but the nature of regional forces is changing all around it. Syrians may now be more willing to embrace Turkey's role in helping lead them out of isolation. That could represent a major new factor in Middle East geopolitics that should be encouraged and watched closely.

Iran

In a striking development, following President George W. Bush's declaration that Iran was part of the "axis of evil," the staunchly secular Sezer visited Iran, calling for new priorities in building economic relations between Turkey and Iran. Additionally, Sezer was the first top Turkish official to undertake a symbolic visit to the Azerbaijan region of Iran. Tehran interestingly acquiesced to this visit, even with all of its ethnic undertones. In another major symbolic concession by Tehran, Sezer gave a lecture on Atatürk's accomplishments at Tehran University; and Iranian president Mohammad Khatami declared that it was in Iran's interests to have Turkey join the European Union.[10]

International relations professor Kemal Kirişçi states that in recent years the threat of Iranian meddling in Turkey's Kurdish or religious issues has

---

10. Mohammad Noureddine, "Is Turkey Turning toward the East?" *Daily Star* (Beirut), June 26, 2002, archives.econ.utah.edu/archives/a-list/2002w27/msg00002.htm.

been much reduced. Further, economic ties between the two countries have increased greatly, particularly in the energy field, and Turkish companies are interested in expanding their involvement in the Iranian economy. Turkey has also established a free-visa policy for Iranian visitors to Turkey, attracting more than half a million Iranian visitors to Turkey each year.[11]

Since Sezer's visit, there have been repeated high-level meetings between Turkish and Iranian officials, including Erdoğan's meeting with President Mahmoud Ahmedinejad in Baku. Further, Iran has offered to help Turkey in developing peaceful nuclear energy—so far without response—and Tehran continues to play a strong game in trying to encourage Turkey's neutrality in Tehran's standoff with Washington. For example, visits to Ankara by U.S. secretary of state Condoleezza Rice and by members of the Senate Foreign Affairs Committee in 2006 were promptly followed by a high-profile visit from Ali Larijani, Iran's national security adviser. In all these exchanges, Ankara's position has not caved in to Iran but has leaned towards useful and friendly pressure on Tehran; it has publicly and repeatedly called for greater Iranian transparency and for Tehran's need to satisfy international concerns over its nuclear developments.

For a long period, Washington did not welcome any development in Turkish-Iranian ties, because it wished to focus heavy pressure on Tehran on multiple fronts. It has even attempted to pressure Ankara to facilitate possible U.S. military action against Tehran if the need ever arises. However, Ankara has resisted such pressure and has begun touting itself as a possible intermediary between Tehran and Washington. Although some critics in Turkey wonder if Ankara could ever deliver results in playing such a role, IAEA director Mohamed ElBaradei, in the course of the West's recent confrontation with Iran over nuclear issues, described Turkey as having an "important and unmatched" intermediary role with its excellent ties with both sides.[12]

Indeed, in early 2006, as the Bush administration found itself increasingly blocked by multiple domestic and international factors in its ability to bring military force to bear against Tehran, it retreated somewhat from a policy of direct confrontation and turned to multilateral instruments, including a willingness to let Ankara do what it could to soften Tehran's stance. For example, a senior Turkish diplomat reported that in late spring 2006 Foreign Minister Gül served as an intermediary between Secretary of State Rice and the Iranians. As a result, Turkey was put on par with other channels to Iran, such as the European Union, Russia, and China.[13] Turkey also took an active

---

11. Kemal Kirişçi, "Turkish Dilemmas," *Bitter Lemons Middle East Roundtable* 4, no. 15 (April 27, 2006), bitterlemons-international.org.

12. "Baradei: Turkey Can Help Ease Iranian Nuclear Crisis," *Daily Star* (Beirut), July 7, 2006, www.dailystar.com.lb/article.asp?edition_id=10&categ_id=2&article_id=73744.

13. Cengiz Çandar, "Turkey's Constructive Role in the US-Iran Situation and Its Domestic Impact, *New Anatolian*, June 5, 2006, www.thenewanatolian.com/opinion-8141.html.

role in trying to explain and defuse the crisis that arose in early 2006 when a Danish newspaper published cartoons insulting to the Prophet. Secular Turkey was well positioned to do so and gained respect from other Muslim countries for its independent views and actions at that time.

Starting in the late spring of 2006, Washington seemed to be adopting a more constructive and realistic approach toward Turkey's foreign policy. It appeared to recognize U.S. limitations on curtailing the type of regional role Turkey wants to play and may have decided to let Ankara play the role it wants and to allow it to pursue whatever benefits might come from its role. There seems to be a belated recognition that a "new Turkey" can sometimes serve as a useful force in the region, even for U.S. interests. But whenever Washington turns up the heat on Tehran, either to fully implement an embargo on Iran or to rally support for a U.S. military confrontation against it, Ankara will find it increasingly difficult to acquiesce.

Palestine

The JDP has demonstrated greater interest and involvement in the Palestinian problem than have previous ruling parties. This is an area of interest to a great extent shared by the broader Turkish public, particularly as Palestinian suffering has grown. In fact, Ankara has worked to position itself as a neutral, balanced intermediary. For example, after the Hamas victory in Palestinian elections in 2006, the JDP government did not shrink from issuing an unofficial invitation to Khalid Mishal, a leading Hamas leader, to visit Ankara—much to Washington's and Israel's dismay since both had sought to entirely isolate Hamas. Although Ankara publicly counseled moderation to the new Hamas government, today Ankara figures more prominently in Palestinian diplomatic calculations. Palestinian president Mahmoud Abbas later visited Ankara for extensive talks and publicly supported Turkey's invitation to Mishal.[14]

Nonetheless, Ankara's actual leverage over both Israel and the Palestinians remains limited, but both parties have sought Turkish support and involvement, a role to which the JDP seems strongly committed despite Washington's periodic misgivings.

In July 2006, for example, Davutoğlu, in his role as Turkish presidential foreign policy adviser, traveled to Damascus in connection with the ongoing military confrontation between Israel and the Hamas government over the kidnapping of an Israeli soldier. Interestingly, Washington reportedly requested the Davutoğlu trip, partly out of recognition that neither the United States nor Israel had any other ally able or willing to undertake the task. If

---

14. "Abbas in Ankara Seeking Stronger Support for Palestinians," *New Anatolian*, April 25, 2006.

true, this request represents a considerable turnaround for Washington and reads as a belated recognition that Ankara's early establishment of ties with the Hamas government and the controversial visit of Mishal to Ankara have their benefits. Indeed, JDP policy toward Hamas seems to have been vindicated and provides the United States a significant long-term venue to Hamas through Ankara.[15]

Israel

Although they have maintained close working ties with Israel, Prime Minister Erdoğan and Foreign Minister Gül have spoken out sharply against the harsh nature of Israel's policies toward the Palestinians, particularly under the strongly right-wing government of Ariel Sharon and later Ehud Olmert. Erdoğan described Israel's assassination of Hamas leader Sheikh Ahmad Yassin as a "terrorist act." Even left-of-center Turkish prime minister Bülent Ecevit warned in 2001 that Israel's retaliatory military strikes against Palestinians risked plunging the region into a war that would be far more dangerous than the U.S. invasion of Afghanistan: "Sharon is determined to implement very excessive, unjust measures against the Palestinian Authority and soil."[16]

Although these critical views are in keeping with general press coverage in most of the rest of the world on Palestinian developments, Turkey has disturbingly witnessed a recent rise in anti-Semitic writings, including broad sales of Hitler's *Mein Kampf*. Additionally, radical elements within the Islamic press have grown much harsher in their rhetoric not only toward Israel but also toward Jews in general—this in a country where anti-Semitism has always been marginal. Some of this reflects a rising level of emotionalism on a global level toward Israel's increasingly harsh policies in the occupied territories in the wake of Likud's (and later Kadima's) electoral success and Washington's Global War on Terrorism.

Even under the JDP, however, Turkey's economic ties with Israel have remained strong: in 2004 Turkey agreed to sell 50 million cubic meters of water annually to Israel, and Turkey also signed an $800 million contract to build and manage three energy plants in Israel.[17] That noted, Ankara did recently freeze some civilian projects with Israel, choosing instead to grant them to European firms to facilitate its membership application to the European Union.[18]

---

15. Rüşen Çakır, "Bush Istedi, Davutoğlu Şam'a Gitti" [Bush Asked For It, So Davutoğlu Went to Damascus], *Vatan*, July 6, 2006.

16. "Turkey Warns of Mideast War Far More Dangerous Than in Afghanistan," Agence France-Presse, December 4, 2001.

17. Soner Cagaptay, *The Turkish Prime Minister Visits Israel: Whither Turkish-Israeli Relations?* Policywatch #987 (Washington, D.C.: Washington Institute for Near East Policy, April 27, 2005).

18. Zvi Barel, "Friend, and Friend of Foe," *Ha'aretz*, January 4, 2005.

Israel and Post-Saddam Iraq

Turkey is aware that some elements of Israeli strategic thinking advocate general support of ethnic minorities in the region, such as the Kurds, as a way to weaken the centralized power of Arab states. Turkey grew particularly concerned in 2004 at the reported presence of hundreds of Israeli intelligence officers actively working in northern Iraq and conducting covert operations within the Kurdish areas of Syria and Iran with the aim of collecting intelligence and causing destabilization in both countries. Ankara was incensed at reports that Israel was providing training to Kurdish *peshmerga* militia forces in Iraq, reportedly to strengthen them against the centralized Iraqi state and to destabilize Iran.[19] Ankara believes that this purported activity contributes directly to broader Kurdish separatism and undercuts efforts to preserve central authority in Iraq.

Lebanon

Following Israel's extensive destruction of Lebanon's infrastructure and its failed effort to eradicate Hizballah in July 2006, Erdoğan took an especially active role as one of the few regional leaders to speak out about Israel's excessive use of force. He also worked for a cease-fire and resolution through a flurry of telephone consultations with George W. Bush, Tony Blair, Kofi Annan, and leaders from Syria, Lebanon, Iran, the European Union, and elsewhere. While Turkey's ability to change the situation on the ground was quite limited, the regional press took note of this high-profile Turkish activism—especially in the face of silence from most Arab leaders.

Organization of the Islamic Conference

Under the JDP, Turkey's long-evolving attitude toward the OIC has reached new heights. In 1993, under the quite secularist prime minister Tansu Çiller, Turkey established a precedent by turning to the OIC for the dispatch of Muslim peacekeeping troops to Bosnia to protect safe havens there. In 1995, all Turkish political parties came to accept the benefits of formal OIC membership. And in 1997, President Demirel himself attended an OIC summit in Tehran but walked out when Turkey fell under public criticism at the conference for its close strategic ties with Washington and Israel.[20]

Then, in June 2003, under the JDP, Turkey for the first time hosted a meeting of the OIC at the foreign minister level in Istanbul. Shortly thereafter, in a symbolic boost to Turkey, Turkey was scheduled to host the second Joint Forum of

---

19. "Seymour Hersh: Israeli Agents Operating in Iraq, Iran and Syria," *Democracy Now,* June 22, 2004, www.democracynow.org/article.pl?sid=04/06/22/148253.

20. Hale, *Turkish Foreign Policy,* 315.

the European Union and the OIC (a meeting that never materialized), under-lining Ankara's dual leadership capacity in both worlds. Turkey also made efforts to gain control of the so-called Jerusalem Committee of the OIC, which oversees discussion of policies on Arab-Israeli issues, meaning Turkey could play a moderating influence in a volatile forum. The committee also plays a key role in the oversight of Islamic sites in Jerusalem, requiring the chair to have diplomatic access to Israel in order to fulfill this function; this role would be facilitated through Turkey's full diplomatic relations with Israel.[21]

In a genuinely dramatic development with considerable long-term impli-cations, Turkey actually assumed the chairmanship of the OIC at the 2004 OIC foreign ministers' summit in Istanbul. Significantly, this marked the first time the chairmanship was decided through an open election, which itself occurred at Turkey's demand. This development was notable for two reasons: first, Turkey actively sought to win the position and to strengthen its role in Muslim world politics, and second, Turkey established a transparent demo-cratic process within the OIC and demonstrated that it enjoyed new-found support and popularity within OIC circles.

Through this process, Ankara hoped to democratize, reform, strengthen, and rationalize the OIC mechanism in order to make it work more effectively. This signaled the first step in a whole series of democratizing and reform pro-cesses that Davutoğlu has advocated in order to strengthen a broad range of regional and Muslim organizations, which to date have largely operated feck-lessly and without tangible result. Erdoğan and Gül have both voiced strong support for the OIC and for a new, open, moderate, and reformist agenda that would make it a stronger, more effective, and more articulate voice for Muslim world issues, including the possible adoption of a permanent secretariat. As Gül has stated, "Turkey continues to voice its opinion that the Islamic world needs to address its problems in a realistic manner and to assume responsi-bility rather than blame others. In this connection we place emphasis on such concepts as democratization, human rights, the rule of law, good governance, accountability, transparency and gender equality."[22]

Davutoğlu, as always favoring broad and multilateral policies, is a strong but not uncritical supporter of Turkish involvement in the OIC and the ECO, which embraces Turkey, Iran, Afghanistan, and now the states of the Caucasus and Central Asia. Davutoğlu attributes the weaknesses of past OIC and Mus-lim organizations to the weak and nonrepresentative character of the unelect-ed regimes that have dominated them and timidly and shortsightedly hobbled and paralyzed their scope of action. This is especially true for organizations

21. Amir Taheri, "Turkey's Bid to Raise Its Islamic Profile and Court Europe May Backfire," *Arab View*, October 6, 2004, www.arabview.com/articles.asp?article=471.

22. Abdullah Gül, *Turkish Policy Quarterly*, February 8, 2005, www.turkishpolicy.com/default. asp?show=fall2004_Abdullah_Gul.

involving Turkish cooperation with the Central Asian states. In his view, all such organizations need to be empowered, strengthened, and reformed. Specifically, they need to be given teeth and an activist executive secretariat before they can fulfill the necessary functions they were created for.[23]

Turkey's increased engagement with the OIC led the organization to call for greater international support for the position of the Turkish communities in Northern Cyprus and in Bulgaria in July 2005.[24] (Interestingly, Russia has been granted observer status at the OIC; Turkish and Russian views tally closely on the handling of most Middle East issues.) Additionally, Turkish scholar Ekmeleddin Ihsanoğlu, secretary-general of the OIC since 2005, is the founding director of the OIC's Research Center for Islamic Art, History and Culture, which produces cultural studies that cover common themes across Islamic civilization. This center has published dozens of volumes on cultural studies in which the Ottoman Empire and the Turkish legacy in the Muslim world occupies a major place, leaving little doubt as to Turkey's importance in Islamic history. With four Turks on its governing board, another Turkish scholar, Halit Eren, took over the leadership of this OIC research center in 2005.

Conclusion

Under the JDP, Turkey has actively sought to play an intermediary role between states that have tense relations with the United States in particular and the West in general. Improving ties with Muslim states and organizations viewed as anti-Western, such as Iran, Syria, and Hamas, strengthen Ankara's hand in the Muslim world and represent a return to traditional Kemalist policies of regional neutrality.

As a high-ranking Turkish diplomat stated in March 2006, "Up to now, another power filled in the grey areas in Middle Eastern politics on behalf of the whole Muslim world, including Turkey. Now its Turkey's turn to fill in these grey areas itself."[25] With his clear reference to the United States, his comment is reflective of Ankara's newfound confidence in playing an activist role in the region, a role that has, for the first time, the support of most states of the region.

Around the same time, Davutoğlu suggested a new term to guide Turkish foreign policy—"proactive peace"—meaning that Ankara should keep its channels open to all political players in the region if it is to possess the needed legitimacy to work among all parties. While in theory such a policy is fine, its

---

23. Davutoğlu, *Stratejik Derinlik*, 281–2.

24. Turkish Press Review, July 1, 2005.

25. Zeynep Gurcanli, "Islamic Diplomacy: The Way to Contain Iran," *New Anatolian*, March 2, 2006, www.thenewanatolian.com/opinion-1936.html.

application must eventually show results.[26] To be sure, Turkey cannot work magic in bringing fundamental change to Iran, Syria, or Hamas; all have strong ideological and policy positions and have continually resisted heavy pressures from both Washington and Jerusalem, much less Ankara. When regional tensions eventually deflate, however, Ankara's leverage may yet be important and valued by others.

Indeed, there are now signs that Washington, in the face of growing regional crises, may be willing to acknowledge that a more independent Turkish role might well have potential advantages worth exploring. Realizing that Turkey's new approach will not be easily changed, Washington may ultimately put Ankara to the test on its ties with Iran, Syria, and Hamas, forcing Ankara to either deliver or face the reality of the impotence of its ties with them. The actual level of Ankara's influence is probably somewhere in between these two poles: if Ankara can exercise an intermediary role and receive regional acceptance in doing so, it will be well on its way to developing a positive regional position unrivaled by any other state. There seems to be a growing consensus in Turkey itself that extends beyond the JDP in support of this type of role.

That said, in the coming years, Turkey's interactions with the Middle East and Muslim world will likely be shaped by

- Ankara's intention to build good relations with all neighbors, including Muslim states;
- Ankara's new vision of Turkey as lying at the "center" between West and East;
- Ankara's willingness to engage with Muslim states on a broad and open basis;
- Ankara's awareness that Turkey's own interests lie in the stability of the region and in finding solutions to volatile problems among states in the region, or between the West and the region;
- Ankara's desire to avoid strategic alliances that limit Turkey's options or create hostility;
- Ankara's interest in developing closer relations with the Gulf states, huge financial centers that have far-reaching international links and increasing financial and investment ties to Turkey and Asia.

In turn, Ankara will no doubt continue to contribute to the shaping of the region through a constellation of strategic, diplomatic, economic, and cultural factors.

---

26. Hüseyin Bağcı, "Proactive Policy in Iraq: How Long?" *New Anatolian*, June 5, 2006.

8

The Foundations of Turkey's Regional Influence

B y any standard except oil, Turkey is the most important country in the Middle East. Its population of 70 million is second only to Egypt (76 million) and surpasses that of Iran (68 million). Among European states, only Germany exceeds Turkey in population; given Turkish population growth rates—modest as they are—this could make Turkey the most populous country in Europe within a few decades. A large population can of course either hinder or facilitate development, depending on the skill of the country in utilizing its human resources. In Turkey's case, it arguably employs its population more effectively than any other Muslim state in the world, particularly when considering the country's general levels of education and professional skills, diversity of economy, and economic and social opportunities.

Military

Turkey is the most important military power in the Middle East apart from Israel. With some 515,000 troops, the Turkish army constitutes the second largest standing force in NATO after the United States. Furthermore, according to the Stockholm International Peace Research Institute (SIPRI), Turkey ranked fourteenth in the world in military expenditures in 2004—with a $10.1 billion defense budget, second only to Israel in the Middle East.[1] (Lest Turkey be thought to spend too much on its military, the government spends more on education than it does on defense.) The importance of Turkey's military is further bolstered by the respected social place of the military in Turkish society.

Turkey's intense program of military modernization that began in 1996 is having a major impact upon the military's overall strength and effectiveness. This modernization program will ultimately allocate some $150 billion over a thirty-year period.[2] As scholar Elliot Hen-Tov notes, "Regionally, Turkey's disproportionate military modernization will further increase the gap between Turkey and its neighbors, since the end of the Soviet Union brought

---

1. *Turkish Daily News,* June, 14, 2005.
2. Elliot Hen-Tov, "The Political Economy Of Turkish Military Modernization," *Middle East Review of International Affairs* 8, no. 4 (December 2004), http://meria.idc.ac.il/journal/2004/issue4/hentov.pdf.

about a decline in Turkey's neighbors' weapons procurement, as well as economic stagnation, while Turkey advanced both economically and militarily."[3] Indeed, as a member the world's most powerful military alliance, Turkey not only has broad access to modern weaponry but also to contemporary strategic thinking and planning and to Western diplomatic support on many strategic issues. This is particularly true as NATO becomes further involved in "out of area" missions in the Balkans and Afghanistan. No other state in the Middle East has this kind of advantage except Israel.

The Turkish airbase at Incirlik has been particularly vital to NATO and U.S. power projection into the Middle East, most importantly during the 1991 Gulf War and the 2003 Iraq War. Although Ankara denied the use of its soil as a land base for the invasion of Iraq in 2003, Incirlik is used by the United States to support military and logistical needs in Iraq and Afghanistan.

Since the collapse of the Soviet Union, Turkey's geopolitical position in the world has grown more central, galvanized by a whole series of other major geopolitical changes in the region. Specifically, nearly all of the potential regional threats that Turkey once faced have either been weakened or eliminated: Russia's geopolitical role in the region has been greatly diminished, and Ankara now enjoys unusually close ties with Moscow; Iran and Iraq were both devastated by the eight-year war they fought with each other; Iraq and Syria lost important Soviet military and political backing; and Saddam and his Ba'th regime are now gone. Although chaos in Iraq has raised new, even more urgent issues of regional instability, Turkish-Greek relations have also undergone dramatic improvement. Thus, Turkey no longer confronts any serious regional military power—a stunningly dramatic change from twenty years ago.

All of these factors taken together have overwhelmingly transformed Turkey into the most important military power in the Middle East after Israel. This fact has broad implications for its foreign policy.

Peacekeeping

An important political-military aspect of Turkey's foreign policy has been its contribution of troops to international peacekeeping operations. Ankara contributed to international observation groups on the Iran-Iraq border (UNIIMOG) and later on the Iraq-Kuwait border (UNIKOM). It also sent peacekeeping forces under UN command to Somalia, Bosnia, Georgia, Hebron (Palestine), and Albania, receiving positive ratings. Ankara experienced some disillusionment in Somalia, which it entered in support of the U.S. mission there, when it was left holding the bag after a precipitate U.S. pullout in 1993. This experience led the Turkish military to veto a subse-

---

3. Hen-Tov, "The Political Economy Of Turkish Military Modernization," 4.

quent peacekeeping assignment to Angola even though the Turkish Foreign Ministry had approved it.[4]

In general terms, however, Turkey has continued to demonstrate its global citizenship in working with the United Nations and other international groups. After the U.S. invasion of Afghanistan following 9/11, for example, Turkey assisted with peacekeeping tasks there at Washington's request. Although it declined to participate in combat operations, Ankara sent ninety elite troops to support the training of the Northern Alliance, to fight terrorism, and to assist with humanitarian efforts.[5]

Economic and Financial Factors

The Turkish experience demonstrates a largely successful transition from a once heavily state-oriented economy under earlier Kemalist policies to an increasingly diversified open-market economy that by the 1990s led Turkey to be included among the top ten newly emerging economies of the world.

In a sense, Turkey has been "blessed" because it lacks oil reserves to drive its economic development, forcing it to develop a broad, diversified manufacturing base whose key industries include textiles, food processing, automobiles, coal, chromite, copper, boron, steel, petroleum, construction, lumber, and paper. Broken down by sector, agriculture makes up 11.7 percent of Turkey's overall economy, industry 29.8 percent, and services 58.5 percent.[6] The strong agricultural base is supplied with abundant water, and the agricultural sector employs 35 percent of the country's workforce. Turkey's key export commodities are apparel, foodstuffs, pharmaceuticals, textiles, metal, and transport equipment, and its automotive and electronic industries are rising in importance. Germany represents Turkey's biggest trading partner in both imports and exports, while the United States ranks fourth as a Turkish export destination and sixth as a source of Turkish imports.

Turkey is currently working to meet economic criteria for admission into the European Union in 2015. The possibility of Turkish accession to the European Union raises hopes among other Middle East countries that Turkey will be the first Muslim country to succeed in breaking the "civilizational barrier."[7] Furthermore, Turkey's experience in its transition to a more export-driven, market economy should be valuable to other largely statist

---

4. Robins, *Suits and Uniforms*, 44–8.
5. Islamonline, "Turkey to Send Troops to Afghanistan," www.islamonline.net/english/news/2001-11/02/article3.shtml.
6. CIA, "The World Factbook—Turkey," https://www.cia.gov/library/publications/the-world-factbook/geos/tu.html.
7. Robins, *Suits and Uniforms*, 207–8.

economies in the region. Today, large Turkish holding companies and contracting firms spearhead Turkey's economic role in the Middle East.

Export of Labor Force

In the 1970s, Turkey began to export its labor force to the Middle East after European immigration doors began to close to guest workers and rising energy costs increased demand for hard-currency earnings. Ankara's strategy of exporting labor was quickly vindicated: in 1965, workers' remittances, primarily from Europe, were $70 million per year; by the early 1990s, this figure had reached $3 billion per year.[8] At a high point in 1982–83, Turkey had roughly three hundred thousand foreign workers in the Middle East.[9] According to the Turkish Ministry of Labor, Turkey still had a total of 1.2 million workers abroad in 2004, more than one hundred thousand of whom were in the Middle East. The vast majority of these workers (95,000) were in Saudi Arabia, while the rest were mainly in Libya (10,000) and Kuwait.[10] This labor export scheme has been augmented by Turkey's new role as a regional contractor in the Middle East, one with growing technical experience and sophistication.

Turkish Foreign Trade with the Middle East

Turkish exports to the Middle East rose nearly fivefold from $1.5 billion in 1990 to $7.2 billion in 2004, accounting for 11.5 percent of Turkey's total exports. (Exports to the Middle East rose in about the same proportion as Turkey's overall global exports.) Meanwhile, Turkish imports from the Middle East in that same period only doubled from $2.5 billion to $5.1 billion, with energy representing a significant portion of that amount.

According to Turkish government foreign trade statistics, the European Union ranks first in exports to Turkey, followed by Russia and the Commonwealth of Independent States, which exports primarily crude oil and natural gas to Turkey. The Middle East ranks third, primarily due to its crude-oil exports, while North America ranks fourth.[11]

Energy

Turkey is a key player in the energy arena both as consumer and as an East-West transit node for regional energy flows. The country's energy needs

---

8. "Turkey Human Resources and Trade Unions," www.photius.com/countries/turkey/economy/turkey_economy_human_resources_and_~11624.html

9. İsmet Koç, "Welfare Status Of Households Headed By Women And Policy Implications In Turkey," *Forum* 5, no. 1 (May 1998).

10. Turkish Ministry of Labor, "Statistics on Turkish Workers Abroad" (in Turkish), www.calisma.gov.tr/yih/yurtdisi_isci.htm.

11. "Foreign Trade of Turkey, 1990–2004," www.dtm.gov.tr/ab/ingilizce/turkeyeu.htm.

have grown at approximately 8 to 10 percent a year since 1993, particularly in support of its ambitious industrialization and modernization projects, and energy continues to drive Turkey's ever-increasing integration into the Middle East.[12]

Gas

Oil still meets more than 40 percent of Turkey's energy requirements, with 90 percent of it coming from the Middle East (Saudi Arabia, Iran, Iraq, Syria) and Russia. But oil is increasingly giving way to natural gas as the energy source of choice in Turkey for multiple reasons, including geopolitical ones. Additionally, gas is less polluting and more readily available to Turkey, and its costs are offset considerably by transit fees for pipelines that transit Anatolia en route to other markets. Turkey's energy supply agreements with Caspian, Central Asian, and Middle Eastern states enhance its geopolitical ties there as well.[13]

Ankara is attempting to diversify its sources of natural gas. By 2010, some 55 percent of Turkey's gas consumption will be supplied by Russia, either directly across the Black Sea, or via Bulgaria; another 20 percent will come from Iran, 13 percent from Azerbaijan, and the remainder from Algeria and Nigeria in the form of liquefied natural gas. Turkey has also undertaken gas-supply discussions with Qatar.[14]

Obviously, such heavy dependency upon Russia for gas supplies has its own significant political implications. But for the near term, supplies from Russian will likely be more stable than those from the Middle East given the turbulence in the region. Although Iran's share of Turkey's gas imports is growing, it has been U.S. sanctions policy toward Iran (and price), more than Turkish reluctance, that has been the primary factor delaying implementation of a $23 billion energy agreement Ankara signed with Iran in 1996.[15] In July 2007 a dramatic breakthrough of strategic proportions occurred when Turkey and Iran signed a memorandum of understanding for a huge joint venture to develop Iranian gas and oil for the Turkish market as well as for onward export via pipeline to Europe. Ankara rebuffed Washington's expression of disapproval of the deal that came at a time of high tensions between Washington and Tehran and U.S. determination to isolate Iran. The gas and

---

12. *APS Review: Oil Market Trends* 62, no. 17, April 26, 2004; and "Turkey" (part 1), *Prospects: The Official Newsletter Of The International Institute For Caspian Studies,* (Tehran: IICS).

13. "Turkey Energy In-Depth Review," *Brief Report of IEA, 2004,* International Cogeneration Combined Cycle and Environment Conference, Istanbul, Turkey, www.icciconference.com/eng/index.asp?t=9&n=82.

14. Ibid.

15. "Turkey-Iran Deal: 'A Slap in the Face to US'," *USIA Foreign Media Reaction Daily Digest,* August 16, 1996, www.fas.org/news/iran/1996/960816-452798.htm.

oil deal had major implications for the geostrategic "pipeline war" ongoing among the United States, Russia, Europe, Turkey and Iran.[16]

Pipelines

Turkey has become a key transit hub for energy, primarily from the Caspian Sea and Central Asia. With the opening of the Baku-Tbilisi-Ceyhan pipeline in May 2005, Turkey will be supplying 1 million barrels of oil a day from Azerbaijan at its Mediterranean outlet. Although present U.S. policies limit Turkey's energy dealings with Iran, Iran's possession of the second largest gas reserves in the world destines it to play a major role in meeting Turkey's future consumption needs; further, it destines Turkey to become a transit point for Iranian gas en route to Europe.

The Kirkuk-Yumurtalık oil pipeline that runs from Iraq to Turkey was closed with Saddam's invasion of Kuwait in 1991 and finally reopened in 2004 after his fall. Since then, it has been regularly sabotaged by Iraqi jihadist insurgency forces and only supplies a fraction of its capacity. Iraq's future stability represents a huge question mark in its ability to guarantee a reliable flow of oil to Turkey.

In May 2005, Prime Minister Erdoğan proposed to Israel the creation of a new pipeline that would provide Ceyhan oil to Haifa via a pipeline through Cyprus. Additional pipelines have been proposed that would carry water, gas, electricity, and even fiber-optic cables and would go on to Jordan and Palestine.[17]

Water Politics

The geopolitics of water and the rivalry and tensions associated with it have played a significant role in Turkish foreign policy for many decades. Both the Tigris and the Euphrates rivers rise in Turkey and eventually flow south: the Tigris enters directly into Iraq, and the Euphrates wends through northwest Syria before entering Iraq. Demands on these rivers are high for both agriculture and hydroelectric power.

Water resources can actually be a source of cooperation between nations rather than conflict, but resolution depends upon the good will of the parties involved. For decades, good will was absent among Turkey, Iraq, and Syria. Water conflict emerged in the 1960s when Turkey, Iraq, and Syria began to increase the use of this water and to build dams in order to expand their respective agricultural output. Trilateral consultation among the states indicat-

---

16 "Turkey returns to energy chess game," *Today's Zaman*, July 16, 2007, www.todayszaman. com/tz-web/detaylar.do?load=tetay&link=116758.

17. Soner Cagaptay and Nazlı Gençsoy, *Startup Of The Baku-Tbilisi-Ceyhan Pipeline: Turkey's Energy Role*, Policywatch 998, (Washington, D.C.: Washington Institute for Near East Policy, May 27, 2005).

ed that planned water usage by all three states would exceed the amount of available water by half, and Turkey's growing energy requirements prompted it to seek exploitation of the hydroelectric potential of these two rivers via new dam construction.[18]

Turkey has proposed a unilateral three-stage plan for future adjudication of water rights among the three countries that would involve need-based distribution but also require maximum ecologically efficient usage of the water. On one occasion, as the massive new Atatürk Dam was being filled in 1990 as part of Turkey's Southeastern Anatolia Project (GAP), Turkey actually temporarily reduced the flow of water to Syria. That act sent a clear message to Damascus: if it continued its support to the PKK, Turkey could expose its water vulnerability.[19] More recently, resolution of key ideological and geopolitical struggles between Turkey, Syria, and Iraq has created an atmosphere far more conducive and amicable solutions than ever before. Additionally, because Turkey's GAP project aims at expanding Turkish agrobusiness in the southeast, Ankara is mindful that it needs a nearby and friendly market for this produce.[20]

Apart from the waters of the Tigris and Euphrates, the large Ceyhan and Seyhan rivers also provide Turkey with valuable water resources. Ankara has suggested that some of this water could eventually be piped to Syria, Jordan, Israel, and western Saudi Arabia or even to the Arab Gulf states—in what former Turkish president Turgut Özal dubbed a "peace pipeline."[21] So far this project remains tabled, its viability hostage to the continuing non-resolution of the Arab-Israeli conflict.

Transnational Ethnic Issues

The Kurdish Problem

In the multiethnic structure of the Ottoman Empire there was no "Kurdish problem" the Kurdish problem. However, with the determination of the new nationalist Turkish republic to create a single ethnic category of "Turk," a Kurdish problem emerged; today it exerts the single biggest impact on Turkey's domestic political life, its security and foreign policies, and its foreign relations in the region. Indeed, for most of the twentieth century, the Kurds within Turkey were engaged in a long struggle for official recognition of their ethnic identity, some degree of cultural autonomy, better economic

---

18. Robins, *Suits and Uniforms*, 229–30.
19. Ibid., 232.
20. Robins, *Suits and Uniforms*, 212.
21. William Hale, *Turkish Foreign Policy, 1774-2000*, (London: Frank Cass, 2002), 174.

conditions in the country's Kurdish region, and the right to use Kurdish in media and education.

There is no formal discrimination against Kurds within Turkey as long as they do not push their own identity: everyone is a "Turk." This is undoubtedly true in terms of citizenship but not of ethnicity or culture. Kurds who simply ignore their Kurdishness can, and indeed regularly do, rise to the highest of offices in Turkey. The roots of the crisis arose in the zeal of the early Turkish Republic to create a ethnically homogeneous nation-state in which the state, for at least half a century, denied the very existence of its large Kurdish minority and suppressed any hint of Kurdish nationalist impulses. This led to repeated uprisings and violence. Kurdish nationalism traditionally turns to either extreme leftist or Islamist ideology as vehicles for expression.

For nearly three decades, this struggle took the form of a violent insurgency dominated by the PKK, a radical leftist group that emerged in the mid-1980s out of Turkish Marxist-Leninist revolutionary movements. Huge amounts of economic and military resources were deployed by the state to crush the movement, resulting in the death of some thirty-five thousand people, the great majority of them Kurds. Turkey's harsh repression of the movement and the decades-long, heavy-handed emergency military rule that came to dominate the country's Kurdish region fostered state-linked corruption and increased the alienation of Kurds throughout the country. Eventually, through the use of widespread repressive measures and massive evacuations of Kurds from their homes in areas of violence, the state brought the movement largely under control. The key turning point was the capture of the PKK's longtime leader, Abdullah Öcalan, who was caught in 1999 in Kenya with U.S. help after he was expelled from his decade-long refuge in Damascus.

For most of the twentieth century, Kurdish policy was always under the strict purview of the military, which treated the problem exclusively as a security issue; the main goal was ending terrorism rather than redressing social and economic grievances. In the late 1990s, however, the seriousness of the problem both within Turkey and at the international level began to push the issue into the civilian sector. Demands grew that the full dimensions of the problem be acknowledged, that is, that the problem be recognized as one of ethnicity and identity and not merely of terrorism. This reality ultimately forced official acknowledgment of the Kurds as a distinct people within Turkey who had cultural and identity aspirations of their own. President Özal, who publicly acknowledged that he himself was part Kurd, played a bold lead in this process. Additionally, the government began expending greater resources in the southeastern region, including the vast GAP project.

As a result, considerable progress was made toward a wiser handling of the problem. This progress was greatly encouraged by the European Union, which made clear to Ankara that it needed to pay attention to human rights issues and to the legitimate grievances of the Kurds before accession talks would begin. Subsequently, the Kurdish movement largely devolved into nonviolent political activism and a cultural renaissance.

Starting in 2005, however, small remnants of the violent insurgency began to show a disturbing revival. This was partly linked to the situation in Iraq and partly provoked by Turkish ultranationalists. Resentment among the Kurds is still high and periodically results in public disorder. The military remains fearful that cultural concessions to Kurds are part of a slippery slope that will ultimately lead to Kurdish demands for secession and independence from Turkey. While the long-range future of Kurdish aspirations in Turkey cannot be known, what is clear is that past denial and harsh treatment of the Kurdish reality only intensified the spread of broad Kurdish self-awareness (*bilinçlendirme*) at all levels of Kurdish society.

Two encouraging developments emerged with the July 2007 parliamentary elections: the Kurdish population gave more votes to the ruling JDP than to their own Kurdish ethnic party, the Democratic Society Party (Demokratik Toplum Partisi - DTP) and the Kurds also elected twenty parliamentarians who ran independently but then formed their own DTP bloc of Kurdish parliamentarians within the parliament—the first such representation in a decade. This means that Kurds increasingly hope to see their grievances handled within the ruling mainstream party and at the same time can take some satisfaction from their own explicitly nationalist candidates also represented in parliament. (There are also many Kurds in parliament affiliated with other parties who do not publicize their Kurdishness or the Kurdish nationalist cause.) These developments place the Kurdish issue within the mainstream of Turkish national politics and will likely weaken the PKK's influence—absent polarizing terrorist operations by the PKK to disrupt such a trend.

The Transnational Dimensions of the Kurdish Problem

The Kurdish problem plays a hugely disproportionate and obsessional role in Turkish foreign policy thinking. Part of Turkey's difficulties with the Kurds lies in the transnational dimension of the problem: Kurds represent the single largest ethnic group in the world without a state of their own, spreading across eastern Turkey, northern Iraq, northwestern Iran, northeastern Syria, and areas of Azerbaijan. Among these states, Turkey possesses the largest Kurdish population, which numbers at least 12 million and makes up at least 20 percent of Turkey's population. Half of the Kurds are located in the east and southeastern regions of the country; the rest are scattered throughout western Turkey: Istanbul is the biggest Kurdish city in the world.[22]

---

22. For a detailed treatment of the Kurdish issue in Turkey, see works by Martin Bruinessen; Henri Barkey and Graham E. Fuller; and Kemal Kirişçi and Gareth Winrow. For a more general treatment of the Kurdish problem at the international level, see works by Michael M. Gunter, David McDowall, and Robert Olson.

The presence and activities of the Kurds have long dominated Turkish bilateral relations with Iraq, Iran, and Syria, often crippling relations. Worse, Turkey's domestic Kurdish issue creates a vulnerability for Ankara that can be exploited by its external enemies. Indeed, over the past seventy years, Kurds in the region have been periodically manipulated against one or another regional state by Great Britain, Russia, Israel, the United States, Iran, Iraq, Syria, Greece, and Armenia.

It can be argued that an "unhappy" Diyarbakir—the unofficial capital of Turkish Kurdistan—constitutes Turkey's greatest Achilles' heel, because it guarantees ongoing domestic strife, encourages potential separatism, and opens the door for foreign exploitation. Conversely, a "happy" Diyarbakir suggests a Kurdish minority well integrated into the country. This would largely foreclose the prospects of external manipulation and make the Kurdish areas of Turkey a large and attractive magnet for all other Kurds in the region. Kurds would then be able to look across the border into Turkey and see a state that has resolved its ethnic issues, that has become an attractive partner for Kurds outside the country, and that is a democratic state offering a gateway to Europe.

The PKK poses a particular challenge to Turkey: it is the first and only Kurdish movement to champion a pan-Kurdish ideal, the union of all Kurds into one single state. It was the first party to rise above localism—the historical bane of Kurdish politics everywhere—tribalism, and even dialectal differences to constitute an internationalized, reformist, secular, leftist, and hence "modern" movement. Despite his theoretical brilliance, Öcalan exercised a harsh Stalinist-style control over the movement, so the PKK was never democratic. Today, he is serving a life sentence in Turkey, although he still commands a considerable emotional following among all Kurds everywhere, even as Kurdish leadership in the country is moving into more democratic and moderate hands.

Although the Kurdish problem remains a volatile issue in Turkish politics, especially among the military and nationalist circles, the harsh reality is that Turkey will never be able to establish normal and stable state relations with Iraq, Iran, or Syria until it has satisfactorily resolved its own domestic Kurdish problem.

Pan-Turkism

The Turkic-speaking world spans Anatolia, the Caucasus, Iran, Central Asia, and western China. This huge linguistic group is quite diverse but well aware of its shared culture. Pan-Turkism has been periodically invoked in the past in various places for various political purposes and could very well be invoked again—potentially strengthening Turkey's clout across the region. However, in view of its broader interests with regional states, particularly with Russia, Ankara will be disinclined to play the pan-Turkist card, but the card will never entirely vanish.

Culture

Turkish music has reportedly become "very popular in the region," according to a Gulf rock star.[23] Turkish Arabesque-style music represents a modern heavy fusion of both Turkish and Arab tradition and is reaching across borders in the Middle East.

Conclusion

Turkey's rise toward clear dominance in the Middle East's military, economic, and diplomatic arenas has increased considerably over the past two decades. Its democratic character and legitimate government provide it with immense strength and resiliency. This stands in stark contrast to nearly all other states in the region that are dominated by unrepresentative, autocratic, and often harsh and incompetent leaders who fear their own populations and must rely on external states to maintain their own hold on power. Turkey is one of the few states whose polity can weather the immense coming storms in the region without revolution, but the not-yet-fully resolved Kurdish problem remains a point of vulnerability to Ankara.

Although Turkey has many sources of influence, to fully understand its current place in the region, one must understand its key bilateral relations across the Muslim world and beyond on an individual basis.

---

23. Jocelyn Elia, "The Rock Sheik," *al-Sharq al-Awsat,* July 5, 2006, www.asharqalawsat.com/english/news.asp?section=7&id=5531.

9

Turkey and Syria

A Transformed Relationship

Right from the founding of the Turkish Republic, Turkey's relations with Syria have been universally poor and often tense. The two countries have come close to war on several occasions. But Turkey's relations with Damascus began to undergo a dramatic shift in 1998, leading to the opening of an historic new era between the two countries and to the creation of a new, positive atmosphere conducive to the settlement of most outstanding issues between them. Furthermore, with their relationship transformed, Turkey is now able to exert a modest but positive influence on Syrian affairs and may be able to broaden Syria's perspectives through frequent and close consultation with it.

Although today the main uncertainty in the Turkish-Syrian relationship stems from ongoing U.S. hostility toward Syria, the relationship between Turkey and Syria has historically been defined by tensions based on identity, territory, ideology and Cold War alignment, the Kurds, water, and Israel.

Identity Issues

The question of identity is often perceived as a "soft" issue in any assessment of bilateral relations, but it might be the most profound one for perceiving the nature of the relationship. As Bülent Aras notes, identity plays a significant role in the construction and application of foreign policy.[1] Foreign policy expresses not only what one wants but also what one is. For the new Turkish Republic, Kemalist aspirations to embrace the West, to reject the Islamic, imperial Ottoman past, and to marginalize the Arab and Muslim worlds served to build a new Turkish identity.

Similarly, with Damascus as the center of Arab nationalism in the years before and after World War I, the creation of a new Arab nationalist identity required rejection of the subordinate role Syria had played within the old Turkish/Ottoman order. As a consequence, the official new national identities within Turkey and Syria created their own particular cultures of security and their own new subjective threat perceptions.[2] In a psychological and so-

---

1. Aras, *Turkey and The Greater Middle East,* 87–8.
2. Ibid., 88.

ciological sense, each state sought to uniquely redefine its own new identity against the other, producing a kind of built-in clash of cultures that easily became a self-fulfilling prophesy. This was perhaps the single most important factor that soured Turkish-Syrian relations over most of the past century; this psychological tension was soon reinforced by further hostile actions on both sides stimulated by the Cold War.

Ahmet Davutoğlu acknowledges the historical existence of major bilateral Turkish-Syrian tensions but also views their perpetuation in some sense as artificial, the product of decades of diplomatic inertia, inaction, and careless neglect; tensions have therefore persisted at the same frozen and unattended level, seemingly impervious to treatment. He views this as a costly luxury for two states that share such a long common border. By perpetuating this stagnating and negative atmosphere, they have even provided openings for other states, including Greece and Israel, to periodically exploit these tensions for their own ends. Davutoğlu points to major opportunities awaiting vigorous bilateral development, most notably in the fields of water, agriculture, trade, and communications. He also believes Ankara must dedicate major attention to the Arab-Israeli issue—of vital concern to Damascus—as it affects Turkey's own potential vision and role in a new Middle East.[3]

Whatever the legacy of their respective postindependence paths, a new willingness on both sides to reach accommodation has led to a reduction and resolution of many long-standing bilateral frictions. As a result, the "identity" crisis may soon be over as both states have begun to readjust their identities through new foreign policies.

Territorial Disputes

The long-standing Hatay/Alexandretta dispute moved toward de facto resolution with Prime Minister Erdoğan's groundbreaking visit to Damascus in December 2004, when both sides publicly acknowledged that there were no longer any border issues between them.[4]

Cold War Rivalry

Turkey's strong support of the Western alliance and Syria's orientation toward the USSR in the Cold War was a key source of ideological tension between them until the collapse of communism. Threats and military tensions were common on both sides. Whatever the substance of various bilateral grievances between Syria and Turkey, the Cold War greatly exacerbated these grievances and all but eliminated any chance for rapproche-

---

3. Davutoğlu, *Stratejik Derinlik,* 402–3.
4. Yoav Stern, "Turkey Singing a New Tune," *Haaretz,* January 9, 2005, www.haaretz.com/ hasen/spages/524517.html.

ment. Each side sought instruments through which to pressure the other, such as through water, the Kurds, and Israel.

Water Problems

President Özal traveled to Damascus in 1987 to try to work out an agreement in which Ankara would guarantee a stipulated flow of Euphrates water to Syria in return for a mutual cessation of support to elements hostile to the other—a clear reference to Syrian support for the PKK. Despite the agreement, Syria did not end its support for the PKK, claiming that the water flow Turkey had offered was unacceptably small over the long term.[5] From the Turkish perspective, Syria failed to honor its proposed commitments. As a result, Ankara did not hesitate to demonstrate Syrian vulnerability to a cut-off of the Euphrates if Damascus continued to pursue policies that Ankara perceived as hostile. With a new atmosphere of good will reigning on both sides, the water issue has since been placed on the back burner. As a result, the continued equitable handling of water from the Euphrates is probable.

The Kurdish Issue

Syria has a Kurdish population of approximately one million, situated mainly in the northeastern corner of the country in the Jazira region. The majority of Syria's Kurds are the descendants of refugees from Turkey in the 1920s, when Kurds escaped over the border from Turkish oppression.[6] They thus have a strong anti-Turkish bias as well as ready access to neighboring Kurdish regions in Iraq.

The leadership of the PKK escaped into Syria in 1980, where it was given state support after a military takeover in Ankara. Syria provided training facilities to the PKK in Lebanon's Biqa' valley and gave Öcalan refuge in Damascus. But with the collapse of the Soviet Union in 1991, Syria's position was promptly weakened; it was isolated and caught between Turkish and Israeli military power. For Turkey, this development provided a great opportunity to put pressure on Damascus, without the risks of broader Cold War confrontation. A showdown was in the making.

Turkish frustration with Damascus had been growing over the years as the scope of PKK guerrilla and terrorist operations inside Turkey reached serious levels in the 1990s. The PKK had also become a magnet for other states seeking to inflict pressure on Turkey, including Greece, Armenia, and Russia; the PKK had built a political base of support in Europe, making it Ankara's number one foreign policy issue with the broader world. By the late 1990s, Ankara's relationship with Israel had grown by leaps and bounds, and

5. Hale, *Turkish Foreign Policy*, 174.
6. David McDowell, *A Modern History of the Kurds* (London: I. B. Tauris, 1996), 3–4.

the Turkish military in this period had taken over de facto control of Turkish security policy. Although Turkish politicians had already been issuing increasingly sharp warnings to Syria for several years, Ankara finally issued a blunt ultimatum to Damascus in 1998, telling it to cease support for the PKK and to expel Öcalan or face a Turkish military invasion. The threat was backed by the movement of ten thousand Turkish troops to the Syrian border. Hafez al-Asad, sensing few options, uncharacteristically caved in and proceeded to completely revise his confrontational policies toward Turkey. This inaugurated a new and important bilateral relationship that has major implications for the region.

Relations with Israel

Turkey's improving relations with Israel in the 1990s was a major irritant to Ankara's relations with the Arab world, placing particular pressure on Damascus. But the strategic threats that once helped stimulate the Turkish-Israeli relationship have receded. As a result, Turkey's ties with Syria continue to blossom.[7] As observers Soner Cagaptay and Nazli Gencsoy note, "The best evidence that Ankara's attitude toward Syria has changed is the nearly 450-mile long, 1,500-foot wide minefield between the two countries (planted in 1952 at the height of the Cold War) which Turkey is now clearing."[8]

Conclusion

With a transformed diplomatic relationship, Turkey and Syria have witnessed positive changes in their economic and civilian interactions as well. Turkey's bilateral trade with Syria totaled $751 million in 2004, amounting to 1 percent of its overall bilateral trade. An agreement was reached for the establishment of a free-trade zone between the two countries in 2005, and with Damascus encouraging Turkish investment in Syria, the two countries have established a joint company for oil exploration. They are also developing a common electricity grid in the border areas. Finally, of particular note, the number of Turkish tourists to Syria underwent a massive nineteen-fold increase from 2000 to 2005.[9]

7. Bülent Aras, "After the Threats, Syria and Turkey Are Fast Friends," *Daily Star* (Beirut), January 4, 2005.
8. Soner Cagaptay and Nazli Gencsoy, *Improving Turkish-Russian Relations: Turkey's New Foreign Policy and Its Implications for the United States,* (Washington, D.C.: Washington Institute for Near East Policy, January 12, 2005).
9. "Number of Turkish Tourists Increasing," *al-Thawra*, August 23, 2005.

10

Turkey and Iraq

From Hostility to Turmoil

Turkish-Iraqi relations since the 1958 Iraqi revolution trace a path from limited, chilly interactions to post-Saddam Turkish involvement in Iraqi affairs. Their relations are now rapidly expanding but are marked by frictions stemming from internal Iraqi chaos. Indeed, turmoil in Iraq poses deep challenges to Ankara, particularly as regards the Kurds, terrorism, regional security, and oil.

In recent years, Ankara's relations with Baghdad have been defined by

- the Iraqi Kurds' political aspirations for autonomy and the status of the city of Kirkuk, its oil, and the fate of the Turkmen population there;
- border issues and the status of the former Ottoman province of Mosul;
- issues related to Iraq's stability and unity after Saddam, such as terrorism, civil war, and Islamic radicalism;
- economic issues, including those related to oil;
- the newly burgeoning Iranian influence within Iraq.

Border Issues: Mosul

After World War I, when the British gained control of Iraq, Ankara perceived the Kurds as an instrument of British imperial designs.[1] With no natural border between the Kurdish regions of Turkey and Iraq, it took eight years of tension-filled maneuvering between Ankara and London before a border settlement was finally reached in 1926, when Turkey reluctantly gave up claim to the Mosul region. But the issue was never fully forgotten and the modern Iraqi state has always remained suspicious of Turkish intentions toward Mosul, particularly under post-Saddam conditions of internal Iraqi turmoil. Ankara, in turn, remains haunted by the vulnerability of the Kurdish region to further external manipulation, including by Washington and Jerusalem—a not unfounded concern.

---

1. David McDowell, *A Modern History of the Kurds* (London: I. B. Tauris, 1996), 118–25.

The Iran-Iraq War (1980–88): "The Beneficial War"

The Iran-Iraq war raised fears in most of the world that global oil supplies would be curtailed and that oil facilities and tankers would be targeted. The Gulf states were (presciently) fearful that whichever state emerged as victor would pose an even greater threat to them. Most states in the world supported Iraq out of fear of revolutionary Iran. Turkey was one of the few countries in the world to adopt a posture of positive neutrality toward both countries and to meet their deep economic needs through trade. As a result, Turkey reaped major revenues from the war: Turkish exports jumped from $220 million in 1981 to $2 billion in 1985, constituting one- quarter of Turkey's overall exports.[2] Turkey also received some $250 million in oil pipeline transit fees from Iraq, and Turkey and Iraq agreed to the integration of their electric grids as part of a broader regional scheme. Additionally, Turkish construction projects in Iraq totaled $2.5 billion between 1974 and 1990. But as the war ground to an end, Turkish exports to both countries dropped off. The developing integration of the Iraqi economy with Turkey was reversed by Saddam's act of monstrous folly—his invasion of Kuwait—and Turkey's response to it.[3]

The one major negative development for Ankara during the Iran-Iraq war related to the war's impact on the Iraqi Kurds. The Iran-Iraq war provided the Iraqi Kurds the opportunity to start developing autonomous institutions free of Baghdad's heavy hand. Furthermore, the PKK was able to develop bases in northern Iraq—often with the tacit sympathies of the Kurdish population there—from which it launched armed insurgent operations into Turkey beginning in 1984. During this period, Baghdad permitted hot pursuit by the Turkish military over the border against the PKK, thereby sanctioning deeper Turkish involvement in Iraq to the dismay of Iraqi Kurds.

The Disaster of the 1991 Gulf War

Unlike the Iran-Iraq war, the 1991 Gulf War and its aftermath was a disaster for Turkey in nearly all respects:
- Saddam's control over Iraq's Ku
rdish region was decisively broken.
- Half a million Kurds fled north toward the Turkish border as a result of Saddam's efforts to reassert absolute control over the Kurdish region, posing a massive refugee problem to Ankara.
- The prospect of a massive flight of Iraqi Kurds into Turkey sparked undesirable political reactions among Turkish Kurds and raised their sense of solidarity with Iraqi Kurds.
- The Kurdish refugee crisis and subsequent international efforts to manage it placed the long-ignored Kurdish question prominently on

---

2. Hale, *Turkish Foreign Policy,* 173.
3. Robins, *Suits and Uniforms,* 58.

the international agenda—a development highly undesirable from Ankara's point of view.

- Iraq's Kurdish region fell under international UN protection and the supervision of the U.S.-sponsored Operation Provide Comfort—offering the Kurds international de jure protection that Ankara could not oppose. Additionally, a U.S. promise not to tolerate Kurdish autonomy was rendered moot by the Kurdish humanitarian crisis. As a result, Operation Provide Comfort, which was loathed by all Turks, became a hot potato within Turkish politics, and the U.S. strategy and tactics that had seemingly brought all this about became a source of broad Turkish suspicion and resentment.[4]
- The Kurdish parties, under U.S. pressure, were forced to cooperate institutionally among themselves at the "national" political level in Iraq for the first time, foreclosing options for Ankara to play them against one another. This represented a decisive turning point in the evolution of Iraqi Kurdish political history.

Iraq's Kurdish zone quickly developed the trappings of a nearly independent de facto state. This reality of a Kurdish authority in northern Iraq compelled Ankara, with immense reluctance, to start dealing with it—first through individual Kurdish leaders, later through their political parties, and later still on a de facto diplomatic level, when senior Kurdish officials increasingly visited Baghdad for formal talks. This marked the beginning of an unofficial diplomatic relationship between Turkey and a "Kurdish entity." (By late 2004, this process had attained the unthinkable: Ankara would have to receive longtime Kurdish leader Jalal Talabani in Ankara, as president of Iraq.) The reality of Kurdish autonomy encouraged regional rivalries to be expressed within northern Iraq, a development long feared by Ankara. Iran, Turkey, Syria, and the Islamists all had favorite Kurdish groups to which they lent support, raising the international stakes there.[5]

Additionally, the Gulf War held disastrous consequences for Turkish-Iraqi economic relationships, which would also impact the Kurds. As Robins writes,

> The international sanctions placed on Saddam's Iraq forced Turkey to close down a great deal of its bilateral trade with Iraq including two oil pipelines; the entire period of the embargo cost Turkey at least $8 billion; Turkey itself claims losses of $5 billion per year. Meanwhile, a debate raged in Ankara over the proper way to handle northern Iraq: doves argued that circumstances offered a golden opportunity to integrate it into the sphere

---

4. Ibid., 320–21.
5. Ibid., 315.

of the Turkish economy; security hawks argued that such a process would only facilitate its separation from Baghdad and propel it along the road to independence.[6]

Both the doves and the hawks were right.

A reminder that the Mosul irredentist issue was still alive emerged when President Özal urged the Turkish military to consider taking back Mosul if Iraq were to fall apart in the aftermath of Saddam's 1993 defeat. However, he was ultimately dissuaded by the military, which recognized that acquisition of this Kurdish area would introduce further massive security and separatist problems that Turkey did not need.

The sole benefit to Turkey of the 1991 war was a cementing of its strategic relationship with Washington, as Turkey solidified the image of a reliable ally. This image was misleading, though, because it ignored the sharp and severe disagreements most of Turkey's policy establishment had with Özal's strategic gamble to support U.S. policy so strongly. These divisions sprang into full light with the U.S. invasion of Iraq in 2003. In fact, Turkey's own suspicions and fears about the dangers of a deteriorating situation in Iraq have been fully borne out by events there since 1980. Every new international incident, conflict, and war within Iraq has only led to a strengthening of Kurdish identity and autonomy, making the ultimate creation of an independent Kurdish state ever more viable and likely.

The 2003 Gulf War—the Unwanted War

Thus, the overthrow of Saddam's regime was the last thing Ankara wanted; to Turkey, it represented the opening of a Pandora's box in Iraq. The only major problem that Saddam had ever posed to Ankara was his unpredictable, aggressive, and erratic character that constantly dragged Iraq into conflict. Saddam had otherwise made huge efforts to keep his own Kurdish population under control.

Observer Henri Barkey and many in Turkey's pro-U.S. camp saw the Turkish parliament's refusal to allow the United States the use of Turkish soil to launch military operations against Iraq as a strategically bad move, costing Turkey "a seat at the table" and any voice in the adjudication of future Iraqi affairs.[7] But there never was a "table" at which Turkey could have wielded influence; the Bush administration ignored even advice from most of the U.S. intelligence community, foreign-policy think tanks, and European allies on how to handle post-Saddam Iraq. The legacy of this Turkish decision, how-

---

6. Ibid., 322.
7. Henri Barkey, *Turkey and Iraq: The Perils and Prospects of Proximity*, Special Report 141 (Washington, D.C.: United States Institute of Peace, July 2005).

ever, still rankles in Washington, even leading some to continue to talk about "payback."

Kirkuk and the Turkmen

One of Turkey's chief stated foreign policy goals in Iraq since 2003 has been protecting the welfare of the Turkmen population in the sensitive oil region in and around Kirkuk. Although this group probably numbers less than a million—the Turkmen insist that they number 3 million—Turkmen have been an important part of the population of the city of Kirkuk. Indeed, the Sunni Turkmen served as a ruling elite in Kirkuk under the Ottomans at a time when the Kurds represented the lower class.[8] Since then, however, the Turkmen have almost certainly suffered a definitive loss of position and influence, particularly in the recent three-way competition for control of Kirkuk and its environs.

Even so, the Turkmen, who themselves are divided evenly between Sunni and Shia, have represented a possible key card for Ankara in its attempts to keep Kirkuk and its oil out of Iraqi Kurdish hands, particularly as the Kurds have taken steps to "Kurdify" Kirkuk. That stated, Ankara's clout is almost exclusively with the Sunni rather than the Shia Turkmen, who share many viewpoints in common with the Arab Shia of the south. Furthermore, the Ankara-sponsored Iraqi Turkmen Front is not supported by all Turkmen.[9] As a result, the Turkmen constitute a very weak reed on which Ankara can base its policies in northern Iraq, and Ankara seems to be gradually dropping them as a possible key card. In fact, Turkey's "red line" has proven to be unrealistically drawn and already crossed. The Kurds are unanimously committed not only to dominating Kirkuk but also to naming it the capital of Kurdistan, however unfair this may be to Arabs and Turkmen living there. Additionally, Kurds are now streaming back to Kirkuk, many of whom had been earlier expelled by Saddam. Few forces on the ground can reverse this process.

Ankara still wants to ensure that all of Iraq's oil is placed under centralized control from Baghdad, in order to prevent the Kurds from using revenues from Kirkuk to strengthen their own autonomy or even future independence, but negotiations are already well underway for some degree of regional oil-revenue control.

New Considerations

In the end, Turkey's quest for EU membership places at least as much of a constraint on Turkish freedom of action in northern Iraq as do U.S. policies there. The United States will eventually leave Iraq, but the European Union

---

8. Ibid.
9. Ibid.

will not tolerate any military intervention by Turkey that is meant to change the political status quo, particularly in the absence of strong legitimating grounds that do not currently exist. Furthermore, other Arab countries and Iran will take strong exception to any Turkish military intervention in northern Iraq, especially if it seeks to establish some kind of permanent presence there. Turkey could easily become bogged down in an unwinnable guerrilla war.

As Barkey points out, internal Turkish political struggle between the Turkish military and the ruling JDP have complicated Turkish policymaking, including in Iraq.[10] The military has no desire to see the JDP do well and has on occasion sought to embarrass it. If there is to be any serious Turkish military intervention against the PKK in northern Iraq, both the military and the JDP would first want to lay the burden of that risky choice on the other. As a result, the JDP has sought to work closely with the military in nearly everything that relates to Iraq and security policy to avoid any disagreements, and has sought to avoid direct confrontation with Washington since the fall of Saddam. (Ironically, this has led to the remarkable charge by most Turkish nationalists and leftists that the JPD represents the "American party" in Turkey.)

Turkey must also think in new terms about the Shia. The Ottomans long saw the Shia as a threat to their own Sunni-based power and legitimacy, especially after Iran took over the Shiite banner in the sixteenth century. But what does Shiism mean to Turkey today? Its own highly heterodox Shiite population, the Alevis, do not represent any orthodox form of Shiism and will find little reason to gravitate toward Iran. Indeed, they are generally intensely secular due to past memories of dominant Sunni repression. But what might Turkey do about the emergence of some new Shiite bloc comprising Iran, Iraq, and Syria, where a Shiite Alawi minority is in power? Need such a grouping be a "threat" to Turkey? Ankara has always sought to avoid any imbroglio into sectarian politics. So even though sectarian politics is what Middle Eastern politics is all about today, Ankara would be quite unlikely to choose sides in an Iraqi sectarian conflict; basing policy on sectarian instincts is not what modern Turkey is about, even if urged to do so by other Sunni states. Either way, such a regional cleavage would present Ankara with serious challenges.

Although Turkey's future role in the Iraqi economy should be quite significant as a provider of agricultural produce, as a source of water and consumer goods, as a consumer of Iraqi oil, and as a transit point for the export of Iraqi oil to the Mediterranean, the Kurdish issue remains a big question mark both for Turkey's relations with Iraq and, indeed, for its own domestic future. Turkey's Kurds have undeniably grown more ethnically self-aware

---

10. Ibid.

and more demanding following recent events in Iraq. PKK guerrilla warfare has been back on the scene for several years, and the PKK still has a stronghold in northern Iraq that Washington, surprisingly and conspicuously, has done little to nothing about. Many Turks believe that consistent U.S. failure to take out PKK bases with air strikes is part of Turkey's payback for closing its soil to U.S. troops. Others argue that Washington cannot afford to alienate the Iraqi Kurds as the only pro-U.S. group in the country. Either way, inaction against the PKK is a foolish luxury by Washington; it remains the single most emotive bilateral issue for many parties.

Although Ankara repeatedly speaks of its right to invade northern Iraq as part of its own war on terror, the Turkish military would pay a significant cost—with Europe, Washington, its own Kurds, and Baghdad—if it used force against PKK bases in Iraq. It may do so yet, if nothing else as a warning shot across the northern Iraqi government's bow. A full invasion of northern Iraq and seizure of Iraqi territory by Turkey is quite unlikely, though, and would result in a damaging guerrilla war in northern Iraq that Turkey could not win.

The Economic Dimension

Turkey's relations with Iraq in the post-Saddam era do not revolve solely around contentious issues such as nationalism and separatism, as high profile as they are. They also include less well-known issues, such as the growing and deepening economic ties between Turkey and Iraqi Kurdistan. With northern Iraq dependent on the Turkish economy, these ties may ultimately help stabilize and limit the rougher exchanges that have characterized Turkish-Iraqi Kurdish relations in the political arena, especially in the volatile run-up to Turkish parliamentary and presidential elections in the summer of 2007. This economic dependence will likely favor a profitable coexistence between the two entities and give Turkey immense voice and influence in Iraqi Kurdistan.

Significantly, the Turkish private sector dominates this important role; it has invested large sums into Iraqi Kurdistan and is the single most dominant economic force there, apart from the oil revenues the Kurds receive from Iraqi oil sales. Turkish exports to Iraqi Kurdistan, particularly of food and building materials, is expected to reach $5 billion for the year in 2007. Turkish companies also expect to land some $10 to 15 billion worth of project work in the area by 2010.[11] Turkish construction firms have already carried out dozens of modern, high-profile projects, including the construction of Kurdistan's "presidential" palace in Irbil, television networks, international airports, universities, bridges, highways, and urban infrastructure. With these

---

11. M. K. Bhadrakumar, "Iraqi Kurds play with Turkish fire," *Asia Times Online*, April 14, 2007, www.atimes.com/atimes/Middle_East/ID14Ak02.html.

increasing ties, Turkish Airlines now maintains regular flights to Kurdish cities in Iraq.[12]

The weight and influence of these bilateral economic relations has been intensified by powerful and developing ties between Iraqi Kurds and major actors on Turkey's political front—not just the JDP but also major opposition parties, including Turkey's anti-Kurdish nationalist party, which are complexly linked with families and corporations that have economic interests in northern Iraq.[13] The economic reality of these new infrastructures may help lubricate political tensions between Turkey and Iraqi Kurdistan and facilitate greater integration of the two economies.

Conclusion

As a result of the 2003 Gulf War, Turkish circles across the ideological and political spectrum are more suspicious than ever of Washington's intentions toward the Middle East. Most now believe that the United States has become a typical imperial power marching in the footsteps of past European imperialism and that it seeks to divide, weaken, and dominate the region. They also believe that they are witnessing the creation of a "poison pill" in the region—a Kurdish state—that will resemble the "imperialist creation" of the state of Israel to be a source of discord, conflict, and struggle, ultimately leading to permanent manipulation and intervention from external powers. A review of European imperial history sadly reveals that such fears are not entirely without foundation. Washington's unwillingness to destroy the PKK presence in northern Iraq has further fueled widespread Turkish paranoia about U.S. intentions to cripple and divide Turkey as a too independent-minded ally.[14]

Turkish fears are hardly groundless. The prospects of an independent Kurdish state are now greater than ever. Furthermore, the world's recognition of identity politics and general calls for democracy and human rights inevitably bolster the Kurdish case for self-determination. Additionally, the increasing divisions within the Iraqi state provide scarce incentive for the Kurds to remain part of a foundering Iraqi state. As a result, no one can predict how the international Kurdish cause across all borders will ultimately evolve. Will there one day be independence for some Kurds and not others, a pan-Kurdish state, or autonomy for all? Or will there be permanent political divisions among the diverse Kurdish groups under a loose confederation, a continuation of the status quo, a Kurdish protectorate under U.S. guarantee,

---

12. Ibid.
13. Ibid.
14. See, for example, Prof. Osman Metin Öztürk, "ABD Türkiye'yi Irak'a İtiyor," April 11, 2006, www.habusulu.com, www.jeopolsar.com.

or an autonomous Kurdistan that will serve as a home for U.S. military bases otherwise unwelcome in Arab Iraq? Many possible scenarios exist, but nearly all are likely to prove volatile in the context of regional state competition.

Even if Iraqi Kurds generally reject the concept of armed insurgency and the terrorism of the PKK, they still retain sympathy and understanding for what the PKK is trying to achieve. Kurdish authorities in northern Iraq oppose any Turkish incursions into their area, but they will try to cooperate with Ankara in resolving the PKK problem.

Turkey's best remaining option is to embrace cooperation with the new Kurdish entity in the hopes of exerting dominant influence over it and co-opting it into the Turkish economy and sphere of Turkish politics. Additionally, Turkey could conceivably develop a quadrilateral confederated Kurdish cooperation zone with Syria, Iraq, and Iran. The absence of manipulation from powers outside the region would greatly reduce regional paranoia and be a boon to creative political and social evolution. Ultimately, only through the resolution of Turkey's own Kurdish problems will the door toward "normal" state-to-state relations between Ankara and Baghdad be opened.

11

Turkey and Iran

A Wary Coexistence

The Turks have no older or more complex cultural interaction than the one they have with the Persians. For more than two thousand years, Iran has been the geopolitical rival of whichever group has ruled Anatolia, including the Byzantines. Although geopolitical tensions between Iran and Turkish Anatolia existed even when Iran was still a Sunni state, only after Iran's stunning religious turnabout and embrace of Shiism as the state religion in 1500 did Iran become the chief theological and ideological rival to the Ottoman state. Beginning in the sixteenth century, this relationship between Shiite Iran and the Sunni Ottoman Empire constituted a religious cold war that included much ideological vituperation and a long struggle over territory in Anatolia and Mesopotamia.

By the seventeenth century serious territorial wars between these two warring states drew to an end, dwindling down to suspicions and occasional skirmishes. Despite periodic cultural and ideological tensions between them and frequent episodes of mutual distrust, frictions were never again to be translated into real territorial conflict. Relations between the two states became characterized by a long and cautious—if sometimes prickly—coexistence and a grudging mutual respect. As a result, the two countries have enjoyed several hundred years of virtual peace, with no significant border disputes other than a few skirmishes. They have not even been allied in opposite ideological camps as the Arabs and Turks were during the Cold War.[1]

After World War I, the newly founded Turkish Republic was eager to establish a business-like working relationship with Iran's new Pahlavi dynasty. Improved relations resulted in a new border agreement between the two states in 1932. The model for Reza Shah in implementing his own reform program of imposed westernization was Atatürk himself, although Reza's reforms were executed with far less brilliance, skill, understanding, or lasting effect.

After the Iranian revolution in 1979 the new Islamic Republic of Iran, as a key center of resistance to U.S. power in the Middle East, began to complicate Turkey's efforts to balance its interests between the region and the West. Even

---

1. For an excellent overview of the complex Turkish-Iranian relationship, see Gökhan Çetin-saya, "Essential Friends and Natural Enemies: The Historic Roots of Turkish-Iranian Relations," *MERIA Journal* 7, no. 3 (September 2003), 3.

so, in the tradition of their historical relationship, both the Turks and the Persians continue to demonstrate a deep and consistent reluctance to go to war with each other.

The modern Turkish-Iranian relationship has been broadly defined by

- the Kurdish issue, which has affected bilateral Turkish-Iranian relations, as well as the triangular relationship among Iraqi, Iranian, and Turkish Kurds;
- ideological tensions over the role of religion in the state—that is, Iranian theocracy versus the Turkish secular state—although this has often been the vehicle rather than the cause of friction;
- Ankara's annoyance with Tehran's periodic propagation of radical foreign policy goals, particularly as relates to Israel and Islam, and anger toward alleged Iranian support for certain assassinations inside Turkey and suspected Iranian encouragement on occasion of the Kurdish Islamist movement Hizballah (unrelated to Hizballah in Lebanon);
- geopolitical rivalry for influence in post-Saddam Iraq, Syria, the Persian Gulf, the Caucasus, and Central Asia;
- Iran's potential quest for nuclear weapons;
- Turkey's need to meet its own energy requirements in the face of international energy politics—especially concerning oil and gas pipelines—and determined U.S. attempts to hobble Iran's ability to export energy;
- latent pan-Turkic motives in Ankara, currently in abeyance, that could lead to a Turkish bid for greater influence within Iranian Azerbaijan;
- Turkey's concern over any prospect of turmoil within or dismemberment of Iran, particularly at the hands of extraregional powers—once Britain and Russia but now the United States, whose policies are perceived as interventionist and destabilizing.

The Religious Factor

Despite the Sunni-Shiite divide, both states have been largely able to overlook their religious differences, particularly in more recent centuries. In the final years of the Ottoman period, for example, Sultan Abdülhamit II readily sought Iran's support in pan-Islamist policies designed to unite all Muslims against European imperial challenges. In fact, Ottoman representatives pointed out that Sunni-Shiite differences were theologically marginal but that their common geopolitical interests were high.[2]

As of the 1920s, both states—Turkey under Atatürk and Iran under Reza Shah—adopted strong secularizing agendas as part of a broader reformist and westernizing program. As a result, the place of Islam in public life was sharply downgraded in both Turkey and Iran. Additionally, both countries shared a

---

2. Ibid.

geopolitical concern over the very real Soviet threat to the north. Only with the Iranian Revolution in 1979, which repudiated the Shah's secularism and pro-Westernism and instituted theocratic rule in the country, did religious tensions between the two countries flare up again. To Ayatollah Khomeini, Kemalist Turkey represented a flagrant case of perfidy to Islam with its abolition of the caliphate, its secularizing policies, and its close alliance with the imperialist West. Iranian state visitors to Ankara regularly refused to make the diplomatically obligatory visit to Atatürk's tomb—a huge affront to Turkey's national ideology. Iranian ambassadors to Turkey have also made outspoken and inflammatory public remarks on Israel, Palestine, and the need to adopt sharia law, promoting radical Islamist views at odds with Turkish policy.

Although today's Islam-oriented JDP has worked to seriously improve ties with Tehran, the Turkish military continues to be far more hawkish about Iran than Turkey's civilian officials. As Bülent Aras notes, the old Kemalist worldview still tends to project the source of domestic problems, such as the resurgence of Islam in Turkey, on "foreign enemies," to use foreign relations as a way to promote domestic ideology, and to turn what are basically domestic issues into "security issues."[3] Thus, Iran as an Islamic Republic has come to symbolize the "Islamic threat" to Turkey's ultrasecularist elite. Nonetheless, in the end, both countries continue to act fairly pragmatically toward each other; despite small periodic diplomatic crises, they usually end up setting aside religious and ideological differences in favor of dealing with shared bilateral concerns and maintaining their wary coexistence.

Iraq Tensions

Most of the key border tensions between Iran and the Ottomans related to the borderlands between Ottoman Iraq and Iran. Although that specific source of tension disappeared with the new borders of the modern Turkish state, Iran's emergent influence in post-Saddam Iraq has opened the possibility for future Iranian-Turkish tension there.

Transnational Minority Interests

Both Turkey and Iran have periodically made efforts to manipulate each other's minority groups for their own advantage, particularly the large Kurdish minority that spills over the border between both states and the sizeable Turkic minority groups within Iran.

Kurds. The Kurdish issue constitutes probably the single most enduring concrete point of friction between the two states, which was triggered by the decades-long uncontrolled movement of Kurdish rebels across the poorly demarcated Turkish-Iranian border. It was not until 1937 that the border was permanently settled after a period of Kurdish uprisings within Turkey that Ankara

---

3. Aras, *Turkey and The Greater Middle East*, 73–74.

accused Tehran of supporting.[4] Later, in the 1970s, the Shah of Iran supported Kurdish rebellions, but only inside Iraq in order to weaken Saddam Hussein. Nonetheless, Turkey was very uncomfortable with Tehran's policy because of the potential encouragement it could give to Kurdish radicals inside Turkey.[5]

The existence of Kurdish tribal and political affiliations across the three-way border of Turkey, Iran, and Iraq creates further problems. The northernmost, more tribal Kurmanji-speaking Kurds under the Kurdish Democratic Party are geographically and culturally closer to Turkey than Iran. The less tribal and more urbanized Surani-speaking Kurds centered in Sulaymaniya are culturally linked with other Surani-speaking Kurds in Iran and historically have closer ties with Iran. Both groups play Turkey against Iran in order to gain maximum room for maneuver.

Turkic-Speaking Minorities. While the large Turkic-speaking minorities in Iran have not posed a significant issue in contemporary Turkish-Iranian relations, they remain a potential instrument of one-way Turkish pressure on Iran. Some 26 percent of the Iranian population is Turkic-speaking, the vast majority of whom are Azeris and culturally and linguistically intimately linked to the Azeris of Azerbaijan. (Some Azeri nationalists refer to "northern" and "southern" Azerbaijan.) But among all the Turkic peoples of the world, the Azeris of Iran tend to be the least mindful of their "Turkishness"; they are quite well integrated into Iran culturally and economically. In fact, the Azeris constitute a huge business class and many key ayatollahs and officials are Azeri. Nonetheless, although sentiments for genuine separatism are minimal, there is an ongoing concern among many Azeris about heavy-handed rule from Tehran, nourishing a desire for greater regional autonomy among them.

The Ottoman state passed through various phases of promoting pan-Turkism, most dramatically under the influence of Enver Pasha during the Young Turk period (1908–18) and later when Enver sought to raise a pan-Turkish rebellion among the Russian Turks of Azerbaijan and Central Asia after the Russian Revolution. The Ottoman state repeatedly intervened in Azerbaijan to strengthen its position there versus Iran at tense points in their bilateral relations. While Atatürk formally abandoned pan-Turkism as an element in the new republic's foreign policy, there remains an active nationalist element within the Turkish political spectrum. It was rejuvenated with the emergence of five newly independent Turkic republics following the collapse of the USSR. These nationalists regularly urge Ankara to employ its pan-Turkic ties to broaden Turkey's influence abroad and to use these ties as pressure points to demonstrate discontent with certain Iranian policies.

Although pan-Turkic issues are not likely to play a major role in future Turkish-Iranian relations, they nonetheless remain latent and open to exploitation

---

4. Çetinsaya, "Essential Friends and Natural Enemies," 27.
5. Ibid., 35.

by Turkey should bilateral tensions deteriorate. Such could be the case in the event of a serious clash of interests between Ankara and Tehran over Iraq, over the nuclear issue, or over the unlikely event that Tehran grossly mishandles its large Azeri minority. In the event of a really serious regional deterioration, one could not rule out a six-way crisis involving Iran, Iranian Azeris, Azerbaijani Azeris, Armenia, Iraq, and Turkey. At present, however, entering into such an imbroglio seems quite unthinkable to Turkey, despite the occasional urgings of some ultranationalist Turkish circles.

Terrorism

Turkish security authorities have in the past accused Tehran of supporting radical Islamic violence in Turkey, especially in the case of a few assassinations of prominent Turkish secular figures. In early 2000, the Turkish National Intelligence Organization claimed that Iran lends support to the Great Eastern Raiders Islamic Front (Islamî Büyük Doğu Akıncılar Cephesi), which has been behind a prominent assassination, and stated that the group was linked with the PKK. In general, the Turkish military has been far more hard-line toward Iran than the civilian foreign policy establishment, particularly due to the Islamic character of Iran's government. Indeed, the military's critique of former prime minister Erbakan's efforts to improve Turkey's ties with Iran was based more on domestic policies toward Islam in Turkey than on the foreign policy itself.

In the past, Turkey periodically claimed that Iran was providing logistical support to the PKK or turning a blind eye to PKK activities across the Turkish border in Iran. This has undoubtedly been true on an occasional tactical basis, but it has not been a long-term Iranian policy. After all, the uniquely pan-Kurdish ideology of the PKK in the end threatens Iran as well. In 2006 and 2007, Turkey and Iran cooperated closely in joint military operations against the PKK and its Iranian equivalent the PJAK (Party for a Free Life). Since Washington is reported to be lending covert support to minority separatist movements inside Iran, including to Iranian Kurds, this close Turkish-Iranian cooperation is a source of irritation to Washington. At the same time, Ankara's perception of Washington's reluctance to take action against the PKK is a key source of aggravation to Ankara.

Economic Factors

Economic factors, especially those related to energy, increasingly tie the two countries together. Turkish-Iranian bilateral trade reached $2.7 billion in 2004, amounting to 3.3 percent of Turkey's overall bilateral trade; Iran ranked third, after Russia and Ukraine, in bilateral trade with Turkey among Turkey's neighbors.[6] By 2006, bilateral trade levels reached $6.2 billion. This level is still rela-

---

6. DEIK, "Foreign Trade Statistics, August 2005, www.deik.org.tr/bultenler/200589173240ft-aug2005.pdf, 11.

tively modest, however, and Turkey so far does not yet figure among Iran's top six import and export partners. This factor is due in part to the similarity of their economies apart from the energy sector and to the absence of smooth working relations between the two countries.

Turkey's biggest import from the Middle East is, of course, Iranian gas. In April 2007, Turkey and Iran announced plans for a strategic alliance based on a joint venture in the field of energy. The project entails drilling new oil and gas wells and the transportation of energy through Greece to Europe via existing gas pipelines currently crossing Turkey. Turkey has pledged $2 billion for marketing and transporting Iranian natural gas, and it is also planning to facilitate the export of Iranian oil via pipelines to the Ceyhan terminal on the Mediterranean. The European Union strongly favors imports of Iranian energy to avoid excessive reliance on Russian energy sources, but Washington is strongly opposed to the project—which is a continuing source of friction with Ankara. Washington also opposes any possible plans to bring Turkmen oil to Turkey via Iran.[7] This process deepened with the signing in mid-September 2007 of a memorandum of understanding between the two states for an extensive joint venture in this area. Turkey now becomes a major hub for the consumption of Iranian gas and oil, as well as for its onward transport to the West. Despite strong U.S. opposition, Europe will welcome this Iranian alternative to exclusive reliance on Russian exports to Europe—also not favored by Washington.

The JDP has strongly encouraged trade increases with Iran. Turkey is keenly interested in investment prospects in Iran, but it nonetheless finds Iran famously devious in its bargaining style and tends to believe that Tehran cannot be trusted, particularly following the collapse of several well-advanced major deals, including one involving the construction of a new airport for Tehran. This has had a negative impact on bilateral relations. Although the JDP is under no illusions about the problems of unreliability in dealing with Iran, it believes that working on the problem and fostering Iranian ties with the West is very important to the broader Turkish posture in the region.

Foreign Minister Gül has made efforts to maintain regular ties with Tehran, but he has also offered some friendly criticism; he has publicly stated that all countries must open themselves up to internal criticism and self-examination in keeping with Islamic values. He has also urged Iran along with the other countries of the region to solve their our own problems before external actors decide to do so for them. Gül's ability to speak frankly on these issues is actually a measure of greater confidence between the two sides than witnessed in the past. Nonetheless, the JDP must tread cautiously in its rapprochement with Iran due to military suspicions that the Turkish Islamists secretly wish

---

7. "US Critical of Turkey's Strategic Partnership with Iran," *Turkish Daily News*, April 7, 2007.

to join Iran in setting up an Islamic state in Turkey.[8] Such a fear is totally alien to Turkish culture and tradition.

Ankara feels itself to be caught in a bind between U.S. strategic demands and the importance of good working relations with Tehran. This kind of dilemma serves to reinforce calls for a more independent Turkish foreign policy and a broadening of ties with Russia, China, India, Africa, and others.[9]

While U.S. military action against Iran would negatively affect Ankara's interests, even U.S. efforts to bring broad economic sanctions against Tehran significantly impact Turkish foreign trade: for example, roughly seventy-five thousand Turkish trucks transit through Iran every year on their way to Central Asia and beyond.[10] Ankara is highly unlikely to yield to Washington's objections to its major new energy initiatives with Iran, given its importance to the Turkish economy as well as to Ankara's efforts to bind Iran closer to Turkey.

International Security Concerns

Both states cooperate meaningfully on issues related to the Kurds and cross-border drug smuggling. They also both joined in opposing the Taliban in Afghanistan and share a common concern over the hazardous and incalculable consequences of a break-up of Iraq. But a Shiite-dominated Iraq positioned between Ankara and Tehran involves totally uncharted strategic waters. Under almost any scenario, Ankara will extend its involvement and influence into Iraq to some degree, but it can never match Iran's huge gains in influence there. An all-out Iraqi civil war could constitute a volatile factor in Turkish-Iranian relations. It is not likely to get out of hand, but on the off chance that it did, it would constitute the first serious geopolitical confrontation between Turkey and Iran in centuries. Under such circumstances, one could imagine Ankara playing the pan-Turkic card against Iran.

Nuclear Issues

Although the prospect of Iranian nuclear weapons is viewed negatively within Turkey, this issue is not a top priority within Turkey when compared to the Kurdish issue, even for the Turkish military. In conventional arms, Turkey is far more powerful than Iran. And despite various sources of tension between them, there is no modern history of serious military confrontation between the two countries. Turkey's main concern lies in how Iranian

---

8. Aras, *Turkey and The Greater Middle East*, 70.
9. See, for example, strategic policy thinker Osman Metin Öztürk, "İran'ın Yeni Dışişleri Bakanı Ve Düşündürdükleri" [Thoughts Stimulated by Iran's New Foreign Minister], August 26, 2005, www.habusulu.com.
10. Mevlut Katik, "Turkey And The United States To Develop 'Common Strategic Vision,'" *Eurasia Insight*, April 26, 2006, www.eurasianet.org/departments/insight/articles/eav042606ru.shtml.

nuclear weapons would impact balance-of-power equations in the region. While Turkish leaders would welcome a curtailment of Iran's nuclear programs in principle, it also fears that U.S. policies will only push Iran to move more rapidly and dangerously in the nuclear direction. In a June 2003 poll on a possible U.S.-Iranian confrontation, 55 percent of Turks stated that they would prefer to remain neutral on the matter, while just under 24 percent actually favored siding with Iran; less than 17 percent would want to side with the United States.[11] Ankara is more likely to follow the EU line than the U.S. line on how to handle the nuclear problem.[12]

Although Erdoğan has reportedly assured Tehran that it would not permit the use of Turkish airspace for an Israeli attack on Iran,[13] Washington made serious diplomatic efforts in early 2006 to enlist Turkey into pressuring Tehran, including through military threat. Ankara has so far resisted and almost certainly would not participate in or even facilitate an Israeli or U.S. attack on Iran unless Iran's actions were to become truly threatening in Ankara's eyes.

Conclusion

Historically speaking, Iran has seemed to either worry about or resent Turkish closeness to the West; even the last Shah sometimes perceived Turkey as a rival for Western attention. For the foreseeable future, then, Iran's attitudes toward Turkey will be powerfully influenced by the degree to which Ankara embraces strategic Western policies against Iran. As late as the 1990s, the Turkish military used its strategic rapprochement with Israel, then at a high point, as a strategic card to play against Iran as needed. But since then, mutual Turkish-Iranian confidence has increased under the JDP, particular in today's post-Saddam environment. To the extent that Ankara is no longer perceived to be acting as a direct instrument of either U.S. or Israeli security interests, Tehran will be much more open to compromise with Ankara. At the same time, the JDP has no ideological problems with Shiism and will continue with its major efforts to improve ties with Iran as part of its "good neighbor" policies and its broadening regional role. As a result, Iran will likely remain a prickly but permanent partner for Turkey under most any future scenario.

---

11. Polls cited in Nasuh Uslu, Metin Toprak, Ibrahim Dalmis, and Ertan Aydin, "Turkish Public Opinion Toward The United States In The Context Of The Iraq Question," *MERIA* 9, no. 3 (September 2005).

12. Jonathan Feiser, "Nuclear Iran: Repercussions for Turkey and Saudi Arabia," *PINR— Power and Interest News Report*, January 28, 2005, www.pinr.com/report.php?ac=view_printable&report_id=261&language_id=1.

13. "Iran Bullies Israel's Strategic Friends—with Eye on Washington," DEBKAfile, August 22, 2004.

12

Turkey and Israel

J ews have a long history within the Ottoman Empire. They found refuge there after they were expelled, along with Muslims, from Catholic Spain in 1492. In fact, as Soner Cagaptay states, "in the seventeenth century more Jews lived in the Ottoman Empire than in the rest of the world collectively."[1] For Jews, the historical experience of life in the Muslim world was generally much more positive than it was in large parts of Europe—at least until the founding of the state of Israel in 1948. In turn, the Ottoman Empire benefited from Jewish knowledge and skills in many professional fields, bringing Western know-how into the developing and transforming empire.[2] The Jews, as a people, never posed any political or strategic threat to the Ottoman state—unlike Christian communities within the empire that ultimately developed strong separatist sentiments—and the Ottomans maintained a tolerant approach to both Judaism and Christianity. In modern Turkey, too, Jews have lived free of persecution, and there is an important Turkish-Jewish community in Israel that remains quite pro-Turkish.

But Turkey has also felt compelled to maintain a delicate balance between Israel and the Arab world in several key respects, causing it to have potentially conflicting interests in the cultural, diplomatic, military, and economic arenas.

The Role of Palestine in Turkish Thinking

Palestine was a part of the Ottoman Empire and the sultan was formally Protector of the Holy Places in Jerusalem. Starting in the late nineteenth century, the growing migration of European Jews to Palestine and their increasing acquisition of land there prompted concern in Istanbul about the broader geopolitical implications of the Zionist movement. In fact, Arab members of the Ottoman Parliament pressed Istanbul to take measures to limit the Zionist expansionism, which threatened to eventually displace the Arab population.[3] The acquiescence of the British—no friends of the Ottoman Empire—to Zionist aspirations created additional anxieties in Istanbul.

---

1. Soner Cagaptay, *The Turkish Prime Minister Visits Israel: Whither Turkish-Israeli Relations?* Policywatch 987 (Washington, D.C.: Washington Institute for Near East Policy, April 27, 2005).
2. Jung and Piccoli, *Turkey at the Crossroads,* 155.
3. Dawn, "The Origins of Arab Nationalism," 17.

After the collapse of the Ottoman Empire, the Turkish Republic was sympathetic to the plight of Jews in Europe, facilitating the transit of Jews from Europe to Palestine before World War II even broke out. With the creation of the new Zionist state, the Turkish elite as a whole showed respect for Israel's military prowess,[4] although this partially reflected the traditional Kemalist lack of sympathy for the Arab world.

But as Aras suggests, there is also an important distinction in Turkish thinking between the Arab-Israeli issue and the Jerusalem issue. Jerusalem is sacred to all three Abrahamic faiths—and the Ottoman sultan historically derived pride in fulfilling his Islamic obligation and responsibility to maintain a just, balanced, and equitable administration of the holy city. Like most Muslims, Turks are extremely uncomfortable that traditional Muslim religious areas of Jerusalem lie under exclusive Israeli control. In a 2000 opinion poll, 63 percent of Turks stated that Jerusalem and al-Aqsa mosque were of importance to them, and 60 percent demanded a more active Turkish role in defense of the Palestinian people.[5] The Muslim world still looks to Turkey to help speak out on behalf of Muslim interests in Jerusalem. During the al-Aqsa intifada in 2000, even Turkey's arch-secular president Necdet Sezer felt compelled to make a not very secular statement: "The Islamic world was deeply upset by the violent deeds against our Palestinian brothers after Friday's prayer in Jerusalem—which Islam deems to be among the most sacred lands—following certain irresponsible provocations."[6]

Thus, the Jerusalem issue in Turkey is not simply an "Islamist issue" but also an abiding part of Turkey's historical, religious, cultural, and emotional ties with Jerusalem—ties that hold sway even during an era of good relations with the state of Israel.

The Military Factor in Turkish-Israeli Relations

By far the strongest advocate in Turkey for close ties with Israel is the Turkish military. For the radically secular army, Israel is significant as an "anti-Islamic" symbol, a source of valuable hi-tech military transfers, a facilitator of access to the U.S. Congress, and a source of strategic intimidation against radical neighbors. A second source of more modest pro-Israeli sentiment tends to be from the pro-American wing within the Turkish foreign policy elite *(amerikancılar)*.

Turkish public opinion itself tends to be more mixed: the population has respect for Israel's democracy and military success, but it has greater sympathies toward Muslim peoples in general, expresses anger at Israel's

4. Jung and Piccoli, *Turkey at the Crossroads,* 157.
5. Aras, *Turkey and The Greater Middle East,* 53, 61.
6. As quoted in Aras, *Turkey and The Greater Middle East,* 61.

regional policies toward Muslim states, and perceives Israel as a bully. Most Turks readily distinguish between Turkey's small (120,000) Jewish population, which they have a high degree of tolerance and respect toward, and the state of Israel, for which they have no popular affection. In a 2004 poll within Turkey, two-thirds of those surveyed believed that Turkey should side with the Palestinians while only 3 percent favored siding with Israel.[7] In a 2007 study conducted by the German Marshall Fund of the United States, Turks viewed Palestinians more favorably as a nationality than any other national group at 47 percent; only 5 percent viewed Israel with favor.[8]

Military cooperation has been the most dramatic and controversial element of Turkey's growing ties with Israel. Cooperation burgeoned in the 1990s as Israel opened the door to a vital source of military technology not readily available from the United States or Europe, whose policies were constrained by concerns about human rights and democracy in Turkey. Joint military training programs with Israel made it possible for pilots of each country to train in the other country. Turkey agreed to establish joint listening posts with Israel on Turkish soil to eavesdrop on Iran, Iraq, and Syria. The strategic implications of joint Turkish-Israeli military cooperation was not lost on Turkey's radical neighbors and excited widespread negative commentary in the region—even from pro-Western Egypt and Saudi Arabia—that Turkey had, in effect, switched over to the Israeli camp.

The Israeli connection was especially valuable to Turkey at a time when the Turkish military had embarked on a major new military modernization project worth some $150 billion over a period of twenty-five years. Both Israeli technology and serious financial investment in Turkey have played a vital role in this effort, bringing the defense industries of the two countries close together. Israeli scholar Efraim Inbar estimates that from 2000 to 2004 total Israeli arms sales to Turkey exceeded $1 billion.[9] At the same time, military and strategic consultation achieved an unprecedented level of institutionalization between the two countries, promising a more durable relationship.[10] Additionally, in 1998, Turkey, Israel, and the United States began engaging in joint naval exercises that were to remain open-ended.

Both Israel and Turkey found considerable strategic value in their potential pincer capabilities against a hostile Syrian state, especially in the mid-1990s when Turkey's ties with Israel reached their high-water mark.

---

7. Soner Cagaptay, "Where Goes the U.S.-Turkish Relationship?" *Middle East Quarterly* (Fall 2004), www.meforum.org.

8. "Turks Become Increasingly More Isolated," *Today's Zaman*, September 7, 2007.

9. Pemra Hazbay, *Political Troubles between Turkey and Israel? Implications of Booming Bilateral Trade for the Two Countries and the Middle East*, PeaceWatch 459 (Washington, D.C.: Washington Institute for Near Eastern Policy, May 26, 2004), www.washingtoninstitute.org/templateC05.php?CID=2150.

10. Jung and Piccoli, *Turkey at the Crossroads*, 163.

In this period, the Turkish military had seized virtual de facto control of Turkish security policy and, as Robins states, "seemed to glory in an assertiveness which almost bordered on truculence."[11] Turkey was actually concerned at one point that a possible peace settlement between Syria and Israel would weaken Ankara's leverage against Damascus, potentially permitting Damascus to redeploy its standing forces northward toward the Turkish border.[12] There is little doubt that the joint pincer power of Turkey and Israel against Damascus contributed significantly to Syria's decision in 1998 to drop its support for the PKK and to entirely revamp its hostile policies toward Ankara.

But Turkey's military relationship with Israel also became a vehicle for the domestic struggle between the Islamists and the Turkish military. During Erbakan's prime ministership, the military found it useful to employ its growing strategic relationship with Israel to embarrass the anti-Israel Erbakan and force him into a closer relationship with Israel. In fact, Islamist hostility to rapprochement with Israel was seized upon as one of the many grounds the military used to justify its decision to extralegally remove Erbakan from office in 1997.[13] Since the late 1990s, Turkey's ties with Israel have lost some of their proxy character in domestic politics. Both Erbakan's Virtue Party and now the JDP have made major efforts to maintain "correct" relations with Israel at all levels.

Civilian Cooperation

Intense military cooperation between the two countries has been matched by major civilian ties in multiple fields. For example, Israeli tourism to Turkey represents a significant part of Turkey's tourism revenue, accounting for $1.85 billion annually. Additionally, Israel has invested in Turkish agricultural development, a field in which Israel commands particular expertise. Trade between the two states quadrupled between 1992 and 1996, and a Free Trade Agreement was signed in 1997 that led bilateral trade figures to reach $2 billion by 2004.[14] This represented an astonishing jump when considering total bilateral trade only reached $54 million as late as 1987. Turkey now ranks thirteenth on Israel's list of trading partners, while Israel ranks ninth among Turkey's trading partners.[15] In 2007, Turkey and Israel provisionally agreed to build a pipeline system connecting the Black Sea to the Red Sea. Going underwater, this pipeline would bypass

---

11. Robins, *Suits and Uniforms*, 267.

12. Amikam Nachmani, "The Remarkable Turkish-Israeli Tie," *Middle East Quarterly* (June 1998), www.meforum.org/article/394.

13. Ibid.

14. Ibid.

15. Hazbay, *Political Troubles between Turkey and Israel?*

Syria and Lebanon and bring both gas and oil from Russia and Azerbaijan through Turkey to Israel.[16]

Turkish-Israeli cooperation has also extended into the Turkic areas of the former Soviet Union. Israel saw Turkey as a valuable bridge to this region following the collapse of the USSR, and Turkey has subsequently facilitated Israeli entry into the region. Israel brings into this region the benefits of its close ties to the United States as well as its technical expertise, while Turkey has developed a good feel for the market there. Washington, Turkey, and Israel signed an agreement in 1994 to launch a common agricultural project in Uzbekistan and Turkmenistan, and Israel remains interested in Turkey's potential to bring energy from the Caucasus and Central Asia that could be used by Israel.[17] The completion of the Baku-Ceyhan oil pipeline from Azerbaijan to Turkey is a first step in this direction.

The Pendulum Swings Back

By the end of the 1990s, the Turkish military had been running roughshod over civilian power for several years, embarrassing it by demonstrating the degree to which the Foreign Ministry was out of the loop on key foreign policy issues. The dramatic improvements in the Turkish-Israeli relationship left the strong impression that the Turkish military was now in near total charge of this policy account. These new policies, while encouraged by Washington, damaged the image of Turkey in the Middle East by suggesting that it was becoming part of a U.S.-Israeli strategic axis and suggested military dominance over civilian policy-makers—a negative mark in Turkey's quest for EU membership. In the end, the partnership of the Turkish military and the Likud Party in Israel overreached in their goal of forming a genuine strategic alliance between the two states. The international perception of the Turkish-Israeli relationship, despite its broad civilian components, was that it was representative of the military's domination in setting policy—a characteristic deemed undesirable for Turkey's democracy, reform process, and EU aspirations. In the end, the Turkish military and the Likud Party in Israel may have overreached in their goal of forming a genuine strategic alliance.

The Turkish military's view of foreign relations had always stressed a threat-based approach to the region, borrowing Israel's line about "living in a bad neighborhood." But most Turkish civilian authorities did not share this view of foreign relations. As Robins comments, "the Turkish generals' ideological defiance, aimed at both domestic and regional consumption, was

---

16. Iaonnis Solomou, "Turkey, Israel to Build Pipelines Connecting Black Sea to Red Sea," *ANI*, January 9, 2007.

17. Jung and Piccoli, *Turkey at the Crossroads*, 165.

critical to [its] public diplomacy."[18] The deputy chief of staff, Gen. Çevik Bir, a swaggering and ambitious man hostile to Islam, figured prominently in the style, verve, assertiveness, and even pugnacity with which the relationship with Israel had been projected. Robins dates the beginning of the decline of the Israeli relationship from 1996,[19] when many in the military itself came to feel that Turkey's ties with Israel had not paid the expected dividends in Washington.

The rise of the JDP to power and its commitment to a "no enemies" regional policy has led to a further relationship shift in which Israel is no longer central to Turkey's foreign policy. Along with JDP leaders, even left-of-center prime minister Bülent Ecevit grew increasingly critical of Israeli policies toward the Palestinians. Further, there has been a rise in anti-Semitism in the Turkish press, in part reflecting broader world dissatisfaction with hard-line Israeli policies under the Likud and later under Kadima—a mood that has opened the door to expressions of cruder and more traditional anti-Semitism.

While the economic and technical aspects of Turkish-Israeli relations remain strong, the strategic aspects of the relationship have undergone significant weakening, particularly with the end of the Syrian and Iraqi (state) threats to Turkey, which considerably reduced Israel's strategic value to Ankara as a pressure point. Turkey's new stake in Syria's welfare further complicates Turkey's ties with Israel. Ankara has likewise been concerned over Israeli activities in post-war Iraq, especially in Kurdistan, where Israel has supported the training of *peshmerga* forces and has used the area as a base for anti-Iranian intelligence operations.

While both Jerusalem and Washington have been uncomfortable with many of Turkey's outspoken criticisms of Israeli policy, neither capital has sought to entirely choke off Turkey's new regional aspirations in the hopes that they might bring some benefit. Turkey is almost the only regional ally of both states that enjoys credibility with most Arab states and Iran. But to the extent that Israel seeks to weaken and divide Muslim states with which it has poor or hostile relations, Israel's interests no longer automatically align with Turkey's interests.

Conclusion

Turkish-Israeli relations are an important element in the broader scheme of Middle Eastern diplomatic and strategic relations. Despite some cooling of ties, Israel still places considerable value on its relationship with Turkey, the only substantive and close working relationship it has with any Muslim state. And where Turkish domestic public opinion also supports it,

---

18. Robins, *Suits and Uniforms,* 265.
19. Ibid., 269.

Turkish-Israeli relations are important as an example of meaningful bilateral regional ties that transcend narrow, purely strategic interests and actually embrace substantive, mutually beneficial economic and technical relationships. Because such a relationship has otherwise been singularly absent in the Middle East, it offers a model of how Middle Eastern countries might operate with one another in a future Middle East.

Ankara is aware, too, that since the overthrow of Saddam, neither the United States nor Israel has shown much concern for Ankara's chief terrorism-related concern, the PKK. Indeed, Israel has always demonstrated some latent sympathy for the plight of the Kurds in the world and has avoided joining Ankara in cooperation against the PKK, treating the situation as essentially an internal Turkish issue.[20]

As remarkable as the flowering of Turkish-Israeli relations has been, the relationship falls well short of what officials in Washington or Jerusalem had hoped for: a solid strategic alliance against states that do not support U.S. policies in the region. As Aras points out, "the Turkish-Israeli-American axis was an extension of the national security apparatuses in both Israel and Turkey and did not necessarily serve Ankara as it embarked on a reform process to achieve democratization, improve human rights and freedoms and establish the rule of law."[21] Israeli observers themselves have long observed a schism in Ankara on these strategic and security issues: the military, intelligence services, and police organizations have taken a hard-line approach more in conformity with Israel's views, while the Foreign Ministry, the Prime Minister's Office, the Finance Ministry, and even public opinion have been more equivocal about the degree of the threat from radical regional states and have sought to maintain a balanced approach to Middle Eastern states as a whole.[22]

The Turkish-Israeli relationship in the economic and material realm is highly advantageous to both parties and is likely to endure. Because of Turkey's military modernization program, Ankara will almost surely maintain a fairly strong military relationship with Israel, even in the absence of strategic cooperation between the two countries. But the nature of the existing relationship could come under additional questioning if Israel is perceived to be moving toward dangerous military confrontations with Syria, Iraq, Iran, or Lebanon, countries that Turkey perceives little threat from. Other states—such as China, Russia, and European ones—could potentially replace certain aspects of Turkey's military relationship with Israel, particularly if Ankara perceives the costs of its close military relationship with Israel to be overly deleterious to its other regional interests. Only if a major Middle Eastern state

20. Ibid, 256.
21. Bülent Aras, "Turks May Look Back with Anger at Israel," *Daily Star* (Beirut), May 6, 2005.
22. Robins, *Suits and Uniforms*, 253.

arose that seriously challenged Turkish security would the importance of the Israeli relationship regain a dominant place in Ankara's strategic thinking. But even under such circumstances, Turkey might opt against dependence upon external protectors in favor of forging a new combination of regional relationships to deal with the challenge.

13

Turkey and Egypt, Saudi Arabia, the Gulf States, and Afghanistan

Egypt

Despite centuries of close dealings between Turks and Egyptians, modern Turkey's relationship with Egypt has never been cordial and has ranged from hostile to lukewarm. This coolness is based not so much on specific historical resentments as on the realities of contemporary geopolitical rivalries. For example, in the 1950s, Ankara was hostile to Cairo's leadership of the Arab nationalist movement against Western power in the Middle East and sought to undercut it. To the extent that Ankara has challenged Arab interests, power, and leadership, particularly in the name of the West, it has incurred Egyptian anger. This has been especially true since the signing of the Camp David peace settlement: Egypt views itself as the key guardian of the broader Arab cause and natural leader of the Arab world, even while increasingly unconvincing in such a role.

That noted, both Turkey and Egypt have shared a few common strategic positions and agreements over the past two decades, helping to keep their relationship correct.

- Both are allies of the United States (Egypt since Camp David).
- Both are among the few Muslim states that have established diplomatic relations with Israel—primarily a function of their relations with the United States—and both make periodic efforts for an Arab-Israeli settlement.
- Both seek to tamp down regional radicalism.
- Both have had strained relations with Iran since the Iranian Revolution.
- In the mid-1990s, Prime Minister Erbakan tried to create a "D-8" bloc of key developing Muslim states that included Egypt, the only proposed Arab member.

- In 1996, Turkey opened negotiations with Egypt over the possible provision of Egyptian natural gas to Turkey, but the project has yet to materialize and its economic feasibility still remains a question.[1]

Despite these modest commonalities, Cairo is consistently wary of Turkish efforts to involve itself in Arab affairs in ways that might shift the region's geopolitical balance or overshadow Egypt's overriding (and foundering) quest to remain the dominant arbiter in Arab affairs. For example, during the Cold War, Cairo spoke out on behalf of any Arab state—including, at various times, Jordan, Syria, and Iraq—whenever there was any potential threat from Turkey. Following the Cold War, Egyptian president Hosni Mubarak was angered at the close personal and party ties between Erbakan and the opposition Muslim Brotherhood in Egypt.[2] Additionally, Cairo has long been uncomfortable with any Turkish policy that strengthens Israel's clout in the region, particularly in the military realm.

In a 1997 study, TESEV, a forward-looking Turkish think tank, argued for the establishment of special ties among a core group of "like-minded" countries—Turkey, Egypt, Jordan, Israel, and Palestine—that share a "greater commitment to economic and political liberalization" than other states of the region and that could set an example for them. Other regional states would then be invited to join this core group once they met "the basic criteria of being democratic, open and market-oriented societies that reject force as a tool of international politics."[3] Turkey has also discussed establishing a free-trade zone with Egypt and a Turkish industrial zone in Egypt, but the TESEV study notes that state domination of the economic structures in Egypt and the Middle East, as well as the heavy-handed security agenda of most regional regimes, severely hinder the development of free-market opportunities. Although bilateral trade between the two countries reached $728.4 million in 2004, the development of formal trade institutions has progressed slowly.[4]

The waning potential of any security alliance between Turkey and Israel and the JDP's more recent policies of rapprochement with all states of the Middle East have smoothed the way to better Turkish-Egyptian ties. Nonetheless, this relationship still remains essentially stalled, primarily due to the sluggish character of the Egyptian economy and its sclerotic, constipated, and jealous political order. Egypt is unlikely to overcome its deeper

---

1. EIA Country Analysis Briefs, "Turkey," July 2005, www.eia.doe.gov/emeu/cabs/turkey.html.
2. Robins, *Suits and Uniforms*, 152.
3. Mine Eder, Kemal Kirişçi, and Ali Çarkoğlu, "Political and Economic Cooperation and Integration in the Middle East: Analysis of Turkey's Mid to Long Term Regional Policy," TESEV, Istanbul, 1997, www.tesev.org.tr/eng/publication/pub6.php.
4. "New Session of Talks to Set Up FTA with Turkey," *ArabicNews.com*, December 25, 2004, www.bilaterals.org/article.php3?id_article=1101; DEIK, www.deik.org.tr.

tendency to view Turkey as a potential regional rival for leadership, but ties could one day be more productive and cooperative under a less authoritarian regime in Cairo.

Turkey and Saudi Arabia

There is a considerable history of antagonism between Turkey and Arab tribal power in the Najd. Wahhabi forces from the Najd challenged Ottoman overlordship of the holy places of the Hijaz and attacked Shiite shrines in Ottoman Iraq, and an Ottoman force from Egypt wiped out the first Wahhabi state in central Arabia. Furthermore, the British used the al-Sa'ud to weaken Ottoman power in the Peninsula before World War I, and the Ottomans, in turn, supported the al-Sa'ud's rivals in the Najd.[5] After World War I, the al-Sa'ud's Wahhabi forces, which had been hostile to Ottoman multicultural expressions of Islam, took control of the holy places in the Hijaz. As a result, modern Turkey retains memories of Arab revolt by both the Hashimites in the Hijaz and the al-Sa'ud against the Ottoman state.

Furthermore, apart from the holy places, Turks have never viewed the Arabian Peninsula with any cordiality, although they do retain some historical emotional attachment to the Levant, Greater Syria, and Egypt. Latent antagonism with the al-Sa'ud resurfaced as recently as 2002, when Turks were outraged at the Saudi razing of a historic Ottoman-Turkish castle in Mecca to make way for a housing project. The Turkish Ministry of Culture stated that "the fort's demolition was the latest attack on Turkish heritage in Saudi Arabia, which had in the past destroyed Ottoman houses, cemeteries and a historic railroad. This is a crime against humanity . . . and cultural massacre." The Saudis struck back, accusing Turkey of abolishing its own heritage and identity as an Islamic state.[6]

The Kemalist establishment has always been suspicious of Saudi Arabia's international Islamic policies. The flowering of Islamic banking in Turkey, bolstered in part by Saudi investment capital, is seen by secularists as a part of Saudi support to reactionary religious forces in Turkey aimed at the overthrow of Turkish secularism. Turkish booksellers carry numerous titles by secularist writers on the "menace" of Saudi Arabia and its efforts to support "religious reaction" in Turkey.

Despite these ideological tensions, starting in the 1970s economic relations between the two countries actually began to flourish as Turkish workers went to the kingdom in considerable numbers and Turkish businessmen won sizeable contracts there. Saudis as individuals probably feel warmer toward

---

5. Nadav Safran, *Saudi Arabia: The Ceaseless Quest for Security* (Cambridge, Mass.: Harvard University Press, 1985), 29–35.

6. BBC Service, "Saudis Hit Back over Mecca Castle," January 9, 2002.

Turkey than their government does, but the feeling is not especially reciprocated. The Turkish street press often carries lurid stories about the kingdom, and the al-Sa'ud enjoy little religious respect from Turks. Saudis nonetheless prize Istanbul as a Muslim tourism destination.

Saudi Arabia was uncomfortable with Turkey's success in imposing an open electoral process on the OIC, weakening Riyadh's traditional management of the organization. Riyadh also has had periodic concerns about potential Turkish expansionism into Iraq and "designs against the Arab world."

Nevertheless, Saudi Arabia and Turkey share some general common interests in the region, particularly as relates to Palestine, terrorism, and regional stability. But these interests are commonplace across the region and do not betoken any particular warmth of relationship. Both also share a concern about Iran—Ankara less so than Riyadh. But should Iran demonstrate a bold, newfound regional aggressiveness in the years ahead, Turkey and Saudi Arabia could well cooperate on certain security issues.

Turkish economic interests in the kingdom are significant and are likely to grow as long as Riyadh maintains interest in improving its economic ties with Ankara—partly as a gesture of Islamic solidarity. Relations between the two countries are likely to remain quite reasonable, correct, and occasionally cooperative even outside the economic sphere, but it is unlikely that they will ever achieve real warmth or substance given the antipathy most Turks feel toward the nature of Wahhabi/Tawhidi Islam in the kingdom. Prime Minister Erbakan reportedly visited the kingdom some fifty times, but most of this was in the capacity of performing the *hajj* or *'umra* as an expression of personal/political piety—or in the interest of developing economic initiatives—and not out of high regard for the kingdom itself. Significantly, in 2006 Saudi King Abdullah paid the first royal visit to Turkey in some forty years, almost certainly in acknowledgment of Turkey's greater sensitivity and involvement in issues in the Middle East including Iraq.

Turkish ties with the smaller Gulf states may ultimately be more important; they are far more relaxed, carry no historical burden, and are not laden with Wahhabi ideology. With large Turkish construction projects across the Gulf and major investments from the Gulf in Turkey, Turkish economic interaction with the Gulf states is increasing dramatically.

Turkey and Afghanistan

Afghanistan, as part of Greater Central Asia, is a region fabled in Turkish myth and historical memory that recall Turkish nomadic migrations across Central Asia and the annals of Turkic foot soldiers serving rulers there. Afghanistan is an intimate part of the broader Turkish geopolitical vision of the world to the East and is in many ways closer to the Turkish psyche than is the Arab world. Afghanistan today includes large and important Turkic Uzbek and Turkmen minorities, and Muslim rulers in the South Asia region in general often looked to Ottoman Turkey for assistance in repelling British imperialism.

Afghanistan was a powerful symbol of Muslim armed resistance and independence against Western imperialists in the nineteenth century and was widely admired across the Muslim world as one of only three Muslim countries that never permitted European imperialists to overtake them. Afghanistan was the second country (after the Soviet Union) to recognize the new Kemalist Turkish Republic, even sending military aid to assist in Atatürk's national liberation war against European imperialists. Indeed, Afghan king Amanullah Khan (1919–29) had a warm personal relationship with Atatürk, was a great admirer of his modernizing reforms, and sought to emulate them in Afghanistan. Officers of a new Afghan air force were trained in Turkey as well as in Europe, and Amanullah took on a number of Turkish military advisers to train his army. Other educational and cultural exchange programs between the two countries were also introduced, such as the establishment of Turkish schools in Afghanistan.[7] The Pakistani elite too, is impressed with the Turkish modernizing experience, admires the historical reforms of Atatürk, and enjoys good relations with Turkey, particularly at the military level. Turkey's close relationship with both Afghanistan and Pakistan puts it in a position to mediate frictions between these two countries—a role Ankara sought after the fall of the Taliban.

With the collapse of the Soviet Union, Turkey's geopolitical vista suddenly opened wide to the East; overnight, Afghanistan and Pakistan became gateways to Central Asia and Kashmir, reopening old associations in the minds of the Turkish peoples. This expanding eastern space has served to instill Turkish policy vistas with new opportunities and a new mindset. Despite zero sympathy for the Taliban, the Turkish public demonstrated widespread hostility toward the U.S. invasion of Afghanistan: some two-thirds opposed U.S. military operations there and any Turkish support to the U.S. operation, including the use of Turkish military facilities by U.S. forces. Nearly 90 percent opposed sending Turkish troops to Afghanistan, and 58 percent were concerned that U.S. attacks on Afghanistan could trigger a war between Christians and Muslims.[8]

Despite Turkish public opinion, the Turkish government agreed to assist the United States in the Afghan operation by providing support and training to Northern Alliance troops for their push south toward Kabul. Additionally,

---

7. "Turkey's Emerging Role In Afghanistan's Reconstruction," *Eurasia Insight,* March 22, 2002, www.eurasianet.org/departments/insight/articles/pp032302.shtml.

8. Steven A. Cook, "U.S.-Turkey Relations and the War on Terrorism," Brookings Analysis Paper 9, *America's Response to Terrorism* (Washington, D.C.: Brookings Institution, November 6, 2001), www.brook.edu/views/ARTICLES/fellows/2001_cook.htm.

because Turkey has had close ties with northern Afghanistan via its support for the opportunistic Uzbek warlord Rashid Dostum, Ankara was able to provide intelligence on this region. It also provided peacekeeping troops to Afghanistan and granted airbase rights for U.S. and NATO support flights to Central Asia.[9] Furthermore, Turkey provided some fourteen hundred troops to the early International Security Assistance Force (ISAF) peacekeeping operation. This represented the largest non-U.S. contingent in the operation and the only one from a Muslim country. In 2006, however, Turkey rejected NATO's call to send troops for operations outside of Kabul.

Some Afghans are concerned that Turkey might seek to exert influence in Afghanistan through the country's Uzbek population, with which Turkey has close ties. Although this would perhaps be to the detriment of other groups, such a fear seems ill-grounded. In January 2006, Afghanistan signed a protocol establishing a Program Coordination Office of the Turkish International Cooperation Agency in Kabul that involves some $11.6 million in Turkish aid funds to Afghanistan.[10] Turkey has since built four schools and two hospitals as part of this aid program. Former Turkish foreign minister Hikmet Çetin is NATO's senior civilian representative in Afghanistan.[11]

Even more impressive has been Turkish private-sector investment in Afghanistan, which has been greater than that coming from any other country and was worth approximately $1 billion dollars as of early 2006. These investments broadly complement Turkish commercial activity in Central Asia, where Turkish companies are the leading investors in many nonenergy sectors. Turkish companies are also working as subcontractors to U.S. firms in highway reconstruction.

Turkey is one of the few regional countries that will feel strongly compelled to provide assistance to Afghanistan over the long haul and that has a permanent interest in its welfare. Emotional ties remain powerful on both sides—although pro-Taliban elements among the Pashtun population will be suspicious of Turkey as a stalking horse for U.S. interests. In turn, Turkey will remain concerned about the rise of radical Islamist forces there, particularly because of their potential longer-term ability to project their ideology into the Turkic world to the north, including among the Uyghur Turks of western China.

---

9. Ibid.
10. Altay Atli, "Turkish Assistance to Afghanistan," *EurasiaNet Commentary*, January 26, 2006, www.eurasianet.org/departments/business/articles/eav012406.shtml.
11. Ibid.

14

Turkey and Eurasia

Alternative Partnerships?

Relations between Russia and Turkey have changed dramatically over the last decade. In fact, in 2005, relations between the two states were probably better than at any point over the last several centuries."[1] So state observers Fiona Hill and Ömer Taşpınar, who make plain the dramatic shift in relations between the two countries following centuries of bitter imperial confrontation between the Ottoman and Russian empires. Russia was a key force in the dismantling of the Ottoman Empire, and Russians as a people have always sensed a visceral cultural threat from Turko-Mongol peoples who ruled Muscovy in the fourteenth century—Russia's classic, centuries-long "yellow peril" other. Both the Russian Empire and Soviet Union always lived in fear of the potential collective power of pan-Turkism and its aspirations to form a united counterweight to Russian power and civilization. But times have changed: none of Turkey's foreign-state relationships has turned around as dramatically as this one, even though latent pan-Turkic issues can never completely disappear off the Turkish political horizon.

New economic and geopolitical factors have forged a historic transformation that displaces the confrontations of the past.[2] The Soviet Union is dead and, more significantly, Turkey no longer even shares a common border with Russia. Russian military aggression against Turkey today seems nearly unthinkable. The great majority of the Turkic Muslims of the USSR, such as in Azerbaijan and Central Asia, achieved independence in 1991. Turkey is reshaping its geopolitical options, and Russia offers major opportunities to it as a partner in the economic, political, and even military spheres.

Yet the reality is that Turkey's historical and ethnic relations with the Muslim (largely Turkic) peoples of the former Russian and Soviet empires can never totally disappear as a potential concern to Moscow. It is almost as if Moscow and Ankara represent alternate poles of influence upon these peoples. Today, the remaining Muslims still within the Russian Federation—the

---

1. Fiona Hill and Ömer Taşpınar, *Russia and Turkey in the Caucasus: Moving Together to Preserve the Status Quo?* IFRI Research Program (Washington, D.C.: Brookings Institution, January 2006), 4, www.brookings.edu/views/papers/fellows/hilltaspinar_20060120.pdf.
2. See, for example, S. Enders Wimbush, "Waiting for the EU, Turkey Draws Closer to Russia," *Wall Street Journal*, January 28, 2005.

Turkic Tatars of the Volga and Crimea, the Chechens, and other peoples of the northern Caucasus—still seek greater autonomy or independence from Moscow and for centuries have looked to Turkey to assist them. But after an initial period of euphoria after the fall of the Soviet Union and the reopening of the Turkic world, Turkey's relationship with these Muslims has proven somewhat disappointing to Ankara. At the same time, the pragmatic benefits derived from Turkey's closer ties with Russia have grown exponentially. The mutual decision by Ankara and Moscow to work with each other is an economic and strategic one; is likely to prove to be of considerable duration, and is supported by most of the Turkish public today.

This turnaround is most dramatically demonstrated in the case of the Chechen struggle for independence in the Caucasus, which has been ongoing for more than two hundred years. The Chechens are deeply committed to their Islamic identity. Although they are non-Turkic, there is a sizeable Chechen diaspora in Turkey, with waves of Chechens having fled Russian repression over the course of centuries. To publicize their cause, Chechens were involved in a few hijacking incidents on Turkish soil in the 1990s. If Ankara played at periodically supporting the Chechens in the past, Moscow demonstratively did the same with Turkey's Kurds. In the end, strong Turkish opposition to terrorism and Islamic extremism ultimately helped link Moscow and Ankara in their fight on these fronts against separatism. In 2004, for example, Erdoğan importantly called for joint action against terrorism and peaceful settlement of the Chechen issue "within the framework of Russia's territorial integrity."[3]

A strong emerging economic complementarity has also come into play in the Turkish-Russian relationship. Moscow is today the second largest importer of Turkish goods in the world after Germany, and Turkey has invested $6 to 12 billion dollars in Russia in the construction field. During Prime Minister Erdoğan's 2005 trip to Moscow, six hundred Turkish businessmen accompanied him with a keen interest in expanding an already booming bilateral trade in the spheres of construction, retail sales, banking, telecommunications, food and beverage, glass, and machine industries.[4] Because of these and other efforts, bilateral trade rose from $10 billion in 2004 to an estimated $15 billion in 2006 and is projected to increase to $25 billion in 2007.[5] By some estimates, Russian-Turkish "suitcase trade" alone was worth up to $3 billion in 2004.[6] Further, the number of Russian tourists to Turkey now rivals the number from Germany; as many as 1.7 million Russians visited in 2004

3. Central Asia–Caucasus Analyst, August 30, 2004, www.cacianalyst.org/view_article.php?a rticleid=2672&SMSESSION=NO.

4. Soner Cagaptay and Nazli Gencsoy, *Improving Turkish-Russian Relations: Turkey's New Foreign Policy and Its Implications for the United States* (Washington, D.C.: Washington Institute for Near East Policy, January 12, 2005).

5. Hill and Taspinar, *Russia and Turkey in the Caucasus*, 6.

6. Ibid.

and Russian can be heard everywhere on the streets of Istanbul and on the beaches of resort towns.

Significantly, massive Turkish importation of Russian natural gas—which comprises at least 70 percent of Turkish gas imports—via the Blue Stream pipeline under the Black Sea creates long-lasting bonds of interdependence between the two countries. In fact, Russia would like to extend the present Blue Stream gas pipeline from Turkey south on to Israel. Additionally, Russia and Turkey are negotiating over a pipeline to carry Russian oil south across Turkey to the Aegean, the so-called Samsun-Kırıkkale-Ceyhan pipeline that would cost an estimated $1 billion. An alternative line under negotiation is a possible trans-Thrace line that would allow Russian oil to cross Turkish soil from the Black Sea into the Mediterranean without going through the sensitive and already overcrowded Bosphorus.

Mustafa Koç, the head of the largest private commercial and financial conglomerate in Turkey and the broader region, foresees Turkey's greatest future economic opportunities as lying mainly in Russian and Middle Eastern markets, although he believes Western markets will remain important.[7] Turkish ties with both Russia and the Middle East will certainly intensify in the next decade, helping shift the center of gravity of Turkish perspectives more to the East.

Strategically, Moscow is in a position to supply military hardware to Turkey that could increasingly complement Ankara's exclusively Western-sourced weaponry. In the mid-1990s, Turkey became the first NATO country to buy arms, rifles, and helicopters from Russia, because Western nations refused to sell it weapons that could be used against its Kurdish rebels.[8] Russia also plans to participate in tenders for the modernization of Turkey's military.

In 2004, Turkey proposed to Russia a new security initiative known as Black Sea Harmony that would entail joint naval maneuvers. In March 2006, the first of these maneuvers was carried out. However, there was some anxiety in the West that this represented a Turkish attempt to maintain its dominance in the area by preventing NATO from extending Operation Active Endeavor, which has similar operations in the Mediterranean, into the Black Sea.[9] Turkey may increasingly seek to make the Black Sea primarily the province of riparian Black Sea powers and to discourage great power rivalry within it. On the other hand, Turkey is simultaneously helping to develop

---

7. Hugh Pope, speech at Merrill House, New York City, March 5, 2005, for Carnegie Council on Ethics and International Affairs.

8. K. Gajendra Singh, *Putin's Visit To Ankara; Russian-Turkish Relations In Perspective,* Paper no. 1101, (Delhi: South Asia Analysis Group, August 27, 2004), www.saag.org/papers12/paper1101.html.

9. "Russian-Turkish Naval Exercise Starts in Black Sea," *Journal of the Turkish Weekly,* March 1, 2006, www.turkishweekly.net/news.php?id=26780.

the militaries of several former republics of the Soviet Union, offsetting their total dependence upon Russia.

Dramatically, Turkish and Russian views have reached considerable consensus in recent years on key controversial and strategic issues, including those related to Iraq, Iran, Syria, Palestine, and questions of stability in the Caucasus. And in each case, their views are largely at variance with U.S. policy. A Turkish diplomat described Ankara's regular political dialog with Moscow as the "most regular and substantial" the Foreign Ministry has with any country.[10] Moscow and Ankara share the view that U.S. policies in the South Caucasus are destabilizing, and they favor preserving the status quo in the region.[11] Ankara tends to view U.S. plans to bring Georgia into NATO as unnecessarily provocative toward Russia; at the same time Turkey's own diaspora of Georgian minorities from Abkhazia and Ajaria are sympathetic to separation of these groups from Georgia. Furthermore, both Russia and Turkey share a joint concern over Islamic radicalism and separatism. Although violent Islamist radicalism inside Turkey is largely a fringe phenomenon and poses no existential threat to the Turkish state, in Russia it is linked to separatist movements. During periods of anger with Washington, some Turkish military officers have even called for a military reorientation toward Moscow rather than the United States. This is, of course, an emotional reaction against many U.S. policies in the region and also reflects a significant anxiety in military thinking that Turkey's reform process in pursuit of EU membership will lead to a sharp reduction of military influence in governance. While the "Moscow alternative" may not be entirely realistic, it finds resonance within an important military segment and represents more than idle thinking; above all it is symptomatic of serious, and now even structural, divergences in strategic vision between Washington and Ankara. Moscow has also made it clear that it supports Turkey's entry into the European Union, no doubt in part welcoming a dilution of Turkey's historic pro-U.S. orientation, and has worked to support Turkey's position on the Cyprus issue. In turn, Turkey has agreed to work to facilitate Russia's entry into the World Trade Organization, which would also further facilitate Russian-Turkish trade. Ankara has also accommodated itself to many aspects of Russia's relations with Georgia, Armenia, and Azerbaijan in ways that do not conform with Washington's policies there. Additionally, Turkey and Russia both share a long-term desire to see the U.S. military pull out from Iraq, even though Ankara remains concerned with modalities.[12]

---

10. Suat Kınıklıoğlu, *The Anatomy of Turkish-Russian Relations* (Washington, D.C.: Brookings Institution, May 2006), www.brookings.edu/comm/events/20060523sabanci_3a.pdf.

11. Igor Torbakov, "Turkey's Strategic Outlook Making Significant Shift," *Eurasia Insight*, March 7, 2006, www.eurasianet.org/departments/insight/articles/eav030706.shtml.

12. Ilan Berman, "Turkey Tilts Eastward," *RFE/RL Newsline*, March 9, 2004.

Russian public opinion toward Turkey is very positive. In a 2005 poll in Russia, 71 percent of Russians displayed a positive attitude toward Turkey, with 51 percent considering it a reliable trade-and-economic partner, 16 percent seeing it as a fraternal country, and only 3 percent thinking that Turkey is an enemy country and probable rival.[13] This is in contrast with a public opinion poll in Turkey after the U.S. invasion of Iraq, in which 83 percent of Turks viewed the U.S. unfavorably, up from 55 percent in 2002. A June 2003 survey by the Pew Research Center found that 71 percent of Turks worried that the United States was a potential military threat.[14]

Thus, the Turkish-Russian relationship now rests on quite new foundations; powerful new ties are emerging, and most contentious issues of the past are fading. Some elements of rivalry will always exist for influence in the Muslim regions of the former Soviet Union, and over alternative courses of east-west energy pipelines to Europe (whether they should traverse Russia or Turkey), but these issues seem manageable, especially to the degree that Russia now views Turkey as an independent competitor to Moscow and no longer an instrument of U.S. policies. Russia will consistently encourage this independence.

The Rise and Fall of the Caucasus and Central Asia in Turkish Thinking

The early euphoria in Turkey after the collapse of the USSR led Turks to believe that they would preside over a new "Turkish century." In that period, then Turkish president Süleyman Demirel declared that Turkey would head up a new Turkic world stretching from the Adriatic Sea to the Great Wall of China. Annual Turkic Summit meetings were launched, as was a Turkic Development Bank. All of this was seen as coming essentially at Russia's expense, for the first time the loser in this massive geopolitical shift. But the cherished pan-Turkic vision was never quite achieved for a confluence of reasons. First, Turkey lacked the economic weight and infrastructure to play a major role in the development and funding of the new, mostly Turkish, republics. Second, tactically and psychologically, Turkey initially behaved somewhat condescendingly as a new "big brother" toward the new republics, whereas in some respects these republics were actually more developed than Turkey. And third, the autocratic leadership of these new states turned out to be exceptionally prickly, paranoid, and unreliable. Uzbekistan's Islam Karimov, for example, remains particularly

---

13. See "Caucasus is No Longer the Source of Discord for Russia and Turkey," an interview with Ruben Safrastyan, director of the Department of Turkish Studies at the Armenian National Academy of Sciences, April 18, 2005, globalpolitician.com/articledes.asp?ID=626&cid=4&sid=35.
14. K. Gajendra Singh, "Boiling Turkey Awaits Rice in Ankara," *Asia Times,* February 4, 2005, www.atimes.com.

obsessed with any hint of internal political opposition and has even accused Turkey of supporting both secular and Islamist forces to overthrow him, rupturing the close relations the two countries had in the educational field and leading to the withdrawal of all Uzbek students from Turkey.

Washington, too, initially made major initial strategic gains in Central Asia at Russian expense, particularly after 9/11 during Washington's bid for broad cooperation in the GWOT; under the circumstances, Moscow reluctantly acquiesced to Washington's new strategic foothold there. But Washington's determination to permanently displace Russia in the southern regions of the former Soviet Union created a backlash in Moscow. And the autocratic nature of Central Asian leadership has increasingly facilitated Moscow's task of keeping the Central Asian states within the Russian orbit, particularly as these leaders came to fear that Washington might destabilize them in democratization campaigns designed, among other things, to weaken Moscow's influence. Moscow has reassured these insecure leaders about its political and military support to them and has adroitly maintained major economic influence over these states, which for so long have been structurally integrated into Russia's economy. In the minds of regional autocrats, Ankara, perhaps unjustifiably, is often linked with the United States. With cooling Turkish ties to the Turkic Central Asian states, Turkey too came to recognize that the stakes in its economic and strategic ties with Russia vastly exceeded any elusive ties with the small, newly independent republics of the Commonwealth of Independent States (CIS).

The heart of the problem lies in the unresolved nature of the character and orientation of the Central Asian republics. Even though their geopolitical orientation remains contested, time is likely on the side of their greater independent-mindedness: the deeper default instincts of the Turkic republics are to remain wary of both Russian and Chinese imperial power and to look to the West and Turkey for balancing support. As of now, however, Central Asian autocrats look to Russia and China for regime protection. Furthermore, the Turkic world is not united; each state has its own priorities and interests, including rivalries among themselves. But pan-Turkic identities may grow stronger with democratization. Should the day come when more democratic governance comes to these former Soviet republics, their ties with Ankara will probably improve. But Turkey's task of balancing its ties between Central Asia and Russia may in turn grow more complex. In the meantime, the story of Turkey's relationship with virtually every single one of these former Soviet republics has been one of disappointing strategic decline since 1991, even though some important ties with them have been maintained.

Moscow, too, needs to reflect on trade-offs and for now seems willing to make certain concessions to Turkey in the Caucasus and Central Asia in order to fulfill other interests. These include (1) weakening U.S. leverage in the region by helping to diminish the overall role of U.S.-Turkish ties; (2) maintaining its new strong and beneficial economic ties with Turkey; and (3) making these ties so attractive and important that they neutralize pan-Turkist influence within Turkish policy, thus weakening potential pan-Turkist trends across the region altogether.

Although Moscow can never serve as a total alternative to Washington or even to the European Union, it is rapidly providing a powerful eastward-oriented pillar in Turkey's new and increasingly complex foreign policy structure.

The Caucasus

Turkey's greatest strengths in its general relationships with the Caucasus and Central Asia have been in building schools and universities, providing military staff college education and training, constructing new energy pipeline networks, and bringing a closer awareness of Turkey and a knowledge of Anatolian Turkish to the area. Turkish Avrasya TV, for example, is beamed by satellite across the Caucasus and Central Asia by satellite and has greatly facilitated the spread of knowledge about Turkey to the region, including a familiarity with Anatolian Turkish. The visitor now regularly encounters considerable numbers of Turkic speakers who at least understand, if not fully speak, Anatolian Turkish, learned via travel, school, and/or the media.

Azerbaijan

Turkey's most important relationship in the Caucasus is with Azerbaijan. Despite its Shiite majority, the state is linguistically and culturally very close to Turkey. The two countries underwent a euphoric pan-Turkic phase that reached a high point in the early 1990s under pan-Turkic-minded president Abulfaz Elchibey and lasted until his overthrow in 1992. Since then, the heart of the Turkish-Azerbaijani relationship has shifted from the cultural realm to the economic—specifically, energy and the important Baku-Tbilisi-Ceyhan oil pipeline that inextricably links the two states.

The economic importance of the line is huge, providing significant transit income for Turkey and an oil outlet for Baku that is independent of Russia. As a result, the geopolitical character of the pipeline is controversial. As initially envisioned by Washington, the first goal of the pipeline was to strategically tie Azerbaijan and its energy into the West and to lessen Baku's dependency upon Moscow and Moscow's ability to control oil flow. Additionally, it was designed to cut Iran out of any regional energy transit role. The first goal has been highly successful, although the second goal is less certain to be fully realized, as Turkey proceeds with its own vital energy projects with both Russia and Iran. The Baku-Tbilisi-Ceyhan oil pipeline is now complemented by the nearly completed South Caucasus gas pipeline from Baku to the Turkish city of Erzurum through Georgian territory; it will carry Azeri gas from the Shah Deniz field for Turkish and European markets.[15]

A new phase of the strategic "pipeline war," however, is just heating up, involving a protean struggle among the strategic and gas interests of Washington, the European Union, Russia, Iran, and China for the favors of Turkmenistan's gas. Washington and the EU hope to persuade Turkmenistan to purvey its gas to Europe via the technically and politically difficult route across the Caspian on to Azerbaijan and Turkey, thereby cutting out both Russia and Iran as alternative pipeline routes to Europe. Tehran hopes to purvey Turkmen gas via Iran into Turkey and onward to the West. Turkey wins either way, but is now committed to Iran for the development of Iranian gas resources for sale to Turkey as well as onward transmission to Europe, despite Washington's displeasure with the idea. China wants Turkmenistan to honor a major tentative agreement to sell the bulk of its gas to China. There exists at a minimum a three-way rivalry among Russia, Iran and Turkey for the privilege of controlling the flow of Turkmen gas to the West. Neither Turkey nor Iran pose a strategic challenge to Russia in this regard in the way that the United States does, but the resolution of the future disposition of Turkmen gas will most likely benefit either Russia or Iran but not both. These complex rivalries will affect—although not decisively—future Russian-Turkish relations. And in the meantime, Turkey will remain heavily dependent on Russian gas until its joint energy project with Iran reaches fruition.[16]

Turkey and Azerbaijan are also deep into negotiations on creating a rail link from Baku to Kars in eastern Turkey via Georgia—the Baku-Alkhalkalaki line—which would link these three states, lay a foundation for a potential China–Central Asia–South Caucasus–Turkey–EU transportation corridor, further integrate the south Caucasus region with Europe via Turkey, and open the Caucasus and Central Asia to direct transport to the Mediterranean. The United Nations Economic Commission for Europe (UNECE) lists this route among its high-priority projects, meaning it could be funded and rapidly implemented by 2010.[17]

In the military field, the Turkish role in Azerbaijan is likewise significant. "Turkish military experts have trained Azeri officers both in Baku and in Turkey, and provided military expertise in the design and development of modern army structures. Hundreds of Azeri officers have graduated from Turkish military schools and starting from 1999, Azeri soldiers participated in the peacekeeping missions in Kosovo and Afghanistan under the Turkish

15. Fariz Ismailzade, "Turkey-Azerbaijan: The Honeymoon Is Over," March 3, 2006, East-West Studies, www.eastweststudies.org/makale_detail.php?makale=202&tur=100.

16. M K Bhadrakumar, "A massive wrench thrown in Putin's works," *Asia Times* September 29, 2007, www.atimes.com/atimes/Central_Asia/II29Ag01.html

17. Taleh Ziyadov, "The Kars-Akhalkalaki Railroad: A Missing Link Between Europe and Asia," *Baku Today*, 2005, www.bakutoday.net/view.php?d=19763.

command," writes Farid Ismailzade.[18] A serious naval confrontation between Iran and Azerbaijan in 2001 over oil exploration in disputed waters led to a show of Turkish military support to Baku, prompting Iran to back off. Turkey's support was greatly valued in Baku.[19]

Turkish businessmen have invested $1.5 billion in Azerbaijan, and Turkish contractors are highly active there, in part directly benefiting from Western infrastructural investments. Bilateral trade in 2004 was $539.5 million, comprised mostly of Turkish exports. Baku is linked to several Turkish cities with regular and busy flights. Turkish entrepreneurs in Baku are visible everywhere, as are Turkish products, but these entrepreneurs complain loudly about Azerbaijan's massive corruption as a barrier to serious trade relations. Most educated Azeris are now fluent in Anatolian Turkish and enjoy ready access to Turkish electronic and print media.

In the sensitive area of Turkish-Armenian-Azeri relations, Turkey's pursuit of good-neighbor policies has extended to a search for improved relations with Armenia. But Armenian victory in a war between Azerbaijan and Armenia over the disputed Nagorno-Karabagh area led both Ankara and Baku to impose trade embargoes against Yerevan due to its occupation of disputed Azeri lands. Baku complains that Ankara is not lending it enough diplomatic support in its territorial conflict, but Ankara is under pressure from the European Union and Washington to end the embargo and establish diplomatic relations with Yerevan. Baku is also aware that it will always need good relations with Moscow as well.

Despite this friction, considerable gray trade takes place between Turkey and Armenia and air routes link the two countries.[20] Additionally, Erdoğan has wisely sought to turn the highly contentious issue of past Ottoman massacres of Armenians over to an international scholarly panel for resolution rather than to leave it to politicians to pass historical judgment. This unresolved historical issue is a continuing albatross around Turkey's neck vis-à-vis the West and the pressures of hard-line Armenian lobbies. The shocking assassination of a leading Turkish-Armenian journalist in Istanbul in January 2007 led to a strong show of public support for the journalist, impressing Yerevan with new signs of growing Turkish maturity toward Armenians. Both sides would like to see a breakthrough in bilateral relations. The considerable Armenian diaspora in the United States and Europe however, works overtime to seek passage of parliamentary resolutions in Washington condemning Turkey for genocide against the Armenians in the late days of the Ottoman Empire; these pressures only complicate a rapprochement between Yerevan and Ankara that both sides seek.

---

18. Ismailzade, "Turkey-Azerbaijan."
19. Ibid.
20. Ibid.

Turkey is currently also caught between Washington and Tehran on the issue of Azerbaijan. The Bush administration's pursuit of a dramatic policy change—or even regime change—in Iran led it to encourage ethnic separatism among Iran's huge Azeri population. However, this fairly well-integrated Azeri community seeks greater regional autonomy within Iran and not separation from it, a country with which it is inextricably intermixed. Turkey has some emotional sympathies for Azeri nationalism inside Iran but does not wish to jeopardize its broader relations with Tehran.

In sum, Turkey plays a significant role in Azerbaijan. The massive and evolving infrastructural projects in energy, communications, and transportation bind the two countries together and intensify Turkey's ties eastward, but generally in ways that need to be calibrated with respect to Russian interests as well.

Georgia

Turkey was delighted with Georgia's new independence following the fall of the Soviet Union and relations between the two countries swiftly warmed. Nonetheless, despite expectations, Turkey's trade with non-Turkic Georgia has remained relatively modest. Total Turkish investment in Georgia was only $165 million, compared to $1.5 billion in Azerbaijan, and recent annual bilateral trade is only $570 million compared to $800 million with Azerbaijan. As in Azerbaijan, Turkish businessmen have been frustrated by corruption, inefficiency, instability, unreliability, and a lack of clear business regulation, making trade in Georgia risky.[21]

An agreement on regional security was signed among Turkey, Georgia, and Azerbaijan in 2002 that included a provision for Turkish assistance in modernizing the Marneuli airbase near Tbilisi. As in Azerbaijan, Turkey has helped build and staff Georgia's United Military Academy. Moscow was displeased with Ankara's move into traditional Russian zones of military influence,[22] as well as with Turkish cooperation with Georgia and Azerbaijan on security measures to protect the Baku-Tbilisi-Ceyhan pipeline.

Turkey has been caught in part between Tbilisi and Moscow over the issue of the separatist Abkhaz region of Georgia, which is supported by Moscow. Ankara sent military observers to the UN mission there to monitor the situation and provided humanitarian aid to refugees from Abkhazia.[23] Turkey is also involved in mediation in the Ajarian separatist movement in southwestern Georgia. There are sizeable Abkhaz and Ajarian communities resident

21. Altay Atlı, "Turkey And Georgia: Opening The Roads For Trade," *EurasiaNet Commentary*, February 8, 2006, www.eurasianet.org/departments/business/articles/eav020806.shtml.

22. Singh, *Putin's Visit to Ankara*, 27.

23. Diplomatik Gözlem, "Brifing Odası," 2000, www.diplomatikgozlem.com/briefing.asp?id=68.

in Turkey interested in resolving these issues, and Ankara is working for a peaceful settlement in both cases.

The Turkish stake in Georgia is far less than in Azerbaijan. While the West would like to see Turkey play a key role in helping strengthen Georgia's entry into NATO, Turkey will be wary of further alienating Moscow and has been more neutral on the Abkhaz separatist issue than Tbilisi would like.

Central Asia

Of the five Central Asian republics in former Soviet space, four are ethnically Turkic: Turkmenistan, Uzbekistan, Kazakhstan, and Kyrgyzstan. Overall, the JDP shows much more interest in Central Asia than did the earlier Islamist Welfare Party. One reason for this is that the JDP received a great deal of electoral support from nationalist strongholds in central Anatolia where the nationalist National Action Party previously dominated; nationalists strongly support close Turkish ties with Central Asia. Turkish military interest in this area remains strong as well.[24] But few Turkish politicians are likely to let ties with Central Asia outweigh ties with Russia.

Turkmenistan

Turkish ties with Turkmenistan are primarily based on potential energy ties. As noted in the section on Azerbaijan above, the future course of Turkmen gas pipelines to Europe is now the subject of intense rivalry among six powers: Russia, the United States, the EU, Iran, Turkey and China. The major geopolitical interests of these states have a lot riding on the outcome of any of these scenarios. Turkey stands to lose the least.

Shortly after Turkmenistan's independence, Turkey signed agreements with the country on trade, rail and air links, communications, education, and culture. Ankara has also built and staffed a military academy in Ashgabat. As long as Turkmenistan was under the quixotic and despotic personal rule of Saparmurad Niyazov, Turkey's relations with the country were unable to proceed smoothly and were not cordial. Nonetheless, Turkey did build some schools there and in the mid-1990s Turkish businessmen were engaged in some sixty joint ventures there, mainly related to the processing of agricultural goods.[25] With Niyazov's death in late 2006, and the assumption of power by the new regime of Gurbanguly Berdimukhamedov, there are signs that Turkmenistan's relations with the outside world are becoming more ra-

---

24. Kemal Kaya, "Turkey's Elections: What Impact For Eurasia?" *Central Asia-Caucasus Analyst*, November 6, 2002, www.eastweststudies.org/makale_detail.php?tur=210&makale=140.

25. Turkmenistan, *Foreign Trade, 1996 Report*, www.country-data.com/cgi-bin/query/r-13872.html.

tional and Turkey's relations with it should improve—largely at the expense of Russia which will lose domination over the state under any scenario that frees up Ashgabat to deal more directly with the outside world.

Uzbekistan

Turkish ties with Uzbekistan have been similarly strained by Islam Karimov's security paranoia. After the development of Turkish ambitions in Central Asia following the fall of the Soviet Union, Karimov himself showed ambitions for leadership of Central Asia and saw Turkey as a potential rival. Additionally, large numbers of Uzbek students sent to Turkey ended up being infected by democratic values and many turned against the Karimov regime. A number of Turkish schools were established in Uzbekistan as well, most of which were affiliated with Fethullah Gülen's movement. As noted earlier, Karimov eventually accused Turkey of plotting against him, brought his students home, and expelled the Turkish schools.

Despite this, Turkey has granted Uzbekistan $2 billion in military assistance, and bilateral trade between the two countries reached a modest $325.9 million in 2004.[26] Furthermore, both countries have agreed to cooperate against terrorism. But with declining U.S.-Uzbek ties starting in 2006 and cool ties with Turkey, Karimov has once again begun to direct his security dependency toward Moscow.

Kazakhstan

Of all the Central Asian republics, Turkey's highest level of bilateral trade is with Kazakhstan, which totaled $797.8 million in 2004. Although there were discussions in 2006 among Turkey, Kazakhstan, and Azerbaijan about shipping oil across the Caspian to feed into the Baku-Tbilisi-Ceyhan pipeline,[27] that plan collapsed with Kazakhstan's commitment to Russia in 2007 to export its energy strictly via Russia. In the educational sphere, Turkey built the Kazakh-Turkish University in Shymkent.

Kyrgyzstan

Perhaps Turkey's most cordial relationship in Central Asia has been with Kyrgyzstan. Although their bilateral trade only totaled $88.1 million in 2004, Turkey has built a number of high schools there that are very popular and competitive, and Turkey has provided military training to the country. Turkey also built the Kyrgyz-Turkish Manas University, where tuition is free. Additionally, there are currently more than one thousand Kyrgyz

---

26. DEIK, www.deik.org.tr/bultenler/2006112818541Cin_kasim2006.pdf.
27. "Kazakhstan to Join Azerbaijan-Turkey Pipeline Project in June, 2006," *RIA-Novosti*, June 8, 2006, en.rian.ru/world/20060608/49203352.html.

students studying in various universities in Turkey.[28] The Japanese Nippon Foundation also annually provides scholarships to sixty students from Central Asia for higher education in Turkey.[29]

China

After Russia, the second key major power with which Turkey is building a significant and growing relationship is China. In this otherwise rapidly improving relationship, the only source of bilateral friction is the oppressed status of the ten million Turkic Uyghurs in China's western province of Xinjiang. The Uyghurs, an important element within broader Central Asian Turkic culture, are subject to heavy pressures of hanization from Beijing through a concerted process of massive Han Chinese inmigration into the Xinjiang area. Ultimately, as with the Tibetans, the Uyghurs' distinct identity and culture will likely be drowned in the relentless hanization of the entire area. Turkish nationalists in Turkey have long been concerned over the fate of the Uyghurs, and various Turkish governments have been torn between a desire for good relations with China and concerns for their Turkic brethren in Xinjiang. In the end, most governments have reluctantly opted for good ties with China at the expense of the Uyghur cause, paralleling the calculus in Ankara's ties with Russia. This is even truer with the JDP as it increasingly turns its geopolitical vision eastward.

Otherwise, China welcomes close ties with Turkey under any conditions and would be delighted if Ankara could help Beijing work with the problem of Turkic separatism and aspirations in the Central Asia region. China offers Turkey major trade opportunities, in both consumer products and military items. Turkey increasingly seeks to be a major player in the future evolution of Eurasia, along with Iran, Afghanistan, and Pakistan, countries with which it has shared strategic and security interests in the past.

Turkey's total trade volume with China more than quadrupled in four years from $900 million in 2001 to $7.4 billion in 2005, about one-tenth of which represented Turkish imports from China.[30] During a November 2004 visit to Beijing, Foreign Minister Gül discussed strengthening cooperation in railways, telecommunications, infrastructure projects, engineering, two-way investment, and tourism. Both sides share an interest in coordination and cooperation on Iraq, the Middle East, and antiterrorism. As with Russia,

---

28. Yasar Sari, "Turkish Schools and Universities in Kyrgyzstan," *Kyrgyz National News Agency,* June 13, 2006, www.kabar.kg/eng/pub/20060614/5.

29. Japanese Nippon Foundation, www.nippon-foundation.or.jp/eng/app/turkey_list.html.

30. DEIK, www.deik.org.tr/bultenler/2006112818541Cin_kasim2006.pdf ; see also Chinese Ministry of Foreign Relations, August 25, 2003, www.fmprc.gov.cn/eng/wjb/zzjg/xybfs/gjlb/2898/t16443.htm.

Beijing has also expressed hope for Turkey's success in seeking EU membership; the Chinese also indicated that they would welcome a more active role
by Turkey on the international scene—code for more independent policies
from Washington.[31] In strategic terms, China is unquestionably interested in
seeing a diminution of U.S. strategic influence over Eurasian states, Turkey
in particular.

In 2005 Turkish minister of national defense Vecdi Gönül visited Beijing,
opening the door to the subsequent visit of Air Forces commander Gen.
İbrahim Fırtına. That visit brought about a set of agreements that envisage
technological cooperation between Turkey and China in the area of space
technologies and medium-range air defense systems. Furthermore, they also
called for training programs for Chinese soldiers under NATO standards in
Turkish facilities.[32] Turkey also seeks to join the important Shanghai Cooperation Organization (SCO), a Russia–China–Central Asian bloc that adopts
an anti-U.S. strategic position. While Washington will be quite unhappy with
such a development, it seems unlikely that Turkey, with its growing Eurasian
ambitions and interests, would turn down a chance for a role in the SCO; the
organization is becoming too important to ignore as the dominant geopolitical bloc in Eurasia—one that is widely perceived as providing the foundation
for an alternative geopolitical power bloc, challenging Washington's aspirations to maintain its unipolar power status in the world.

Along with Russia, China now represents another new and important strategic pillar in Turkey's increasingly differentiated foreign policy. These new
ties will complement and even offset to some extent Ankara's ties with the
United States and the European Union. Furthermore, China is the economic
and strategic giant of coming decades, so it is only natural that Turkey, as a
Eurasian player, will seek good working ties with it. China's role in the Middle East and in the energy field is also growing rapidly and will inevitably
intersect with Turkey's interests in those areas. Indeed, as with Russia, Turkey
and China share common views on the areas of crisis in the Middle East.

The Balkan Muslims

The early 1990s Bosnian crisis remains important for Turkey in three key
respects: first, Turkey gave de facto support to a Muslim minority in the
Balkans; second, the crisis led to early Turkish frustration with Western
and U.S. policies, institutions, and "solutions" that did not meet Turkish
expectations or needs; and third, the crisis demonstrated strong Turkish
domestic political opposition across the political spectrum to its govern-

---

31. "China, Turkey Agree to Enhance Economic, Trade Cooperation," *Chinese People's Daily Online,*
    November 10, 2004, english1.people.com.cn/200411/21/eng20041121_164618.html.
32. Ardan Zenturk: "Message to Washington From Beijing," *Istanbul Star,* April 6, 2005.

ment's weak and cautious deference to Western policies. This ad hoc coalition of interests and attitudes within Turkey is arguably stronger today and only serves to bolster a more distinct and assertive Turkish approach to regional issues.

During the Bosnian crisis in 1993, Turkey took the lead within the OIC to press for the dispatch of Muslim peacekeeping troops to protect Bosnian safe havens, and Erbakan called, unsuccessfully, for a unilateral force of ten thousand Turkish troops to be sent to Bosnia.[33] In the end, the reality is that Balkan Muslims have long looked to and continue to look to Turkey as their historic Muslim protector against Balkan Christian power. However awkward this situation is for secular Turkey today, it represents an irrefutable religious legacy of the past. There is also a large Bosnian (Boşnak) and Kosovar community within Turkey dating from Ottoman days that is naturally sympathetic to the Bosnian and Kosovar cause, thus injecting a domestic element into Turkey's Balkan policies. Turkey will not stand on the sidelines in future crises involving Balkan Muslims, even if it strives to maintain good ties with all parties and states there. Turkey today is a Balkan power once again. In this respect Turkish policy is now again at odds with Russian policies in the Balkans that has historically supported the Eastern Orthodox Serbians and has sought to prevent Bosnian and Kosovar separatism. Again, because Turkey's new policies are no longer viewed by Moscow as simply an extension of US anti-Russian policies, Turkey and Russia will most likely agree to disagree on this Balkan question rather than permit it to color a broad range of other ties.

Conclusion

Given its frustrations with the long, tendentious, and querulous entry process into the European Union, Turkey is consciously developing an alternate geostrategic strategy that is oriented toward Eurasia and the Middle East. With the dramatic new economic and strategic rise of China and India, global power now demonstrates a major new eastern dimension. Turkey is keenly aware that it cannot ignore the huge new markets of the East, including the burgeoning Gulf region. Association with these markets also implies a more independent position for Turkey in which it represents its own interests and is no longer dependent upon the United States or Europe for security ties. While Turkey will never cut its important economic and strategic ties to Europe and the United States, it now has meaningful alternatives that allow it to diversify its strategic orientation. These realities are evident to the entire political class of Turkey and are not a function of new JDP thinking alone.

---

33. Robins, *Suits and Uniforms*, 364–65.

15

Turkey and Europe

Turkey's overall position in the West is increasingly affected—not always positively—by the presence of a large number of Turkish immigrants in Western Europe, some going on third generation. Today, there are approximately 3.8 million Turks who live in the countries of the European Union, of whom 1.3 million are citizens. The vast majority are in Germany (2.6 million), followed by France (370,000), the Netherlands (270,000), Austria (200,000), Belgium (110,000), and the United Kingdom (70,000), with most of the rest in Denmark and Sweden.[1]

Statistics show that the Turkish community's overall labor productivity has contributed significantly to the EU economy: 1.2 million employed Turks (0.75 percent of the working population of the European Union) have contributed twice as much money to the European Union's gross national product (GNP) as Luxembourg and just over half as much as Greece. Turkish entrepreneurship within the European Union is growing, and the amount of capital repatriated back to Turkey by Turks in the European Union is dropping sharply, especially among new generations whose economic ties to Turkey are weakening and who seek to employ their capital locally.[2]

The degree of Turkish integration into EU society varies considerably from country to country, with Germany among the most problematic and the United Kingdom the least. This discrepancy has at least as much to do with the "ideology of immigration" in each EU country as it does with the particular metrics of Turkish integration in each.

Generally speaking, Europe has traditionally devoted little attention to an overall policy of immigration and integration and hence has been less successful in assimilating newcomers than have full-fledged immigrant societies, such as the United States and Canada.[3] The process of integration is, of course, a two-way street. While there are legitimate European concerns about problems of unemployment, the extension of expensive social services to immigrants, and the frequent failure of immigrants to actively seek integration, immigrants often do face discrimination and hostility from the ethnic natives of each state, particularly from those who are nervous about the cultural implications of immigration.[4]

---

1. Greg Austin, Kate Parker, and Sarah Schaefer, *Turks in Europe: Why Are We Afraid?* (London: Foreign Policy Centre, 2005), 32–35, fpc.org.uk/fsblob/597.pdf.
2. Ibid., 35.
3. Ibid., 35.
4. Austin, Parker, and Schaefer, *Turks in Europe*.

Today, with the GWOT and the spread of terrorist activities beyond the Middle East, there are ever-growing anxieties about Muslim immigration into Europe. This is especially so as a new sense of "Muslim identity"—as distinct from ethnic or national identity—is widening among Muslims, particularly among immigrant Muslims. This new sense of identity among immigrant Muslims is partly in response to loosening ties with their countries of origin and partly a reflection of their ambivalence toward secularism (the meaning of which varies widely), causing them to become objects of European suspicion. A European insistence on imposing some kind of elusive monoculturalism upon the increasingly multicultural nature of European society is also part of the problem.[5]

The reality is that Turks have created a diverse but strong body of local institutions and connections that have served them well in preserving their communities in "foreign lands" *(gurbet)*. Going back to the late 1950s, Turkish labor migration to Europe originally entailed a highly rural and uneducated population that felt great social vulnerability in industrial urban areas. As a result, these Turks sought to recreate Turkish social conditions within their new Western environment. They created, in effect, small and inward-looking Turkish communities bolstered by the maintenance of traditional Turkish religious and social values. "This population has recreated in Europe all of the social, political, religious, and ethnic cleavages of Turkey by setting up a true web of immigrant associations, from local associations and local mosques to Europe-wide federations," writes Ural Manço, a sociologist in Europe of Turkish origin.[6] This preservation of local cultural modes has had both positive and negative repercussions: on the one hand it provided a social discipline and backup that enabled the early communities to survive and function without deracination and social deterioration; on the other hand, it slowed considerably their integration into European society.

Perhaps the largest and best organized of the Turkish immigrant organizations in Europe is the Islamist Millî Görüş (National Vision) movement, which, like so many other Islamist movements, offers social, cultural, religious, educational, and commercial services across Europe.[7] Millî Görüş reportedly has hundreds of separate chapters across European cities that are closely linked to the long-standing Erbakan movement. It often espouses quite traditional Islamist views—anti–European Union, anti-Jewish, antisecular, pan-Islamist—that do not represent the JDP; but the Millî Görüş movement undoubtedly lends financial support to the remnants of the old Erbakan movement and perhaps to elements within the JDP as well. The

---

5. Ibid., 41.
6. Ural Manço, *Turks in Europe: From a Garbled Image to The Complexity Of Migrant Social Reality* (Brussels: Centre d'Études Sociologiques), www.flwi.ugent.be/cie/umanco/umanco5.htm, 8.
7. Ibid., 8.

views of Millî Görüş are obviously viewed negatively by Europeans and, after 9/11, the group itself is seen as a potential security threat—falling under suspicion as so many other Muslim organizations in Europe have. Yet the movement enjoys widespread Turkish immigrant support not because of its specific policies but because it speaks in the name of Turkish Islam and provides broad social services. Increasingly, however, younger generation Turks in Europe no longer share the movement's views, and the movement itself is evolving and differs considerably from country to country.[8] With the rising prestige and success of the JDP, the Millî Görüş movement appears to be losing ground to it, as traditional Turkish religious views even in Europe evolve into the more modernist Islamist JDP views.

There are some indications that German internal security organizations view Millî Görüş as an "extremist" organization. In the context of today's spectrum of global Islamist organizations, it would be difficult to call Millî Görüş "extremist," even if ideologically immoderate. It does not seem to have ever advocated or been involved in acts of violence, although Millî Görüş is obviously anathema to the Turkish secular order.

In 2004, Germany extradited to Turkey Metin Kaplan, a renegade preacher who did represent a highly radical organization that may have been involved in planning terrorist activities against Turkey. Additionally, in earlier years, violence occasionally flared between Turks and Turkish Kurds resident in Europe, and the PKK did attack certain Turkish installations in Europe, helping give the Turks an unfairly generalized reputation for importing violence.

Unfortunately, the Turks have a somewhat negative image in the European Union, not because of any sociopathic behavior but because they reflect, or seem to reflect, negative Western images of Islam. They are seen to oppress their women through the use of the veil and honor killings, to lack an interest in education except religious, and to depend upon social welfare. Additionally, their presence recalls past and present conflicts and violent events, such as the Ottoman Empire's sieges of Vienna in the sixteenth and seventeenth centuries, the 1915 Armenian massacres, the Cyprus conflict, the Kurdish problem, Turkish military coups, Turkey's conflict with Greece, and Turkish mafia involvement in drug trafficking.[9]

Yet some 6 million EU tourists visit Turkey annually, creating positive impressions about the more "advanced" character of Turks in Turkey compared to those in Europe; this helps "normalize" the face of Turkey to Europe. Turkey also moved with astonishing swiftness toward meeting the EU Copenhagen criteria for membership, demonstrating seriousness of intent. Europe-

8. Martin van Bruinessen, "The Millî Görüş in Europe" (notes from an ISIM workshop, Leiden, January 9, 2004), www.let.uu.nl/~Martin.vanBruinessen/personal/conferences/Milli_Gorus_workshop_report.htm.

9. Manço, *Turks in Europe*, 10.

ans have also been impressed with Turkish accomplishments in the field of sport, such as the Turkish national soccer team's third place finish in the 2002 World Cup and the presence of Turkish players on European soccer teams. In the field of entertainment, meanwhile, a Turkish singer recently won the Eurovision contest, a German-Turkish director won the top prize at the Berlin Film Festival for a film about the life of Turks in Germany, and another director, Nuri Bilge Ceylan, won the critic's prize at the Cannes Film Festival for the second time in 2004.[10] In the field of politics, there is an elected Turkish member in the German Bundestag.

Turkey's negative image is overdrawn and today represents something of a throwback to certain realities of earlier decades. With each new generation, the Turks living in Europe are gradually becoming better educated, more professionally skilled, and more integrated into European life. Furthermore, they are developing a clear European identity that complements but does not eliminate their parallel Turkish identity. While they still have a long way to go and mostly live in close-knit communities in a few key cities, by objective measures the profile of the Turkish reality in Europe is on the rise and encouraging.

But "objective" reality is not all that matters. Europe itself is in the throes of a painful reassessment of questions of identity and change. European anxieties about Turks in Europe—which vary depending on the particular conditions of each given country—increasingly reflect the deeper angst of European society in the face of major challenges from the forces of globalization and multiculturalism. The violence and chaos of the broader Middle East may at most only marginally involve the Turkish population in Europe, but all it takes is only a handful of incidents involving Muslims, even non-Turkish ones, to cause yet deeper European fears.

The Turkish government is highly committed to supporting the Turkish community in Europe, which it perceives as the nucleus of an economic and intellectual elite down the road who will be strong and positive advocates for Turkish integration into Europe and the European Union.[11] And in the long run, the Turkish reality in Europe should facilitate European access to the Middle East and an understanding and treatment of Muslim world problems.

Europe inevitably must develop a Muslim face as well as Christian, Jewish, and Hindu ones, and the Turks are likely to be the most advanced of all Muslim communities in Europe. Turkish skills acquired in Europe also strengthen the overall emergence of Turkey into mainstream Western politics. While the outlook for rapid Turkish entry into the European Union does

---

10. Faruk Şen, interviewed by Özgür Sağmal in "The Changing Face of Turks in Europe," *Turkish Time*, August 15, 2004, www.turkishtime.org/30/4_2_en.asp.

11. Manço, *Turks in Europe*, 10.

not look bright in 2007, times and circumstances can rapidly change. A decade from now, Turkish membership may look much less daunting to a Europe that has already passed through a serious identity crisis under the onslaught of multiculturalism. Regrettably, European misgivings about Turkey have already begun to sour and even anger much of the population in Turkey that feels its European calling is being rebuffed on ethnic, cultural, and even religious grounds. A U.S. German Marshall Fund survey made in Turkey in mid-2007 reported that support for EU membership among Turks had fallen to less than half of the population, a mere 40 percent, in 2007—as compared to 54 percent in 2006. The survey found that Turkish support for NATO had also continued on a declining trend that began in 2004, with only 35 percent of respondents seeing the alliance as being essential to Turkey's security, as compared to 44 percent last year and 53 percent in 2004.[12]

Should U.S. military confrontations in the Muslim world increase, terrorism markedly rise in the West, or the whole Middle Eastern region tumble into deeper chaos, Turkey's EU membership application, however unrelated to Middle East events, will unquestionably suffer and propel Turkey further in the direction not toward the United States, but toward the Middle Eastern, Eurasian alternative.

---

12. "Turks Become Increasingly Isolated," *Today's Zaman,* September 7, 2007.

16

Turkey and the United States

A Chronicle of Growing Wariness

The broadly positive character of a great portion of the U.S.-Turkish relationship has been heavily documented over the years and is the focus of most studies of Turkish foreign policy; detailed analysis of it lies outside the purview of this study. Clearly, U.S.-Turkish relations over a fifty-year period have been generally close, substantive, and important to both parties. The Cold War cemented the relationship, but Washington also facilitated Turkey's entry into the Western alliance and security structure, securing its position as a "Western" state and beneficiary of Western largesse. It has also consistently supported Turkish entry into the European Union. Additionally, the United States has institutionalized many of its close military relationships with Turkey in significant ways that cannot be readily dismissed by any Turkish government, and the U.S. contribution to Turkey's new role as an energy hub has been invaluable.

But many of the drivers that once cemented the bilateral relationship in the past have weakened or disappeared, while new factors are entering into both the American and Turkish calculus. Despite the long annals of basically good relations, it is instructive to devote special attention to the nature of key long-standing and underlying frictions between the two countries, many of which have intensified since 9/11.

Sources of U.S.-Turkish Tensions

Past U.S.-Turkish tensions have followed a specific pattern and generally involved

- Turkish concerns over divergences of interest between Washington's goals and policies in the Middle East and Turkey's own interests;
- Turkish concerns over loss of sovereignty due to the impact of U.S. political, economic, military, and strategic actions in the Middle East that lie beyond Turkish control;
- Turkish concerns over a perceived U.S. disregard for Turkish national honor and dignity;
- Turkish concerns that close strategic ties with the United States foreclose other options for it in the region;
- Turkish concerns over alliance entanglements that could drag it into unwanted regional conflicts;

- Turkish concerns over the degree of reliability of U.S. security commitments, especially when they run counter to U.S. interests at a given moment.

Many of these Turkish concerns are intertwined and interrelated, and most involve frictions inherent in any alliance between unequal powers. But today, Turkey's concerns also reflect the gradual maturation, broadening, and diversification of a foreign policy that is moving out from under long-term U.S. "tutelage."

Turkey's admission into NATO in 1952 was without doubt an extraordinary strategic gain, bringing the country more deeply into the Western order and institutional structures. Turkey became, in effect, a full-fledged "Western country"—an event of immense psychological importance to the westernizing Kemalist elites, bolstering their identity and power. Although NATO membership provided vital security against a Soviet threat, over the next two decades Turkey came to reconsider the implications and extent of its commitment following a series of emerging crises.

To begin, the collapse of the Baghdad Pact in 1958 presented significant problems for Turkey because its successor organization, CENTO, contained no Arab members, was weak in its provisions, and did not satisfy Turkish concerns about pro-Soviet activity in the Arab world. More important, Turkey was left diplomatically isolated. For example, the Arab world demonstrated consistent support for Christian Greece over Muslim Turkey on the vital Cyprus conflict throughout this period, which was a dramatic demonstration of the cost of Ankara's strong pro-Western alignment.

Although Turkey lost diplomatic support in the Muslim and developing world following its admission into NATO, two crises in particular raised serious doubts in Turkey over the actual reliability of its alignment with Washington. The 1963 Cuban missile crisis between the United States and the Soviet Union created serious levels of concern in Ankara over the potential of being dragged into an unwanted war with the USSR. Most disturbing for Ankara was the United States' willingness to pull out its Jupiter missiles from Turkey in return for a Soviet pullout of missiles from Cuba. Although the Jupiters were obsolete, their removal had symbolic importance to Ankara: that they were removed without any consultation with Turkey demonstrated how much Washington's interests as a great power could and did override Turkish national interests. This event produced a severe shock and provoked some reconsideration in Ankara about the nature of the alliance and its relationship with the United States.[1]

Then, the crisis over the notorious "Johnson letter" and Cyprus in 1964 raised further doubts about the value of the U.S. alliance. In the let-

---

1. For a discussion of this crisis, see Hale, *Turkish Foreign Policy,* 134–36.

ter, U.S. president Lyndon Johnson warned Ankara that it could not count on NATO support if Turkish policies toward Cyprus brought Ankara into conflict with Greece or even with the USSR. This incident opened a major discussion in Turkey over the very cost and value of its alliance with the United States and NATO, sparking serious internal debate about whether Turkey should even withdraw from NATO. Many serious establishment figures argued for the benefits of a return to traditional Kemalist policies of neutrality.[2]

In fact, this crisis inaugurated a dramatic new era of rapprochement between Ankara and Moscow in which, by the end of the 1970s, Turkey eventually became the largest recipient of Soviet Third World aid. Additionally, Moscow dramatically shifted away from its pro-Greek position on Cyprus to lend a more sympathetic ear to the Turkish position. Turkey also moved to place greater restrictions on the United States' use of Incirlik airbase and the number of U.S. personnel stationed there. It was primarily the fear of losing spare parts from NATO and very considerable U.S. financial aid that ultimately prevented a more serious deterioration of relations. But the high point of Turkey's near-total pro-U.S. orientation had irrevocably passed.[3]

In 1972, Turkey was unhappy at U.S. pressures to ban all poppy production in Turkey—an entirely legal and supervised production process for Turkey's significant pharmaceutical industry and a source of Turkish governmental income. Turks saw the imposition of the ban as a reflection of U.S. panic over its own domestic narcotics problem that was little related to Turkey's domestic poppy production.[4]

Turkey witnessed firsthand the fickle nature of U.S. domestic politics intruding on "hard" foreign policy relationships in 1975. Following Ankara's invasion of Cyprus in 1974 to protect the status of Turkish Cypriots after a hard-line Greek coup, the Greek lobby successfully convinced Congress to ban all U.S. military sales and aid to Turkey until Ankara proved more malleable on reaching a settlement with Athens. Ankara retaliated by suspending the U.S. Defense Cooperation Agreement of 1969 and placing limitations on all U.S. military activities in Turkey except those directly related to NATO. The U.S. arms-sale ban was not lifted until three years later.[5]

This congressional crisis was only the first of several: the Armenian lobby comes ever closer to getting Congress to pass a resolution recognizing Turkish massacres of Armenians during World War I as genocide—an exceptionally volatile and complex issue. As a result of these experiences Turkey decided to place priority on developing its relations with Israel in the belief that this

---

2. Ibid., 149–252.
3. For a detailed description, see Ibid., 149–52.
4. Ibid., 154.
5. Ibid., 160–61.

would placate and win over the powerful pro-Israeli lobby in Washington—
an experiment that, in Ankara's view, produced only disappointing results.

By the late 1970s, Turkey reached a turning point in its once-solid strategic
orientation toward the United States, sparking a decade of new Turkish
foreign policy initiatives and an expanded foreign policy horizon well
before the collapse of the USSR. Turkey, under the left-of-center government
of Bülent Ecevit, formally acknowledged an easing away from its strong
orientation toward the United States and the development of a more variegated
set of defense and foreign policies.[6] Ecevit explicitly articulated a concern
that Turkey was too dependent on the United States and was spending too
much on NATO-related defense, and called for opening its own defense
industries and lessening regional tensions through improved relations with
its neighbors.[7] Even though there was some discussion of possibly pulling
out of NATO as the French had done earlier, Turkey decided that NATO still
represented a valuable tie. Nonetheless, Ankara signed a "Political Document
on the Principles of Friendly Cooperation" with the USSR, which represented
a significant gain for Moscow but still fell short of Moscow's hopes for an even
more neutral Turkey.

But even the new cordiality of Turkish-Soviet relations in the 1970s was
marred by the Soviet invasion of Afghanistan in 1980, an act that highlighted
potential problems for any neutral nation along the Soviet border. The United
States also stepped up its aid to Turkey in this period and recovered the use
of its bases; U.S. military aid to Turkey peaked at $715 million in 1984. Ronald
Reagan's presidency in the 1980s also intensified the atmosphere of global
confrontation with the USSR. By the late 1980s, however, Turkey's relations
with the Soviet Union had again smoothed out but at no direct loss to Ankara's ties with Washington.[8] Ankara was learning to develop a more nuanced
and balanced foreign policy.

The 1991 Gulf War, a disaster for Ankara, inaugurated a new phase of
friction with Washington, quickly revealing underlying sources of tension
that have remained central to the U.S.-Turkish relationship ever since. The
war created a Kurdish refugee crisis for Ankara and launched the beginning
of de facto Iraqi Kurdish autonomy that has broadened and deepened to this
day, much to the intense chagrin of Turkey. Although the United States was
highly instrumental in Turkey's tracking and spectacular capture of PKK
leader Abdallah Öcalan in Kenya in 1999, suspicions within Turkey of U.S.
intentions vis-à-vis the Kurds have not disappeared.

The U.S. invasion of Iraq in 2003 only intensified existing Turkish fears
about the direction of Iraqi Kurdish politics. These fears were not ground-

---

6. Ibid.
7. Ibid.
8. Ibid., 163–67.

less: with the fall of Saddam Hussein, the prospects of permanent Kurdish autonomy and the nucleus of a potential independent Kurdish state were well established. U.S. policies are perceived in Turkey as the primary cause of these developments. They unleashed predictable Turkish paranoia that deeply infects many levels of Turkish society; even the military and the Kemalist nationalists regularly nurture gnawing suspicions about the true nature of U.S. intentions. Many Turks fear that the United States seeks to strengthen its own position in the region through a divide-and-conquer policy that supports minority rights across the region, thereby weakening the centralized character of Arab states and even Iran. (The idea is not entirely fanciful: there are thinkers in both the United States and Israel who regularly and publicly propose such a strategy to weaken unfriendly Muslim regimes.)

An immense shock to the bilateral relationship came with the decision of the Turkish parliament in 2003 to deny the United States use of Turkish soil for its invasion of Iraq. Many observers in Ankara stated that they saw such a rejection coming given earlier abrasive and heavy-handed U.S. pressure tactics on Turkey to acquiesce to U.S. war plans. Turkish anxiety vis-à-vis developments in Iraq were not, of course, conjectural. Turkey had witnessed not only the huge Iraqi Kurdish gains made toward autonomy in the 1991 Gulf War, but also the loss of up to $8 billion dollars in cross-border trade with Iraq.

As relations with Washington deteriorated, the neoconservative press in the United States launched a series of articles asking "who lost Turkey?" It blamed Turkey and the JDP for what it perceived as an orgy of anti-American emotionalism. In 2004, for example, the arrest and rough handling of a team of Turkish Special Forces in Iraq by U.S. Special Forces on suspicion that they were on an assassination mission against Kurdish activists raised a fire storm of Turkish nationalist anger. This act was taken as an affront to the national dignity in Turkey; three years later it has still not subsided, having become a subject of films and novels. As a result, Turkey's relations with the United States continued to drop to an all-time low. A Turkish thriller novel titled *Metal Storm*, which depicts a U.S. invasion of Turkey and a retaliatory Turkish nuclear suitcase bombing of New York and Washington, has even been a bestseller read at all levels across the country.

A 2004 German Marshall Fund poll taken in Turkey found that one in three Turks believed that suicide attacks against U.S. occupation forces in Iraq were justified and that 67 percent of the population had a negative view of the Bush administration—the highest of Western countries polled.[9] Meanwhile, in a poll that asked Turks to make a choice between ties with the European Union or the United States, 51 percent chose the European Union while only 6 percent chose the United States. (The Turkish Foreign

---

9. Şahin Alpay, "Türkiye ABD'den Niçin Soğuyor?" [Why Is Turkey Cooling toward the United States?] *Zaman*, September 28, 2004.

Ministry currently endorses 95 percent of EU policy decisions.) The same poll showed that one-third of those Turks questioned identified the United States as the greatest threat to world peace.[10] In the summer of 2006, Pew Research similarly showed that only 12 percent of Turks approved of U.S. policies[11]; in mid-2007, a second poll showed that only 9 percent of Turks hold a favorable view of the United States, compared to 13 percent of Palestinians.[12]

Given the long annals of imperialist forces active in the Middle East, large numbers of Turks today perceive the United States as seeking to dominate the Middle East for its natural resources and strategic bases without regard for others' interests. Many secularists in Turkey believe that the United States is actually trying to impose a moderate Islamist regime on Turkey in order to make it a political model of moderate Islam for the rest of the Muslim world. As a result, many Turkish nationalists ironically perceive the Islamist-rooted JDP as a tool of U.S. power—and this while the JDP has taken the most ideologically neutral posture on foreign relations of any government in Turkey since World War II. Furthermore, large numbers of Turks also believe that the United States is seeking to weaken Turkey by providing support to the Kurds and even to the PKK.

Strikingly, in a series of polls taken in Turkey in 2002 and 2003, JDP supporters consistently held *more moderate* views toward the United States than did supporters of two other major Turkish parties: the right-wing National Movement Party (MHP), a strong nationalist party, and the left-of-center Republican Peoples Party (CHP), the oldest national party and stronghold of classical Kemalist thinking. As a whole, this suggests that the reservoirs of hostility toward the United States and a desire for greater national independence are found across a broad spectrum of society.[13]

Attitudes of this sort must of course be seen in some perspective. These emotions have flared during a long ongoing bloody war in Iraq; they may partially recede after a U.S. withdrawal from Iraq and the end of Bush administration–style policies. Furthermore, the once relatively high Turkish expectations over EU membership have been partially diminished in accordance with the European Union's own mixed signals and shifting fortunes. This EU coolness toward Ankara's application reduces some of the admiration the Turks have had for the European Union at the expense of the United States. There is also the inevitable "blame-America" factor, which sees all

---

10. Cagaptay, "Where Goes the U.S.-Turkish Relationship?"
11. Brian Knowlton, "Global Image of the U.S. Is Worsening, Survey Finds," *New York Times*, June 14, 2006.
12. Pew Global Attitudes Project, pewglobal.org/reports/display.php?ReportID=256.
13. Nasuh Uslu, Metin Toprak, Ibrahim Dalmış, and Ertan Aydın, "Turkish Public Opinion toward The United States In The Context of The Iraq Question," *MERIA* 9, no. 3 (September 2005).

problems attributed to the world's reigning superpower. Nonetheless, this level of deterioration far transcends normal alliance spats; it reveals deep and increasingly institutional and structural change in the strategic relationship between Turkey and the United States.

A more independent Turkish course of action does not mean outright rejection of U.S. ties by any means, but it spells the end of ready Turkish acquiescence to U.S. goals in the region and demonstrates a desire to strongly diversify Turkish foreign policy. Washington should no longer consider Turkey an "ally"—an increasingly meaningless term in today's world, where few countries truly wish to be "allied," and especially not Turkey. A Turkish government bulletin recently stated that "the EU membership process, relations with the US and its position in NATO are primary on Turkey's foreign policy agenda. Meanwhile, it is necessary for Turkey to have a wide and balanced foreign policy parallel to its geostrategic position and historic-cultural ties within the wide area that surrounds its territory."[14] In fact, Turkey will need heavy convincing that its own interests are still well served by U.S. policies. It is telling that in September 2005 Turkey joined other European states to block U.S. efforts to meld the NATO-manned ISAF with U.S. peacekeeping forces under U.S. control in Afghanistan.[15]

Are Turkish and U.S. Interests Compatible?

One long-standing mantra about U.S.-Turkish relations has been that both countries share a "common vision." They indeed hold a common appreciation of certain broad and generalized values—all unexceptionable in principle—but these values are hardly unique to Washington and Ankara: these values are shared by any number of other countries. Furthermore, this bland assertion takes on real meaning only at the level of details and tactical implementation. Turks still question where U.S. policies coincide with specific Turkish interests and where they are likely to diverge.

What, then, are the theoretical shared interests between Turkey and the United States in the Middle East—at least in principle? They include

- a peaceful, centralized Iraq;
- a nonmilitant, nonnuclear Iran;
- an end to the Arab-Israeli dispute;
- an end to terrorism in the region, particularly as it affects Turkey;
- an end to the development and spread of radical Islam;
- a continuation of good ties with Israel, especially in material goods;

14. Turkish Directorate General for Press and Information, May–June 2005, www.byegm.gov. tr/YAYINLARIMIZ/newspot/2005/may-jun/n2.htm.

15. Laurent Zecchini, "Several European Countries Oppose the United States on NATO's Mission in Afghanistan," *Le Monde*, September 15, 2005, translated by the Truthout Web site, www.truthout.org/docs_2005/091505H.shtml.

- the realization of broader stability in the Middle East;
- the development of Caspian and Central Asian oil pipelines to Turkey, making Turkey an energy hub;
- the maintenance of de facto independence for Georgia, Armenia, Azerbaijan, and the Central Asian republics.

All but the last two of these shared interests need to be sharply qualified. In the Turkish view, *how* these interests are pursued is of extreme important. It is at this level where the United States and Turkey often have sharply different understandings on key issues.

Terrorism: What Are Its Main Sources?

Of course Turkey and the United States share a concern for terrorism—almost every country in the world does. Turkey sees itself as having been the victim of at least four different types of terrorism in the past: domestic Marxist-Leninist; extreme right-wing nationalist *(ülkücüler)*; ethnic Kurdish leftist-separatist (PKK); and radical Islamist. Currently, PKK secularist terrorism is by far the greatest threat to the Turkish state because of its ethnic and separatist character and the intensity and magnitude of its violence, which has persisted on and off for more than two decades.

Although the Kemalists are quick to link violence to religion, actual Islam-inspired terrorism has been relatively minor in Turkey when compared to the scope of violence originating from ethnic and secular ideological groups. Furthermore, the nature of Islamist violence in Turkey differs dramatically from Islamist violence in other countries. In most Muslim states, Islamist terrorism against the state is viewed with ambivalence by a large portion of the population: while it does not like terrorism, it sympathizes with those who feel compelled to attack harsh and dictatorial political orders or perceived U.S. imperial ambitions. Yet in Turkey, almost no one feels ambivalent about terrorism; even those with grievances against the state view violence with horror, simply because the state generally enjoys a *large degree of legitimacy* among the public. Thus, while al-Qaeda and other international jihadist organizations might be able to recruit a few individuals to commit a few violent acts in Turkey, Islamist terrorists cannot "swim in the public sea" there in the way they can in autocratic countries shaken by widespread political dissidence. This means in the end that Islamist terrorism in Turkey is mostly a police problem, not a political or social one, and hence is manageable. The same cannot be said for most other Muslim countries.

An August 2005 public opinion poll revealed an interesting Turkish perspective on Middle East terrorism-related issues: 91 percent of those polled characterized Osama bin Laden as a terrorist; 75 percent stated al-Qaeda does not represent Muslims; and 86 percent did not condone the attacks of 9/11.

But 66 percent stated that U.S. policies were the major source of global terrorism, and when asked who is the world's leading actor in the expansion of global terrorism, 54 percent named George W. Bush, 22 percent named Ariel Sharon, and only 17 percent named bin Laden. When asked what the United States and the West should do to combat global terrorism, 41 percent said that they should not encourage tensions between Christians and Muslims and 21 percent said that they should retreat from Iraq. Interestingly, when asked why al-Qaeda attacked Istanbul, 40 percent said it was because Turkey offers the best alternative to al-Qaeda and 36 percent said it was because Turkey is an ally of the West.[16]

Turkey is particularly adamant about bringing an end to PKK nationalist violence, in which Kurdish guerrillas do, in fact, "swim in a Kurdish sea." Ankara demands action from all states to curtail any political or media activity by the PKK, particularly in Europe, and expects Washington to move against any PKK presence in northern Iraq. While Ankara will certainly cooperate to the fullest extent in trying to eradicate al-Qaeda and other international jihadist movements in the region, these groups do not constitute Turkey's biggest terrorist problem. The real terrorist threat facing Turkey, the PKK problem, stirs only limited response from the U.S.

The Status Quo: Sharply Differing Turkish and U.S. Perspectives

Turkey has almost always been a strong proponent of maintaining the status quo in international relations: Turkey has strong respect for multilateral institutions, the importance of international norms of conduct, and the sanctity of states.[17] Yet from the Turkish perspective, the United States under the Bush administration has been moving away from these norms, causing drastic change in the Middle East's status quo and showing a disregard for international institutions and even for the sanctity of states with its interventionist—even preemptive—policies. Ankara is extremely uncomfortable with all of this, both in principle and in implementation. More precisely, Ankara is quite unhappy with Washington in a number of specific areas and believes the following:

- the U.S.-led GWOT is exacerbating tensions in the Muslim world and polarizing Muslim-Western relations;
- the war in Iraq has damaged Turkish interests there, stimulated the Kurds toward independence, facilitated the breakup of the country,

---

16. International Strategic Research Organization (ISRO), *Terrorism Perception Survey* (Ankara: ISRO, August 2005), www.turkishweekly.net/pdf/USAK_ORG_UK-TerrorismPerception-Survey.pdf.
17. Robins, *Suits and Uniforms*, 8.

and created a new center of radical Islamist terrorism that is spreading out across the region;

- Washington has not significantly worked to solve the PKK problem in Iraq;
- Washington has restricted Turkish freedom of action in Iraq;
- U.S. policies toward Iran immensely complicate Turkey's access to Iranian energy supplies and have only served to intensify Iranian nationalism and its spirit of resistance to the West and to strengthen hard-liners there;
- any U.S. attempt at a military solution to the Iranian nuclear issue will not be effective and will only destabilize regional conditions against Turkey's interests;
- Washington does not treat Turkey with sufficient respect and does not seriously consult with Turkey on major strategic and military actions that have immense impact on Turkey's own security and interests;
- Washington's unwavering support of Israel's policies consistently exacerbates the Palestinian problem and serves to polarize Muslim-U.S. tensions in the region—all of which harm Turkey's interests;
- U.S. unilateralism and policy choices are creating negative reactions elsewhere in the world, including in Europe, making it harder for Turkey to identify with those policies or to cooperate with them;
- an agenda of U.S.-imposed democratization in the Muslim world will only serve to destabilize the region further.

On balance, when it comes to the specifics of U.S. policies, Ankara believes that the negatives greatly outweigh the positives; furthermore, the negative concerns touch directly on core Turkish interests much more so than do most of their nominally "shared interests." Thus, Turkey will remain wary of supporting most U.S. actions in the region. It may feel compelled to support some actions simply to avoid confrontation with Washington as a potentially necessary ally *in extremis*, but as of now Ankara's cooperation with Washington can at best be understood as an attempt to limit damage to its national interests.

This situation was clearly exemplified in a hurried patch-over meeting between Gül and Rice in Washington in July 2006, when they signed what was touted as a "new beginning," a document that underlined a "common vision" between Ankara and Washington. Both capitals seem to have felt the need for such a highly publicized gesture in order to stem the hemorrhage in their bilateral relations. Significantly, although much use was made of the term "common vision," Washington did not refer to Ankara as a "strategic partner."

In fact, the document represented the first major U.S. acknowledgment that things have changed in Turkey and that Turkey must be allowed greater latitude in pursuing its chosen role as chief intermediary in the immediate region. It also indicated some awareness by Washington that its efforts to check Turkish initiatives that complicate the U.S. agenda have in fact been increasingly counterproductive. Furthermore, the document indicated a growing U.S. acceptance that Turkey's access to all parties just might on occasion be helpful in crisis situations and that Turkey's intervention would generally be preferable to potential intervention by Russia, China, or even Europe.

Although the document repeated familiar shared grand "principles" that have been invoked before, it did not address the details of policy implementation, which is where grand principles have consistently broken down in the past. The Turkish press was largely skeptical about the document, believing that it did not reflect any genuine situational change, that it only papered over or partially legitimized Ankara's own policy goals, and that it only served to help avoid further mutual irritation between the two countries.

Indeed, vague, declarative, rhetorical ideals between the two countries will inevitably fall short in implementation. Ankara does not want a nuclear-armed Iran but fears the U.S. approach will be counterproductive and will negatively affect Turkey's overall relations with Iran—its neighbor in perpetuity. Turkey wants regional stability, but it fears that an activist U.S. presence in the Middle East may only serve to undermine regional stability. As evidence of this, even after 9/11—and before the JDP came to power—Turkey moved away from participation in a joint defensive ballistic missile arrangement with Israel and Washington, largely out of concern for how the region would react. Turkey also feared that the suffering of civilians in Afghanistan as a result of the U.S. invasion would intensify radicalism in the region.[18]

As a result, the JDP's relationship with Washington is one of intense ambivalence. On the one hand, the JDP favors a more independent Turkish foreign policy and a broad good-neighbor policy. On the other hand, many in the JDP believe that maintenance of decent relations with Washington is the JDP's chief insurance policy against overthrow by the Turkish military—that is, it wants to preclude Washington from giving the green light to the military to move. Indeed, some within the military anticipated a more radical JDP posture that would have served to justify such a military move against it. Thus, the JDP struggles to avoid using excessive anti-U.S. rhetoric, even while trying to pursue quite independent policies in the Middle East. And even the JDP has its "American wing." Ironically, the JDP has actually come under heavy attack from the nationalist movement, which labels it as the

---

18. Steven A. Cook, "U.S.-Turkey Relations and the War on Terrorism," Analysis Paper 9, *America's Response to Terrorism* (Washington, D.C.: Brookings Institution, November 6, 2001), www.brook.edu/views/ARTICLES/fellows/2001_cook.htm.

"American party" and as part of a CIA-sponsored strategy to spread "moderate Islam" in the region with Turkey at the helm. Although the very term "moderate Islam" infuriates the military as a whitewashing of the Islamist threat, today the JDP is probably more moderate toward Washington than most other political elements in Turkey.

But now that the European Union plays an increasingly significant role in Turkish political, economic, and strategic calculations, there will be a certain new tension between Ankara's ties with Washington and its ties with Brussels. In fact, its ties with Brussels may help Ankara—intentionally or perhaps even inadvertently—to wean itself away from Washington on numerous fronts. However, as Philip Robins states, "Turkey is also profoundly suspicious of Western Europe and what it regards as the political agenda of neo-imperialists, Christian Democrats, and liberal humanists alike, which it fears will risk, if not result in, the weakening if not dismantling of the Turkish state."[19]

Either way, multiple new regional and global factors are opening the door to a considerable shift in all of Ankara's relationships—especially with Washington—and a new strategic Turkish calculus is emerging with which Washington will be increasingly uncomfortable and will not be able to do much about it.

---

19. Robins, *Suits and Uniforms*, 100.

Part III

Turkey's Future Trajectory

17

Turkey's Future Foreign Policy Scenarios

At some point in the future, Ankara will likely choose one of three overarching foreign policy directions. Alternatively, they are

- a Washington-centric foreign policy in which Turkey's primary priority remains close geopolitical association with the United States;
- a European-centric foreign policy based on the primacy of EU membership;
- an Ankara-centric foreign policy that stresses independence of outlook and action, that balances cooperative and strategic interactions with a broad range of other powers, and that has a strong Eurasian and Middle Eastern bent.

Although none of these policy directions are mutually exclusive—and both Turkish domestic politics and global events will strongly affect the direction Turkey takes—the ultimate grand orientation of Turkey's policies will significantly affect Turkey's decisions and actions on the ground.

A Washington-Centric Policy

For roughly six decades, Turkey's Washington-centric foreign policy orientation was motivated by a multitude of factors: the Soviet threat, the overall weakness of Europe after World War II, the reality of U.S. world dominance, Washington's relative lack of historic baggage compared with Europe's imperial baggage, and Turkey's lack of serious economic ties to the East and South.

But today, much has changed:

- The Soviet Union is gone, and Turkey is developing an important new relationship with Russia.
- A pattern of U.S. interventionism in the region now uncomfortably crowds Turkey's options.
- U.S. regional policies and interests are increasingly divergent from Turkey's.
- New social classes within Turkey view their Islamic and Ottoman heritage with greater respect and pride, diluting the country's old, elitist, strictly Western orientation.

- Turkey increasingly shares in the rising global opposition to U.S. policies and perceived hegemonic drives.
- Russia and China have moved, among others, to create an alternative power balance to U.S. unipolarism and perceived hegemonic aspirations.
- With its long-term strategic shift toward good-neighbor relations with all, Turkey no longer has an "enemy" in the region.

Despite these major shifts, a Washington-centric orientation for future Turkish foreign policy still remains possible. Continuation of such an orientation, however, would probably require the presence of several of the following factors:

- A significant new regional security threat to Turkey would need to emerge:
  - Russia seems to be the only major power that could represent such a threat, but trends are currently moving the other way. Russia's perception of Turkey as a rival will be in part a function of how much Turkey is identified with Washington's policy agenda.
  - Serious threats to Turkey could otherwise emerge only from an aggressive, chaotic Iraq or an Iran in possession of nuclear weapons intent on checking Turkish influence in the Middle East and engaged in manipulating Turkey's Kurds. Turkey otherwise faces no serious regional threats.
- Turkey would need to be subject to serious and persistent strategic long-term targeting by international jihadist forces.
- Turkey's EU membership bid would need to be rejected outright by the European Union, Turkey would need to be dramatically alienated from Europe in the process of trying to meet EU requirements, or, however unlikely, the EU project would need to collapse as a whole.
- Turkey would need to turn to the United States to help in its military modernization, particularly in the absence of any attractive alternative military suppliers. If Turkey does so, the United States must be willing to cooperate closely with Turkey on this matter and to provide to Turkey virtually all the weaponry it wants.
- Turkey would need a reason to seek a strong rock on which to base its security, such as if the Middle East were to descend into major turmoil, violence, and radicalism that directly threatens Turkey.
- Turkey would need to rely only on the United States via the International Monetary Fund to meet its economic assistance requirements (the current trend, however, is moving in the opposite direction).
- There would need to be a resurgence of moderate Kemalist thinking that insists on (1) close ties with Washington as the natural primary foundation of Turkish security and (2) a new ideological rejection of significant

Turkish involvement in Middle East affairs except on a defensive security basis. Such a scenario might be accompanied by a crushing of Islamist political gains in Turkey by the military, possibly as the result of
Islamist political overreach, significant political failure of Islamist policies, or the emergence of aggressive Islamist regimes in the region.
- Turkey would need to continue to rely on U.S. energy policies in the
  region that benefit Turkey—such as the present Baku-Tbilisi-Ceyhan
  pipeline—but there would need to be a lack of friction with Washington over increased Turkish importation of Iranian gas and Turkish cooperation with Iran on energy projects.

A European-Centric Policy

A new strategic orientation within Turkey that looked mainly toward Europe
would require most of the following conditions to be present:

- Gradual progress toward Turkey's ultimate integration into the European Union would need to continue.
- The European Union would need to continue with its generally successful ongoing evolution, making the prize of membership worth
  having. Although the progress of the EU project may be erratic, it has
  shown dramatic progress over the past sixty-year period.
- There would need to be a severe weakening of anti-EU forces in Turkish politics.
- The European Union would need to be able to meet Turkey's high degree of economic and military needs.
- The European Union would need to appreciate the value of an active
  Turkish role in the Middle East.
- There would need to be ongoing Turkish irritation and disagreement
  with the United States over Washington's strategic goals and tactical
  policies in the region, particularly those that are seen to be at odds
  with Turkish interests.

Although a strong Turkish shift toward Europe would not exclude good
working relations with Washington in certain areas, Turkey's relationship with
the United States would definitely take a back seat to a strong relationship with
the European Union.

In fact, economically speaking, Turkey is already deeply involved with
Europe. Of Turkey's top six export partners in 2004, for example, five were
EU members; the United States ranked number three with 7.7 percent mar-
ket share.[1] Furthermore, the European Union represents an equally important

---

1. CIA, "The World Factbook—Turkey."

share of Turkish imports: four of Turkey's top seven import partners were from the European Union in 2004, while the United States ranked only fifth with 4.8 percent of the market share.[2]

Thus, many economic trends are already moving Turkey toward a European-centric policy. Even though the future evolution of the European Union itself over the next decade contains many unknowns, its function as a common market is not seriously in question, and individual European states have their own growing bilateral ties with Turkey. Although Turkey's future relations with the European Union are partly conditioned by the large Turkish population resident in several EU states, the symbolism of a Muslim country joining the union would be powerful. As a result, this process is viewed with immense and positive interest in the adjacent Arab world.

However, as Hill and Taspinar note, "Interestingly, there is also an anti-EU political and economic lobby within Turkey, which, on the basis of [flourishing trade with Russia], argues that the Turkish economy would be better off pursuing free trade agreements with countries such as Russia, Iran, China, and India, instead of indexing all its trade policy to the existing customs union with the EU."[3]

The present trajectory of Turkey's bid for EU membership is slow, bumpy, and frustrating; Turkey is faced with foot-dragging and, in the case of France, even outright opposition to its membership, all of which creates an anti-EU backlash in Turkey. While Turkey's EU future is not good. Today, multiple factors can and will change over a ten year period. The logic of Turkish membership in the EU is still likely to grow rather than recede over time.

An Ankara-Centric Policy

An Ankara-centric orientation would be characterized by a confident new approach to foreign policy that seeks to build maximum independence and to maintain positive and active relations with a broad range of world states in the East and West and in the North and South.

The Strategic Vision of Ahmet Davutoğlu

Although an impulse toward greater independence has been present in Turkish foreign policy circles for several decades, the intellectual and conceptual underpinnings of a genuinely independent Turkish foreign policy has only recently been systematically set forth by Turkish scholar and chief foreign policy adviser to the JDP Ahmet Davutoğlu. Davutoğlu's concept of "strategic depth" specifically focuses on Turkey's need to have variegation in its foreign policies and a deepening of relations with all states, which in

---

2. Ibid.
3. Hill and Taspinar, "Russia and Turkey in the Caucasus."

turn would lessen Ankara's vulnerabilities to great power domination. Davutoğlu's as yet untranslated volume titled *Strategic Depth: Turkey's Place in the World (Stratejik Derinlik: Türkiye'nin Uluslararası Konumu)* is perhaps the most systematic, substantial, and comprehensive vision of Turkey's strategic position yet written.[4] It is based on a sophisticated and complex—if controversial—reading of history, political cultures, geography, geopolitics, global balances, and national interests. Davutoğlu's critics accuse him of shaky historical readings on many issues, but the importance of the book lies in its broad thrust and comprehensive vision and not as a history of the world.

While many have described Davutoğlu's view as "neo-Ottoman" due to his reference to Turkey as the inheritor of one of seven great historic world empires, the book contains a much wider vision that transcends the Ottoman Empire's territorial reach and extends Turkey's historic ties and interests into Asia, Africa, and the West. Davutoğlu speaks of restoring geopolitical axes along which Turks have historically operated, such as in Asia. Turks have traditionally been deeply engaged there as a result of their East Asian/Central Asian origins and the existence of a Turkic world there. For example, Turco-Mongols formed the Golden Horde that ruled Russia and held sway in much of Eurasia in its time, and Turks formed the founding ethnic nucleus of the great Mughal dynasty in India and in the Delhi Sultanates that preceded it. Turkey also has links to Eurasian Islam, which is reemerging with the rising Islamic consciousness of Chechens, Tatars, and Chinese Uyghur Turks. Davutoğlu recognizes that important state-to-state relations with Russia and China conflict with Turkish support for these embattled Muslim minorities, but this is one of the conflicts Turkey must reconcile, particularly given its historical ties with these groups.[5]

The historic interests and experiences of the Turkish people made them look eastward along southern Russia for more than a millennium. Thus, in Davutoğlu's view, it entirely behooves Turkey today to seek membership in the Shanghai Cooperation Organization, which, under Russian and Chinese direction, seeks to guide the security and development of the Central Asian region. Davutoğlu's vision is at once independent, nationalistic, Islamic, pan-Turkist, global, and Western; the challenge is to integrate and reconcile these various interests with specific policies. He sees democratization and modernization as the key liberating and empowering instruments for many of these regions and peoples, particularly for those that are currently weak.

In turn, Davutoğlu strongly believes in the vital importance of a solid Turkish role within the Arab world. But he does not flinch from recognizing at least two key problems there that hinder progress: (1) the lack of legitimacy

---

4. Davutoğlu, *Stratejik Derinlik.*

5. Ibid., 250.

of most Arab regimes, with which Turkey must work patiently to encourage reform and change and (2) the contradictions of pan-Arab nationalism. That is, although there exists a general Arab yearning for greater unity, it has been exploited by Arab autocratic regimes as a tool to be used against others—a problem that Davutoğlu refers to as "imposed Arab unification" and that has been exacerbated by the arbitrary colonial nature of existing borders.[6]

Davutoğlu is quite critical of past Turkish failure to exercise its own independent global options and its earlier tendency to drift into what he sees as limiting and sometimes unproductive security alliances—particularly with the United States. In his view, this state of affairs has sharply curtailed Ankara's strategic options and broadly damaged its image as an independent power. He argues that, as late as the 1990s, these policies helped foster a nascent Greek-Syrian-Iranian axis against Turkey.

Since his vision advocates a bold move away from a U.S.-centric policy orientation in order to cut a wide swathe of independent Turkish policies toward the West, the Middle East, Russia, Africa, and Asia, some observers in the United States have accused Davutoğlu of being anti-American. Although he does not want Turkey's position in the world to be limited and dominated as it has been in the past by a U.S. alliance, any characterization of Davutoğlu as "anti-American" is simple-minded. Additionally, it ignores the broad range of sophisticated and searching arguments he makes that justify a restoration of Turkey's long-absent place across the Muslim world and elsewhere.

Davutoğlu's strategic vision has undoubtedly had major impact on current JDP foreign policy, but his outlook finds resonance among many non-JDP thinkers, including among Kemalists and leftists who similarly favor maximum Turkish flexibility and independence in foreign policy. Davutoğlu's particular formulation for a systematic and broad vision of the Turkish national interest in foreign policy can indeed be debated, but it is unmatched in its scope and depth and has already had major impact on Turkish foreign policy thinking. His legacy cannot be overestimated.

The Strategic Vision of Sedat Laçiner

Sedat Laçiner, who is a journalist, scholar, and director of the International Strategic Research Organization in Ankara, has spelled out another alternative agenda for an independent Turkish foreign policy in the Middle East. His views too are in harmony with some JDP and Turkish left-of-center thinking and quite independent of the "Americanist" group in Turkey's foreign policy community. According to Laçiner,

- Turkey cannot rely on the United States, the United Kingdom, or Israel to meet its strategic needs. These powers are only stirring up the

---

6. Ibid., 250.

region, have no real answers to Turkey's problems, and are damaging Turkey's own interests. As a result, Turkey must go it alone; its Ottoman heritage equips it to do so. The United States will find it has no real alternative to Turkey and will be forced to accept Turkey's new independent role.

- An integrated approach that meets the social, economic, and cultural needs of the countries involved can resolve security issues far more effectively than a military approach.
- Communications and dialog must be broadened in the region, not just among the governments but also among the peoples of the Middle East, whose views are rarely heard or known to world leaders. This absence of meaningful communication fosters suspicions and tense relations.
- Turkey should create more bilateral and multilateral regional organizations on common issues related to drought, irrigation, medical services, education, and disarmament. A truly "regional mentality" must be fostered.
- Independent regional media must be strengthened and free of domination by Western media and its interpretation of world events.
- The sweeping nature of regional Middle Eastern problems requires a multilateral approach to reach solutions on issues ranging from border security and terrorism to disarmament and smuggling. In turn, genuine cooperation will help bring about psychological transformation.
- Middle Eastern students must be brought to Turkey to study to increase person-to-person contacts and to promote Turkey's own contributions to the region.
- Regional education and its infrastructure must be improved, such as through the building of schools in the Middle East.
- Turkey must work toward gradual disarmament in the region.
- Turkey must work for the protection of regional minorities and their rights.
- Turkey must support human rights and democratization in the region and get regional regimes to clean up their act before the United States does it for them.
- Turkey must work for regional economic integration.[7]

Conclusion

The thinking and rationale for a new, more independent Turkish posture toward the United States is already well in place and percolating deep

---

7. Sedat Laçiner, *Irak, Küresel Meydan Savaşı ve Türkiye [Iraq, Global Warfare, and Turkey]* (Ankara: Roma Yayınları, 2004), 162–63, 301–7.

within Turkish society. Furthermore, not only has the JDP shown particular interest in pursuing such a policy, but this interest is also shared by many other elements of the Turkish political spectrum.

- Turkey's socialist left has long been hostile to the United States, which it views as an imperial power bent on exploiting Turkish resources for its own globalization project and interests. Even with the collapse of the USSR, the Turkish left still exists and is quite vocal, even if not widely popular at the moment. It broadly shares its views with the Kemalist left.

- The Kemalist left has traditionally been highly suspicious of great-power motives toward Turkey and the region. Although this dates from the Sèvres Treaty, it remains suspicious of U.S. motives today; it sees current U.S. actions as being designed to strengthen the Kurds and Islamists, and to weaken Turkey and bend it to U.S. will. It is hostile to U.S. free-market preferences, which it perceives as an opening wedge to U.S. domination of the Turkish economy, and champions Turkish independence above all else. The Kemalist left still represents an important and vocal ideological minority trend with ties to the military.

- The Kemalist mainstream feels much ambivalence about the United States. On the one hand, it recognizes the need for good ties with the United States in economic and security terms, but it is under no illusions about the United States' own self-interest and its willingness to sacrifice Turkish interests as U.S. interests dictate. For the Kemalist mainstream, good ties with Washington help symbolize Turkey's Western vocation. This group will maintain selective cooperation with Washington when possible but will be on guard against any indication of divergent interests. There is little ideological sentimentality for the United States within this dominant elite group, which has been alienated considerably by U.S. policies since 9/11.

- The Turkish military values the United States in security terms and does not wish to endanger the practical benefits of that relationship, but it shares the general Kemalist mistrust of U.S. motivations and strategic intentions. Its ties with the United States are viewed in strictly pragmatic and largely unsentimental terms. Ties with the United States symbolize Turkey's "Westernness," and, in the past facilitated Turkish access to Western institutions. That facilitating role is less necessary today. While the United States is important as a key arms source, the military also wishes to diversify arms sources to avoid dangerous dependence upon the United States. In the event that the requirements of the EU process severely threaten to cripple the guiding role of the military in "supervising" Turkish politics, the United States does not represent the alternative to the EU. Instead a Eurasian orientation, with less emphasis on the Arab world, becomes the major alternative.

- Turkey's fierce nationalists strongly share the suspicions of the Kemalist left about U.S. intentions. They are often paranoid and xenophobic and quick to take offense at any slight they might perceive from Washington. The nationalists have been highly negative toward the U.S. role in Iraq and believe Washington is supporting Kurds and Islamists to weaken Turkey's powers of resistance and independence. They believe Turkey is now being encircled and even besieged by Washington. While the nationalists do not like the Islamists, they share a cultural distaste and suspicion of Western motives with them.

- The Islamists are highly ambivalent about Washington. On the one hand, the ability of the JDP to deal effectively with Washington symbolizes the new acceptability of the Islamists on the Turkish political scene. The JDP thus wishes to keep Washington on its good side to keep political enemies, especially the Kemalists and the military, at bay. U.S. and EU support for democratization and liberalization in Turkey directly strengthens the position of the Islamists within Turkish politics. At the same time, the Islamists definitely seek a more independent foreign policy and feel they have the grudging support of most other elements on the Turkish political spectrum in pursuing one. Ironically, across the Turkish spectrum, the Islamists of the JDP are tactically more tolerant of Washington's policies than most of the other groups listed above. Once out of power, however, they will likely resume a more critical stance toward the United States.

In terms of a Eurasian alternative for Turkey—intimately linked with an independent, Ankara-centric view—it is easy to see how nationalist, Islamist, and radical secular views can all look to this alternative, differ on chief focus, and yet share several overlapping tendencies. Roughly speaking, all three groups at least share a distrust of the West as they look to differing types of Eurasian futures for Turkey.

- Nationalists tend to stress *pan-Turkic* ties in Eurasia, and hence are cool toward Russia and China. For some nationalists for whom the racial aspects of pan-Turkism are central, cooperation with Russia or China is anathema. But for others for whom distrust of the West is a key factor, certain pragmatic compromises with Russia and China are possible in the interests of forging maximum Turkish strength across Eurasia.

- But many nationalists also share with the Islamists a pride in Turkey's past greatness in both the Ottoman period as well as in the pre-

Islamic period; they often acknowledge Islam as one major element of the Turkish identity—even as they look down upon Arabs and Persians from an ethnic point of view. The nationalist orientation is based primarily upon ethnic rather than religious considerations.

- Rigidly secular nationalists blend into the Kemalist camp in sharing a deep distrust of Islam even while distrusting the West. They have no respect for the Ottoman period and instead cherish the *pre-Islamic* Turkish past. In the post-Soviet period the centrality of Russia in a Eurasian orientation tends to be strongest among these secularists, especially in the military.
- Islamists look to Eurasia but emphasize Islamic ties and the importance of the Middle East element. It is Islam, rather than pan-Turkism, that links Islamists to Eurasian Turks, but Islamists are not devoid of national pride in Turkic history and tradition either. This is a major factor in the thinking of Fethullah Gülen. Moderate Islamists readily accommodate the West among their significant political relationships but the West is not central to their identity and orientation; Western ties are a question of pragmatism and a pride that Turkey has "made it" into the Western club.

One should be wary of drawing clear and sharp distinctions between these various groups; only at their extreme polarities are these distinctions most evident. The key point is that Turks can approach the "Eurasian strategic alternative" from several different vantage points and find coincidence of interest among themselves even as they represent different ideological points of departure. Distrust of the West as well as a fierce loyalty to Turkey characterize them all.

On balance, the trend toward an increasingly independent Turkish foreign policy is the most powerful force in Turkey today and is increasingly supported by domestic, regional, and global events.

18

Conclusion: What Can Washington Do?

To significantly alter Turkey's outlook toward the United States and its current policies, many key U.S. policies would likely need to change. In particular, there are three high-impact policy changes that would immediately catch Ankara's attention:

- In the short term, a determined U.S. push to eliminate the PKK presence in Northern Iraq and to compel the Kurdish government there to permanently bar the area to PKK forces would have significant impact on one of the most immediate and emotional sources of U.S.-Turkish friction. While such a step will be welcome, the issue runs deeper: any longer term U.S. commitment to, or support of, de facto autonomy or the quasi-independence of the Kurds in Northern Iraq will perpetuate Turkish distrust of American intentions, even if the PKK presence is removed from Iraq.
- Ankara would respond to a new U.S. willingness to reduce tensions in the region by engaging with states with which it has an adversarial relationship, by abandoning intimidation and counterproductive confrontation, by opening up formal dialog with Iran, and by improving ties with Syria. Presently, however, Washington employs few carrots and many sticks in dealing with Iran and Syria.
- Ankara would respond positively to efforts to bring about a settlement of the Palestinian problem, particularly one perceived to be just by a majority of Palestinians and Muslims who have genuine grievances at stake. This would immensely lower the temperature of the supercharged atmosphere that currently dominates the Middle East and affects Turkish public views.

The benefits of these changes would not, of course, be limited to U.S. policy goals vis-à-vis Turkey; they would likely enhance the overall policy goals of the United States in the broader Middle East and Muslim world.

With regard to Iraq, many of Washington's policy disputes with Ankara may not be readily reconciled because of fundamental differences on concrete policies, such as those that affect the power and degree of independence of the Iraqi Kurds, the position and role of the Turkmen, the status of the city of Kirkuk, and the disposition of Kirkuk's oil revenues.[1] Thus, to bring about greater U.S.-Turkish concord on the handling of Iraq, these key areas of disagreement would need to be addressed. Although none of these disagreements may be fully or successfully bridged, they can be better managed.

Whether Washington will actually opt to change any of these policies is an open question. If it chooses not to, the only option left for it would be to explore ways to offset Turkish concerns. Specifically, it would need to raise the value of the United States' current associations with Turkey in ways that would lead Ankara to recalculate the balance of trade-offs. Such a recalculation by Turkey would likely be stimulated if Washington were to

- lower the threshold on the level and cost of military technology transferred to Turkey to ensure that the United States overwhelmingly becomes the most important and reliable source of military procurement to Turkey;
- ensure that the International Monetary Fund meets Turkey's economic needs;
- continue to effectively facilitate Turkish entry into the European Union;
- facilitate a settlement on Cyprus through the use of greater pressure on Greece;
- offer Turkey better trade terms with the United States, particularly with regard to tariff agreements and optimal free-trade access to U.S. markets.

Additionally, Washington should raise its current level of consultation with Ankara and include it in its Middle East policy planning. After all, Turkey is a key political and military power in the region and should be part of regional thinking and U.S. policy planning. U.S. and Turkish interests may not be identical, but Turkish concerns need to be taken seriously—not simply as a courtesy but because Turkey might actually have something of value to say and even contribute.

Ultimately, a failure by the United States to cooperate and consult closely on regional affairs with Turkey—a unique, strongly grounded, legitimate, and activist state in the region—will cost the United States far more dearly than neglecting consultations with various Arab states. Although the views of friendly Arab rulers may often be more welcome to Washington's ears than Turkish bluntness, these Arab rulers are often timid and unrepresentative of their own populations views, and therefore unreliable gauges of the regional mood. And, lacking legitimacy, they are often paralyzed when

---

1. Henri Barkey, *Turkey and Iraq: The Perils (and Prospects) of Proximity* (Washington, D.C.: United States Institute of Peace Press, 2005).

it comes to taking independent or decisive action against the popular will, whereas the legitimacy of the Turkish government strengthens its ability to speak and act decisively.

Impact of U.S.-Turkish Relations on the Region

Turkey has great potential to become a major regional player in the Middle East, particularly as it begins to demonstrate a new interest and concern for the region and its peoples. Turkey's successes in its own national development can and are attracting the attention of others. Conversely, to the extent that Turkey continues to be perceived as an instrument of U.S. policy and power, Ankara's credibility and access to the region will be highly diminished—as past experience has shown. The respect given to Ankara rises almost in direct proportion to the extent to which it is perceived as an independent power. For example, the symbolism of Turkey's "no" to Washington over the Iraq invasion hugely contributed to sparking new Middle Eastern interest and respect for Turkey. It also facilitated serious new discussions between Turkey and most Muslim countries, which feel isolated, fearful, and angry over the use of U.S. military power and policies.

Turkey's reputation in the Muslim world and in Russia stands higher today than ever before in the republic's history. If a demonstrably independent Turkey advocates certain policy courses to the Arab world, it will be listened to with greater attention than would its old strictly Western-aligned self. This would not simply be a matter of the Arabs trying to neutralize Turkey but of them gaining a friendly partner who can lessen the Muslim world's sense of isolation and siege and who can facilitate communication with both Washington and Jerusalem. A Turkey that truly spans both the Eastern and Western world would be a valuable commodity for both the East and West.

Ankara has already publicly conveyed independent messages to Syria, Iran, and the Palestinians, not only on foreign policy issues but also on domestic reform issues that would affect their own respective political orders. Furthermore, if "Turkish Islam" has regional credibility, it can affect regional discussions and alter debate about the role of Islam in public life. The model would not be the old, secularist Kemalist one in which the state suppresses Islam. Rather, it would be of a vital, proud, and moderate Turkish Islam that is capable of comfortable coexistence with non-Muslim states.

This all may, in effect, be an argument for "letting Turkey be Turkey"—with the key proviso that until Ankara has comfortably resolved its own domestic Kurdish issue, its relationships with Iraq, Syria, and Iran will remain colored and skewed. This may also be an argument for the long-range value of an independent Turkey to the United States, as opposed to a Turkey with diminished regional clout and respect because it has been pushed into meeting short-term U.S. policy needs.

No matter what the future holds, one thing is certain: Turkey as the old, predictable, and loyal American ally is a thing of the past.

Postscript

In the summer of 2007, Turkey underwent a series of crucial political events. The JDP, publicly warned by the military not to attempt to elect the JDP foreign minister, Abdullah Gül, to the presidency of the country, responded by calling a snap election in which its share of votes rose to almost 47 percent—a near landslide in terms of Turkish electoral politics. This was also the first time in Turkish history that a party already in power actually gained votes in a subsequent election. The public's message to the military was clear: while it respects the military as an institution, it does not support its intervention into politics.

Immediately following the election, Abdullah Gül was elected by parliamentary vote to assume the presidency of the country—the first time an Islamist has ever assumed this post, which has always been regarded as a stronghold of Kemalism. What was particularly noteworthy about these events was the maturity and stability of the process as it unfolded, albeit under somewhat tense circumstances, in accordance with the rule of law.

In addition, the JDP strikingly received a higher proportion of Kurdish votes than the ten Kurdish candidates of the official Kurdish party who ran independently and won. This is the first time in a decade that a Kurdish party is represented in parliament. More importantly, the Kurdish population demonstrated a belief that the JDP is capable of broadly representing their interests in parliament. Thus, the Kurdish issue has now fully entered into mainstream Turkish politics, thereby offering hope that it can gradually be adjudicated in a less volatile atmosphere.

The military and hard-line Kemalists suffered a considerable setback at the hands of the electorate in this July 2007 election. Significantly they could not rally a meaningful following within the country willing to threaten the country' stability with a coup against the ruling party. Equally importantly, the power of new economic elites demonstrated their independence from former state-linked sectors and offered the JDP a vote of confidence, carrying most of the economic sectors of the country along with them.

President Gül, whose wife wears the first headscarf ever seen in the presidential palace, has moved carefully, skillfully, and sensitively on the public scene to allay deep-set military fears and to avow his commitment to secularism—that he defines as no longer denoting state *domination* of religion, but state *neutrality* on religious issues. Thus the trends for adjudication of both the Islamist issue as well as the Kurdish issue—Turkey's two most visceral political questions—are moving in positive directions.

Undoubtedly there will be further challenges and tensions within the political arena in the years ahead as other sensitive issues are addressed. But a major watershed has been crossed that bodes well for the future stability and maturity of the country and that has strengthened the rule of law.

In foreign policy, the Turkish government, now backed by a large public mandate, is likely to move more deeply and confidently in the direction of an ever more independent foreign policy that emphasizes good neighbor relations with all its neighbors and substantive engagement in Middle Eastern and Eurasian issues. This bodes well for Turkey's future. And although this process may cause Washington to yearn for the good old days of an "allied" Turkey, the new Turkey will, in fact, probably better serve the interests of itself as well as the cause of regional stability overall. Surely enlightened American observers will come to appreciate the presence of this new Turkey, strengthened and rooted in democratic process, as an anchor of stability in the troubled and tempestuous region of the Middle East.

Index

About the Author

Graham E. Fuller is currently an independent writer, analyst, lecturer and consultant on Muslim World affairs and adjunct professor of history at Simon Fraser University in Vancouver. He served for fifteen years as an intelligence officer in various countries in the Middle East and Asia, is a former vice chairman of the National Intelligence Council at the CIA, and later as a political scientist at RAND. He is the author or coauthor of numerous books, including *The New Foreign Policy of Turkey: From the Balkans to Western China* (with Ian Lesser), *A Sense of Siege: The Geopolitics of Islam and the West* (with Ian Lesser), *Turkey's Kurdish Question* (with Henri Barkey), *The Arab Shi'a: the Forgotten Muslims,* and *The Future of Political Islam.* He also has authored articles for *Foreign Affairs, Foreign Policy, National Interest, Washington Quarterly, Orbis,* and *Harvard International Affairs* on-line.